In the strange South Seas

Travel and adventures of an Irish woman
in the South Pacific

by

Beatrice Grimshaw

Trotamundas Press

Trotamundas Press Ltd.
The Meridian, 4 Copthall House, Station Square, Coventry
CV1 2FL, UK

"In the Strange South Seas" by Beatrice Grimshaw

First published in 1907

copyright © 2007 of this edition, Trotamundas Press Ltd.

ISBN: 978-1-906393-01-4

Trotamundas Press is an international publisher specializing in travel literature written by women travellers from different countries and cultures.

Our mission is to bring back into print great travel books written by women around the world which have been forgotten. We publish in several languages.

It is our privilege to rescue those travel stories which were widely acclaimed in the past and that are still relevant nowadays to help us understand better the diversity of the countries and the world.

The travel stories also make an enjoyable reading, full of adventure and the excitement of discovery.

We are proud to help preserving the memory of all those amazing women travellers which were unjustly forgotten and hope that you will enjoy reading about their interesting experiences as much as we have enjoyed researching them.

www.trotamundaspress.com

Beatrice Grimshaw 1871-1953

Beatrice Grimshaw was born a few miles outside Belfast, Ireland in a big country house. She was an adventurer at heart since childhood and an independent soul who longed to travel to far away places.

When Beatrice was 21 years old, she went away to Dublin to work as a journalist. She was a keen cyclist and broke the women's world 24 hour record by five hours. As a journalist in Dublin from 1891 she became sub-editor of "Irish Cyclist" and from 1895 edited the "Social Review" for four years. Later on she moved to London, where she continued working as a journalist. However, her dreams of travel persisted and although in those times travel was not only uncommon for a single woman but also expensive, she managed to get a commission to write newspaper publicity for the shipping companies in return for travel around the world. She provided for her other expenses by commissions for articles from various newspapers.

Until 1903 Beatrice had been a freelance journalist, a tour organiser and an emigration promoter but her dream was to go to the South Pacific islands. She sailed in early 1904 with the Union Steamship Company of New Zealand. Embarking from San Francisco, she sailed first to Tahiti, followed by a four month voyage through the South Pacific and an additional two months on the island of Niue. During this trip, she visited Tonga, Samoa, Fiji, Rarotonga and some of the Cook islands. She returned to London with enough material to publish "In the Strange South Seas" and "From Fiji to the Cannibal Islands" in 1907.

In these books, Grimshaw not only recounts her adventures in the South Seas, but she also describes the customs and lifestyles of the native populations as well as giving an exhaustive picture of the region's fauna and wildlife. The books also contain accounts of cannibalism, head-hunting, poisoning and tribal magic. She managed to skilfully mix tales of exotic jungle adventure with romantic descriptions of the South Sea allure.

Now established as a professional travel writer, Beatrice left in November 1907 for Papua New Guinea where she lived for many years and where she owned two plantations as well as being the manager of one. During those years she also wrote 37 books, mainly novels which were inspired by the many interesting people she met.

Eventually, Beatrice settled in Bathhurst, Australia where she died in 1953 at the age of eighty two with no descendants. In her book "Isles of Adventure" she provided an accurate epitaph for herself: "I have written as a traveller, a wanderer, to whom new and strange things are the chief happiness of my life".

Beatrice Grimshaw's books had a large readership but were unjustly forgotten in later years. Trotamundas Press is bringing back into print some of the travel books that so well describe the allure of the South Pacific islands that she dreamt of when she was a young woman in Ireland and that she loved so much.

Mercedes López-Tomlinson
Director
Trotamundas Press

CONTENTS

	PAGE
INTRODUCTION	1

CHAPTER I

Fate and Her Parcels—How It All came true—The First South Sea Island—Coleridge and the Tropics—The Spell of the Island Scents—What happens to Travellers—Days in Dreamland—A Torchlight Market—The Enchanted Fei 4

CHAPTER II

The History of Tahiti—Drink and the Native—In the Old Wild Days—The Simple and the Civilised Life—What an Island Town is like—The Lotos Eaters—Cocoanuts and Courtesy—A Feast of Fat Things—The Orgy on the Verandah—Schooners and Pearls—The Land of Tir-n'an-Oge 20

CHAPTER III

Is It the Loveliest?—How they deal with the Beachcomber—Cockroaches and Local Colour—The Robinson Crusoe Steamer—Emigrating to the South Seas—The Lands of Plenty—How to get an Island 46

CHAPTER IV

Where are the Six Thousand?—Calling on the Queen—A Victoria of the Pacific—The Prince sleeps softly—The Mystical Power of the Mana—How Islanders can die—A Depressing Palace—Round the Wonderful Roadway—The Home of Queen Tinomana—A Princess's Love Story—Once on Board the Schooner!—The Incredible Crabs—Depravity of a Mor Kiri-kiri . . 66

CONTENTS

CHAPTER V

Feasting and Fun on Steamer Day—The Brown People of Raratonga—Who sent back the Teeth?—Divorce made easy—Climbing a Tropical Mountain—A Hot-water Swim—Out on the Rainbow Coral Reef—Necklaces for No One 89

CHAPTER VI

The Simple Life in the South Seas—Servant Problems again—Foods and Fruits of the Country—The Tree that digests—Homemade Vanilla—The Invaluable Lime—How to cook a Turtle—In an Island Bungalow—The Little House on the Coral Shore—Humours of Island Life—Burying a Cycle—a Network of Names—Mr. Zebedee-Thunderstorm-Tin-Roof—The Night-dress that went to Church—The Extraordinary Wedding—South Sea Musicians—A Conductor's Paradise—Society Journalism in Song 105

CHAPTER VII

The Schooner at last—White Wings *versus* Black Funnels—Not according to Clark Russell—The Marvellous White Woman—The Song of the Surf—Why not?—Delightful Aitutaki—Into an Atoll—A Night in the House of a Chieftainess—The Scarlet Devil—Nothing to wear—How to tickle a Shark—The Fairy Islets—A Chance for Robinson Crusoe 121

CHAPTER VIII

Jumping a Coral Reef—The Great Wall of the Makatea—Makaia's Wonderful Staircases—A Clothing Club of the Pacific—Cool Costumes in Atiu—The Lands that lie waste—Mystery of a Vanished Tribe — Fashions in Hair-Dressing — The Sign-Language of the Sex—Invited to a Feast 146

CHAPTER IX

Islands and Adventures—What about the Missionary?—The Lotus Eaters—How to Hunt the Robber-Crab—The Ship that would not sail—Proper Place of a Passenger—One Way to get wrecked—The Pirate and the Pearls 164

CONTENTS

CHAPTER X

How not to see the Islands—Lonely Niué—A Heathen Quarantine Board—The King and the Parliament—The Great Question of Gifts—Is it Chief-like?—The New Woman in Niué—Devil-fish and Water-Snakes—An Island of Ghosts—How the Witch-Doctor died—The Life of a Trader 192

CHAPTER XI

A Life on the Ocean Wave—Where they kept the Dynamite—How far from an Iced Drink?—The Peacefulness of a Pacific Calm—A Golden Dust Heap—Among the Rookeries—Sailing on the Land—All about Guano 226

CHAPTER XII

Pearl-fishing at Penrhyn—The Beautiful Golden-Edge—Perils of the Pearl Diver—A Fight for Life—Visit to a Leper Island—A Godforsaken Place—How they kept the Corpses—The Woman who sinned—A Nameless Grave—On to Merry Manahiki—The Island of Dance and Song—Story of the Leper and his Bird—Good-bye to the *Duchess* 248

CHAPTER XIII

The Last of the Island Kingdoms—Fashions in Nukualofa—The King who was shy—His Majesty's Love Story—Who got the Wedding-Cake?—The Chancellor goes to Jail—Bungalow Housekeeping—The Wood of the Sacred Bats—By the Tombs of the Tui-Tongas—A "Chief" Kava-party—The Waits!—Mariner's Cave—The Cave of the Swallows—To Samoa . . 274

CHAPTER XIV

Stevenson's Samoa—What happened when it rained—Life in a Native Village—The Albino Chief—A Samoan "Bee"—The Tyranny of Time—Fishing at Midnight—Throwing the Presents—My Friend Fangati—The Taupo Dances—Down the sliding Rock—"Good-bye, my Flennie!" 303

CONTENTS

CHAPTER XV

Southward to New Zealand—Into the Hot-Water Country—Coaching Days come back—The Early Victorian Inn—The Fire and Snow of Ruapehu—A Hotel run wild—Hot Lakes and Steaming Rivers — The Devil's Trumpet — The Valley of the Burning Fountains—Waking up the Champagne Lake 338

CHAPTER XVI

From Heaven to Hades—Gay Rotorua—Where One lives on a Piecrust—The Birth of a River—Horrible Tikitere—In the Track of the Great Eruption—Where are the Pink and White Terraces?—A Fountain fifteen hundred feet high—Foolhardy Feat of a Guide—How the Tourists were killed—A Maori Village—Soaping a Geyser—The End 359

APPENDIX 379

IN THE STRANGE SOUTH SEAS

> In desire of many marvels over sea,
> When the new made tropic city sweats and roars,
> I have sailed with young Ulysses from the quay,
> Till the anchor rattled down on stranger shores.
>   KIPLING.

MOST men have their loves, happy or hopeless, among the countries of the earth. There are words in the atlas that ring like trumpet calls to the ear of many a stay-at-home in grey northern cities—names of mountains, rivers, islands, that tramp across the map to the sound of swinging music played by their own gay syllables, that summon, and lure, and sadden the man who listens to their fifing, as the music of marching regiments grips at the heart of the girl who loves a soldier.

They call, they call, they call—through the long March mornings, when the road that leads to everywhere is growing white and dry—through restless summer nights, when one sits awake at the window to see the stars turn grey with the dawn—in the warm midday, when one hurries across the city bridge to a crowded eating-house, and the glittering masts far away down the river must never be looked at as one passes. Of a misty autumn evening, when steamers creeping up to seaport towns send long cries across the water, one here, and another there, will stir uneasily in his chair by the fire, and shut his ears against the insistent call. . . . Why should he listen, he who may never answer?

(*Yokohama, the Golden Gate, Cape Horn, the Rio Grande, Agra, Delhi, Benares, Bombay, the Amazon, the Andes, the South Sea Islands, Victoria Nyanza, the Pyramids, the Nile, Lhassa, Damascus, Singapore, the tundras, the prairies, trade-winds, tropics, and the Line —can't you hear us calling?*)

Love is not stronger than that call—let sweetheartless girls left alone, and the man of cities who has loved the woman of the wandering foot, give bitter witness. Death is not stronger—those who follow the call must defy him over and over again. Pride of country, love of home, delight in well-known faces and kindly hearts that understand, the ease of the old and well-tried ways, the prick of ordinary ambitions hungering for the showy prizes that every one may see—these are but as dead leaves blown before the wind, when the far-off countries cry across the seas. Not one in a hundred may answer the call; yet never think, you who suppose that love and avarice and the lust of battle sum up all the great passions of the world, that scores out of every hundred Englishmen have not heard it, all the same. "In the heart of every man, a poet has died young"; and in the heart of almost every Briton, a wanderer once has lived. If this were not so, the greatest empire of the world had never been.

So, to The Man Who Could Not Go, I address this book—to the elderly, white-waistcoated city magnate, grave autocrat of his clerkly kingdom (never lie to me, sir—what was your favourite reading in the sixties, and why were you a very fair pistol shot, right up to the time when you were made junior manager?)—to the serious family solicitor, enjoying his father's good old practice and house, and counting among the furnishings of the latter, a shelf of Marryats, Mayne Reids, and Michael Scotts, wonderfully free of dust—to the comfortable clergyman, immersed in parish cares, who has the oddest fancy at times for standing on dock-heads, and sniffing up odours of rope and tar—to all of you, the army of the brave, unwilling, more or less resigned Left Behinds, who have forgotten years ago, or who will never forget while spiring masts stand thick against blue skies, and keen salt winds wake madness in the brain—to all I say: Greeting! and may the tale of another's happier chance send, from the fluttering pages of a book, a breath of the far-off lands and the calling sea.

CHAPTER I

Fate and Her Parcels—How It All came true—The First South Sea Island—Coleridge and the Tropics—The Spell of the Island Scents—What happens to Travellers—Days in Dreamland—A Torchlight Market—The Enchanted Fei.

LIKE an idle messenger-boy, Fate takes a long while about her rounds, but she will get through with them and deliver all her parcels, if you give her time enough.

She has so much business that she confuses orders very often, and you are never sure of getting what you sent for. Still, you will certainly get something, if you wait, and it may even be the thing you demanded.

The morning she called at my door, with a very full basket, she had already been to my neighbours, and given them, in a big assortment of goods—a failure on the Stock Exchange, a hunting accident, and a broken engagement. What they had ordered was a seat in Parliament, and a winter at Monte Carlo, with anything good that might come in in the way of new-laid motor-cars. But Fate was, as usual, in a hurry, and she never changes any goods, once delivered. So they had to take them in.

I had given up expecting her when her knock came to my door, because my order had been sent in some years ago, and so far had remained unacknowledged. But she fairly emptied her basket into my hands, once she was admitted.

"Goods all right, and none the worse for keeping; couldn't find time to see to you before, I've been so busy attending to an order from Japan for a new army and a gross of assorted victories," she panted. "Had to serve the Czar of Russia with a lot of old defeats I've had lying by since the Crimea, instead of the new empire he sent for; and can't get time to fill more than half the German Emperor's order for fireworks. You private people are lucky to get anything at all. Count the goods, please—one journey round the world, two-and a-half years of mixed adventures, a hundred South Sea Islands, threescore new friends, first quality, one large package luck. That's all, I think—sign the book, and let me go; I've got seven attacks of appendicitis, a foreclosed mortgage, two lawsuits, and a divorce, to deliver in this square before lunch."

So, like the fairy tales, "it all came true," and one bright winter afternoon a Cunard liner bore me away from the streets and shops and drab-coloured, huddled houses of Liverpool, down the muddy Mersey—off round the world.

There were thousands of people on the quay, come to see the famous boat away, for it was Saturday afternoon, and the town took holiday. They had a few hours of freedom before them—then, the airless office room, the stuffy shop, the ledger and the copying-press, and the clattering typewriter, the grim window giving on the dark wet street, for six long days again. Next year, and the year after, just the office, the frowsy lodging, the tram car, the pen in the strong young fingers, the desk to stoop the broad young shoulders, the life foreseen, eventless, grey for ever and for ever. And I was going round the world.

It is three weeks later, and the big " A and A " steamer is ploughing along in the midst of a marvellous dazzle of diamond-spangled, pale-blue tropic sea and scorching, pale-blue tropic sky. The passengers, in cool white suits and dresses, are clustered together on the promenade deck, looking eagerly over the port railing, while the captain, telescope in hand, points out something lying only a mile away, and says: " That's Tiki-Hau, so now you've seen a South Sea Island."

We are on our way to Tahiti, a twelve-day run from San Francisco, and are not stopping anywhere, but as Tiki-Hau is the only glimpse of land we shall get until we cast anchor in Papeëte, every one wants to look at it. Not one of us has ever seen a South Sea Island, and we are all eager to realise this little fragment of our rainbow-coloured childish dreams.

Is it as good as we dreamed it? we ask ourselves and each other. The verdict, given unanimously, is: " Yes —but not the same."

Here is no high green palmy peak, overhanging a waveless sea, with sparkling waterfalls dashing down from crag to crag, like the coloured illustrations in our old school prize books. There are, indeed, just such islands in the Pacific, we are told—many hundreds of them—but there are still more of the kind we are now looking at, which is not half so often mentioned. All South Sea Islands are either high or low; the high island, with lofty mountains and dark, rich volcanic soil, is the familiar island of the picture book, while the low type, composed only of coral, is the variety to which Tiki-Hau belongs.

What we can see of the island, however, is enough to set at rest any tendency to comparison. None of us want anything better; none of us think there can

THE FIRST CORAL ISLAND 7

be anything better, among the wonders that the Great South Seas yet hold in store.

Tiki-Hau is an island of the atoll or ring-shaped type, a splendid circle of seventy and eighty-foot palms, enclosing an inner lagoon clear and still as glass. Outside the windy palms, a dazzling beach runs down to the open sea all round the island—a beach that is like nothing the travellers ever have seen before, for it is made of powdered coral, and is as white as salt, as white as starch, as white as the hackneyed snow-simile itself can paint it. All the island—the whole great ring, many miles in length—is coral too, white, branching, flowering coral under water, white, broken-coral gravel above, with here and there a thin skin of earth collected by a century or two of falling palm-leaves and ocean waste. Outside the magic ring the sea-waves tumble, fresh and blue, upon the cloud-white sand; within, the still lagoon glows like a basin of molten emerald. Above, the enormous palm-trees swing their twenty-foot plumes of gaudy yellow-green to the rush of warm trade-wind, high in the burning sky. A glorious picture indeed—but one before which the painter well might tremble.

Here, for the first time, we begin to understand why pictures of tropical scenes are so few and so unsatisfactory. Paint! what combination of coloured grease that ever came out of a box could hope to suggest the pale green fire of those palm-tree plumes, the jewel-blaze of the lagoon, the sapphire flame of the sea, the aching, blinding whitenesses of spray and sand? Who could paint the sun that is literally flashing back from the light dresses of the passengers, making of every separate person a distinct conflagration, and darting lightning rays out of the officers' gold shoulder-straps and buttons? Does any dweller in the dim grey North really know what light and colour are? did we know, with our tinselled April days, and gentle blue and white August afternoons, that we were so proud of once? Well, we know now; and, alas, in the dim prosaic years that are yet to come, we shall remember!

The ship steams on, the atoll fades away in the distance, and once more comes the changeless level of long blue empty sea. But we have seen a coral island, and the picture is ours for ever.

Flying-fish, skimming and "skittering" over the surface of the waves, we have all become used to now. The first day we met them was a memorable one, all the same—they were so exactly what one had paid one's money to see. Sharks have disappointed us so far; never a sight of the famous "black triangular fin" have we yet enjoyed, and the passengers have an idea that something ought to be said to the steamship company about it. Nor have the equatorial sunsets quite kept up their stage character. Books of travel, and sea literature in general, have led us to expect that the sun, in the tropics, should go out at sunset as though Poseidon had hold of the switch down below the water line, and turned off the light the instant sun and horizon met.

> ... The sun's rim dips, the stars rush out,
> At one stride comes the dark.

They don't, Mr. Coleridge, and it doesn't, and you never were there to see for yourself, or you would not have talked beautiful nonsense and misled countless travellers of all ages who did see, but who have refused to look, save through your illustrious spectacles, ever since. Even on the equator, the sun gives one time to dress for dinner (if the toilet is not a very elaborate one) while it is setting, and after it has set. So dies one more illusion. Yet it can easily be spared, in the midst of a thousand wild dreams and strange imaginings, realised to the very utmost, as ours are to be ere long.

Tahiti comes at last. In the pearly light of a sunrise pure as a dawn of earliest Eden, we glide into the shadow of a tall, rose-painted peak, spiring eight thousand feet up into heaven, and anchor in the midst of a glassy mirror of violet sea. Papeëte, the loveliest, sweetest, and wickedest town of all the wide South Seas, lies before us—just a sparkle of red roofs looking out from under a coverlet of thick foliage, a long brown wharf and a many-coloured crowd. Across the water steals a faint strange perfume, unlike anything I have ever smelled before—heavy, sweet, penetrating, suggestive. . . . It is cocoanut oil scented with the white tieré flower, and never, from Tahiti to Samoa, from Raratonga to Fiji, Vavau, Manihiki, or Erromanga, will the South Sea traveller lose the odour of it again. Cocoanut oil, and the nutty, heavy smell of copra (dried cocoanut kernel) are charms that can raise in an instant for any old island wanderer, in the farthest corners of the earth, the glowing vision of the wonderful South Sea world.

> . . . Smells are surer than sounds or sights
> To make your heartstrings crack,
> They start those awful voices o' nights
> That whisper : " Old man, come back ! "

(*Old island wanderers in all parts of the world—settled down to desks in the E.C. district—tramping through the December glare of Pitt Street, Sydney, for " orders "—occupying a tranquil, well-bred billet, and a set of red-tape harness, in the Foreign Office—do you smell the tieré flower, and hear the crooning of the reef, and feel the rush of the warm trade wind, and the touch of the sun-baked sand, under the utu trees once more?*)

So I landed in Papeëte, and found myself in the South Sea Islands at last.

All that afterooon, like "Tommy" in Barrie's *Thrums*, I kept saying to myself: "I'm here, I'm here!" ... There was no mistake about Papeëte. It was not disappointing or disillusioning, it was only more lifelike than life, more fanciful than fancy, infinitely ahead of all past imaginations.

There were the waving palms of picture and story, laden with immense clusters of nuts; there were the wonderful bananas, with broad green leaves ten and twelve feet long, enshrouding bunches of fruit that were each a good load for a man; there were the greenhouse flowers of home—the costly rare stephanotis, tuberose, gardenia—climbing all over the verandahs of the houses, and filling half-cultivated front gardens with stacks and bouquets of bloom. And the dug-out canoes, made from a single hollowed log supported by an outrigger flitting about the glassy lagoon like long-legged waterflies—and the gorgeous, flamboyant trees, ablaze with vermilion flowers, roofing over the grassy roadway in a series of gay triumphal arches—and above all, beyond all, the fiery-gold sunlight, spilling cataracts of flame through the thickest leafage, turning the flowers to white and red-hot coals, painting the shadows under the houses in waves of ink, and bleaching the dust to dazzling snow—how new, how vivid, how tropical it all was!

The native population was out in full force to see the steamer come in. So, indeed, were the white residents, in their freshest suits and smartest muslins,

NATIVE DRESS

but they met with small attention from the little band of newcomers. It was the Tahitians themselves who claimed all our interest—the famous race who had been so well liked by Captain Cook, who had seduced the men of the *Bounty* from allegiance to King George of England, a hundred and sixteen years ago, who were known all the world over as the most beautiful, the most amiable, and the most hospitable of all the South Sea Islanders.

Some of the passengers, I fancy, expected to see them coming down to the shore clad in necklaces and fringes of leaves, eager to trade with the newcomers, and exchange large pearls and thick wedges of fine tortoiseshell for knives, cloth, and beads. . . . Most of us were better prepared, however, having heard a good deal about Papeëte, the Paris of the South Seas, from the people of the steamer, and having realised, on our own account, that a great deal of water might run under a bridge in a hundred years, even here in the South Pacific.

So the smartness of the native crowd surprised only a few, of whom I was not one. On the contrary, I was surprised to find that here, in this big island group, with its fortnightly steamer, its large "white" town, and its bureaucratic French Government, some kind of a national dress did really still exist. The Tahitian men were variously attired, some in full suits of white, others in a shirt and a brief cotton kilt. The women, however, all wore the same type of dress—a flowing nightdress of cotton or muslin, usually pink, pale green, or yellow, and a neat small sailor hat made in the islands, and commonly trimmed with a pretty wreath of shells. Most of them wore their hair loose, to show off its length and fineness—Tahitians have by far the most beautiful hair of any island race—and not a few were shoeless, though nearly all had smart parasols. The colour of the crowd was extremely various, for Tahiti has more half and quarter castes than full-blooded natives—in Papeëte at all events. The darkest, however, were not more than tea-coloured, and in most instances the features were really good.

So much one gathered in the course of landing. Later on, during the few days I spent in an hotel waiting for the Cook Island steamer—for, alas! I was not staying in Tahiti—there was opportunity for something further in the way of observation. But——

But—— It happens to every one in Tahiti, why should I be ashamed of it? There was once a scientific man, who came to write a book, and took notes and notes and notes—for two days and a half. Then, he thought he would take a morning's rest, and that is five years ago, and he has been resting ever since, and they say in the stores that he has not bought so much as a sheet of letter paper, or a penny bottle of ink, but that his credit for cigars and ice, and things that go with both very well, and for pyjamas to lounge about the back verandah in, and very cheap novels, and silk-grass hammocks, is nearly run out in Papeëte. There was a Government official—perhaps it was two, or three, or sixty Government officials—who came to Papeëte very full of energy and ability, and very much determined to work wonders in the sleepy little colony. . . . He, or they, is, or are, never to be seen awake before three in the afternoon, and his clerks have to type the signatures to his letters, because he will not trouble to write his name; and their people think they died years and years ago, because they have never carried out their intention of telling some one to find some one else to

IN DREAMLAND

send a message to say they are alive. And there are a dozen or fourteen gentlemen who keep stores in Papeëte, and if you go in to buy things in the morning or afternoon or evening, mayhap you will find the gentleman or his understudy asleep behind the counter, but mayhap you will find the door shut, and the proprietor away at breakfast, which takes him an hour, or lunch, which takes from two hours to three, or dinner, which occupies him from six till nine inclusive. After that, he may open again for a little while, or he may not.

Must I explain now what happened to me in Papeëte, or why I am not in a position to add anything to the scientific or ethnological, or geographic knowledge of the world, concerning the Society Islands in general?

A duty, obvious, immediate, and unperformed, is perhaps the best of all spices to a dish of sweet laziness. And there is not on earth's round ball such a spot to be lazy in as pleasant Papeëte. One is never fairly awake. It is dreamland—and what a happy dream! The golden light on the still lagoon is surely the "light that never was on sea nor land"—before we sailed in under the purple peaks of Orohena. The chanting of the coral reef far out at sea, unceasing, day and night, is the song the sirens sang to strong Ulysses, in the dream dreamed for all ages by the old Greek poet, long ago. The languorous voices of the island women, sweet and low as the "wind of the western sea"—the stillness of the island houses, where feet go bare upon the soundless floors, and music waxes and wanes so softly now and then in whispering songs or lightly swept piano keys, that it only blends with the long mysterious murmur of the wind in the rustling palm trees, to lull the senses into perfect rest—these, too, are of the world of dream.

Something out of dreamland, also, is the little hotel where most of the travellers stay—a rambling bungalow in a grass enclosure, overrun with vivid flowers and splendid leafage. That the proprietress should welcome her guests in a long lace and muslin nightgown-dress, her pretty brown feet bare, and her flowing wavy hair crowned with a wreath of perfumed gardenia and tuberose, seems quite a natural part of the dream; that the chambermaids should be beautiful island girls clad in the same garb, and that they should sit in the drawing-room playing the piano and singing wild melancholy island songs, like the sighing of the surf on the shore, when they ought to be making beds or serving dinners, is also "in the picture." That the Chinese cook should do elaborate Parisian cookery, and that the coffee and the curry and the bread (or at least the bread-fruit) should be picked in the garden as required, and that there should be no visible means of shutting the door of the bathroom, which is very public, until a carpenter is called in, and that L——, the charming proprietress, should explain with a charming smile: "Only the house been using it all this time," to account completely for the deficiency—all this belongs unmistakably to the irresponsible dream-country. And when the warm tropic night drops down, and one goes wandering in the moonlight, to see for the first time the palm-tree plumes all glassy-silver under the radiant sky, flashing magically as they tremble in the faint night wind, it is more than ever the land of dream that is thus lit up in the soft clear dusk. So vivid is the moonlight, that one can even see the scarlet colour of the flamboyant flowers fallen in the dust, and distinguish the deep

EARLY MARKETING

violet and hyacinthine hues of the far-off mountain peaks across the bay. . . . How, in such a place, can one waste the night in sleep?

It is certainly not like any sort of waking life one has hitherto known, to find that the market of Papeëte—one of the principal sights of the place—is held on Sunday mornings before sunrise. One might have supposed that such a supremely indolent people would scarcely choose the most inconvenient hour of all the twenty-four for a general gathering. But they do choose it, and the visitor who wants to see the market must choose it also.

L—— calls me, herself, at some unearthly hour, not much after four, and I get up and dress in the warm darkness. It is the hot season at present and the air, night and day, is very like a hot bath, and not far behind it in temperature. I have been loafing about the town during the previous day in rather thin shoes, and my feet have been almost blistered by the heat of the ground striking up through light soles, so that I cannot walk very far, and am glad to find the market close at hand.

L—— in a fresh muslin nightdress (she has something like fifty or sixty of them), acts as guide. She has put a new coronet of flowers in her hair, and before we reach the market she proceeds to dress me up Tahiti fashion, with long necklaces of sweet white blossoms round my neck, falling all over my dress, and a heavy crown of closely woven gardenias on my head, instead of my hat, which she removes, and politely carries. She wants to pull my hair down as well, but in a temperature of eighty degrees the idea does not sound tempting, so I decline to follow Tahitian custom further. Besides, there is really no knowing where she would stop!

There is not yet a glimmer of daylight when we enter the market-place, and flaring lamps and torches cast huge flickering shadows all over the gay assembly. Fruit and fish for the most part are the wares—but such fish, and such fruit! Where one would look at home for white and grey turbot, pallid plaice, zinc-coloured herrings, here one may see the most gorgeous shapes of gold and scarlet and green ; of iridescent rose, silver, orange ; of blue, brilliant as a heap of tumbled sapphire, and pearl as bright as the lining of a shell. Tahiti is famous for its beautiful fish, and indeed these in the market look almost too poetically lovely to eat.

Then the fruit ! bananas as big as cucumbers, as small as ladies' fingers (after which, indeed, this little sugar-sweet variety is named), dark red bananas, flavoured like a peach, large bloomy ones, tasting and looking like custard within ; smooth yellow ones, like those exported to other countries, whither the daintier fruits will not safely go—pineapple in rough-skinned heaps (one learns soon in Tahiti how to eat a pineapple, and that is to peel it, cut it into largest possible lumps, eat the latter undiminished, even if they make you speechless, and never, never, slice the fruit)—oranges of several different kinds, custard-apples, rose-apples, paw-paws, melons, avocado pears, guavas, mangoes, and other fruits the name of which I have never heard—all lying together in masses under the lamplight, costing not as many halfpence to buy as at home they would cost shillings.

The native beauties are here in a merry crowd, intent quite as much upon enjoyment as on business. Scarcely one but wears a flower behind her ear—and if you have ever been in the South Seas, you will know what that pretty little signal means, but if you have not, why then I shall not tell you—and all are so wreathed, and crowned, and necklaced with woven blossoms, that the air is heavy with scent, and the market-place looks as though the transformation scene of a pantomine were just about to begin, with a full chorus of flower-decked nymphs appearing for the dance.

One exceedingly pretty girl, with a perfect cataract of black hair overflowing her pale green gown, and a pair of sparkling dark eyes that could never be matched outside the magic lines of Cancer and Capricorn, is making and frying pancakes with something fruity, nature unknown, inside them. She has half a dozen French officers about her, enjoying breakfast and flirtation at the same time. Another, who is selling a number of the oddest little parcels imaginable, made out of cut-up joints of bamboo, carefully sealed, is doing a good trade among the coloured and semi-coloured ladies. L—— says she is selling ready-made sauces, to be eaten with fish or meat, and adds that she herself will show me what Tahitian sauces are like later on, because there is no one in the whole group fit to act as scullion to her in that important matter—or words to the same effect.

Strange-looking mountain men are here, dressed in shirt and kilt of cotton cloth, patterned in flowers and leaves as big as soup-plates. The former garment is a concession to Papeëte—outside the town, the "pareo" or kilt alone forms the Tahitian full-dress suit. These men have come in to sell the "fei," or wild banana, which is only found on the highest and most perilous of the mountain precipices. To get it, the Tahitian must climb where not even a goat would venture to go, and make his way back, having secured the fruit, carrying a bunch that is a heavy load, even on level ground. Many are the lives that have been lost gathering the "fei," but the Tahitian, like all islanders, is something of a fatalist, and the death of one fruit gatherer never stops another from going a-hunting in the very same place next day.

There is something about the same "fei" that is worth noting. It is one of the standing dishes of the islands—a cooking banana, large, and well-flavoured when baked, but not so attractive on the whole as many of the other kinds. The Tahitian, however, ascribes to this variety a certain magic property, not unlike that of the fabled lotus. If you eat of the "fei," he says, especially if you eat freely of it, you will fall under the spell. For ever, in its working, it binds you to Tahiti. You may go away, and without any intention of returning, say goodbye to the islands, and place many thousand miles of land and sea between yourself and sweet Tahiti, saying to yourself that you and Papeëte have no more to do with one another for ever. . . . Yet by-and-by—some day, one knows not when ; it may be soon, or it may be late, but it will surely come—you will return to Tahiti. The spell of the fei will work, and draw you back again.

So the natives said, and I thought the fancy a pretty one, and wondered whether it had really any connection with the lotos myth, and then forgot all about it.

That is three years ago, and since those days I have travelled the whole world over, leaving Tahiti behind as one leaves a station passed long ago on a railway journey, upon a line that one never expects to traverse again. As I write, the snows of winter Britain lie thick outside my window, and a sea of Arctic coldness breaks in freezing green and grey upon a desolate shore. Nothing on earth seems farther away than the warm blue waves, and flowers that never fade, and shining coral sands of Tahiti. But . . . there is a steamer running southward before long, and a great sunny city on the other side of the world where the island boats lie waiting at the quays. And one of those island boats, in a month or two, will carry a passenger back to Tahiti—a passenger who ate of the fei three years ago, and went away for ever, but on whom the spell of the magic fruit has worked—after all.

CHAPTER II

*The History of Tahiti—Drink and the Native—In the Old Wild Days—
The Simple and the Civilised Life—What an Island Town is like—
The Lotos Eaters—Cocoanuts and Courtesy—A Feast of Fat Things
—The Orgy on the Verandah—Schooners and Pearls—The Land of
Tir-n'an-Oge.*

ALTHOUGH I certainly did not use the few days of my stay in Tahiti to the best advantage— although I saw none of the public buildings of Papeëte, never set eyes on any of the officials of the place, and did not collect any statistics worth mentioning, I gathered a few crude facts of a useful kind, which are herewith offered as a sop to the reader, who must be informed and improved, or know the reason why. (If he would only go to Tahiti, that dear reader, whom all travellers know so well and fear so much ! if he would just spend a week lying on the coral beach, and strolling in the moonlight, and listening to native songs, and feeding fat on native dainties—he would never want to be informed of anything any more, and as to being improved . . . O Tahiti, loveliest and least conventional of the siren countries of the dear South Seas, can you lay your hand on your heart, and honestly declare you are improving ?)

Tahiti was discovered, not by Captain Cook, as is rather commonly supposed, but by Captain Wallis of H.M.S. *Dolphin*, in 1767. Captain Wallis formally took possession of the group in the name of His Majesty King George III., and Captain Cook, in the course of his different visits to the islands, laid the foundations of all the civilisation they afterwards acquired. Nevertheless, the islands are French property to-day. There is nothing in the Pacific better worth owning than the Society group, more fertile, more beautiful, more healthy, richer in valuable tropical products—and the construction of the Panama Canal, an event which has been foreseen for several generations, will obviously add much to the importance of the islands. Because of these, and other excellent reasons, Great Britain, acting on the principles by which her colonial policy is commonly guided, allowed the Society Islands to slip gradually into the hands of a power better able than herself to appreciate their value, and the group, after thirty-seven years of "protection," was finally taken possession of by France, in the year 1880. The native Queen, Pomare IV. (Pomare being a dynastic name like Cæsar, but, unlike the latter, applied to both sexes), was allowed to retain her state and possessions under the French protectorate. Her successor, King Pomare V., who succeeded in 1877 and died in 1891, only reigned for three years. After the formal annexation he retained his title of king, and much of his state, but the power was entirely in French hands. Prince Hinoe, his heir, who would in the ordinary course have occupied the throne, lives in a handsome European-built house near Papeëte, and enjoys a good pension, but is otherwise not distinguished in any way from the ordinary Tahitian.

Under French rule, the islands have done fairly well There were at first many regrettable disputes and troubles between opposing camps of missionaries, but these have long since been made up. Commerce is in rather a languishing state. The group exports copra, vanilla, pearl-shell, and fruit, but the trade with America was so much on the down-grade during the time of my visit, that steamers were leaving the port with empty holds. The natives are well treated under the present system; the liquor laws, however, are defective, and no Tahitian, apparently, has any difficulty in obtaining as much strong spirits as he wants and can pay for. The disastrous effects of such carelessness as this need no mention to the reader who knows anything of dark-skinned races. For the benefit of the reader who does not, however, it may be remarked that all colonial administrators agree concerning the bad effects of intoxicants on coloured races of every kind. It matters not at what end or part of the scale of colour the man may be—whether he is a woolly-haired, baboon-jawed nigger from Central Africa, a grave, intelligent, educated Maori of New Zealand, or a gentle child-like native of Tahiti, barely café-au-lait as to colour —all the same, and all the time, spirits are sure to convert him, temporarily, into a raging beast, and, in the long run, to wipe out him and his kind altogether. It is not a question of temperance principles or the reverse, but merely a matter of common-sense policy, in dealing with races which have shown themselves unable to withstand the effects of the liquors that our hardier northern nations can use with comparative safety. One may lay it down as a general principle that nothing with a coloured skin on it can take intoxicants in moderation—it is not at all, or all in all, with the "native" when it comes to strong drinks. Scientific folk would probably set down the comparative immunity of the white races to the protection that lies behind them in the shape of centuries of drinking ancestors. The coffee-coloured islander's great-grandparents did not know whisky, just as they never experienced measles and other diseases, that do not usually kill the white, but almost always put an end to the "man and brother." Therefore, the islander's

CAUSES OF DECADENCE

body has not, by inheritance, acquired those points of constitution which enable the white to resist whisky and measles, and other dangerous things; and when they touch him, he goes down at once. A parallel may be found in the case of opium, which the white man, broadly speaking, cannot take in moderation, although most of the yellow races can. Europeans who once acquire a liking for the effects of opium will generally die as miserable wrecks, in the course of a very few years. A Chinaman, under similar circumstances, may, and often does, live to a good old age, without taking any harm at all from his constant doses. His ancestors have been opium takers, the Englishman's have not. It is the case of the islander and the spirits over again.

After which digression, one has some way to come back to the fact that the French Government does not prevent the Tahitian from drinking gin nearly so effectively as it should, and that, in consequence, the diminution of the native population receives a downward push that it does not in the least require. In the Fijis, British rule keeps spirits strictly away from all the natives, with the exception of the chiefs, and something, at least, is thereby done to slacken the decline that afflicts the people of almost every island in the Pacific. The Fijian chiefs, as a rule, drink heavily, and do not commonly live long, thus providing another argument in favour of restriction.

The population of Tahiti is indeed much less than it should be. Captain Cook's estimates of native populations are now understood to have been mistaken in many cases, owing to the fact that he calculated the entire numbers from the density of occupation round the shores. As most Pacific islands are inhabited about the coasts alone, the interior being often unsuitable for cultivation, and too far removed from the fishing-grounds to suit an indolent race, it can easily be understood that serious errors would arise from such a method of estimate. The diminution, therefore, since ancient times, is not quite so alarming as the first writers on the Pacific—and, indeed, many who followed them—supposed it to be. If the sums worked out by the travellers who visited Honolulu in the sixties, or Tahiti a little later, had been correct, both of these important groups would long since have been empty of all native population. But the Hawaiian group has still a very fair number of dark-skinned people, while Tahiti, including all its islands, had a population, according to the census of 1902, of over thirteen thousand, one-eighth of whom are said to be French, and a smaller number Chinese and other foreigners.

Still, it cannot be said that this is a large, or even a fair population for a group of islands covering 580 square miles, nor can it be denied that the numbers of the Tahitians are steadily on the decrease. The exact causes of the decline are disputed, as indeed they are in connection with every other coloured race in the Pacific. European diseases of a serious kind are extremely common in the group, and consumption also is frequent. These are two obvious causes. Less easily reckoned are the unnamed tendencies towards extinction that follow the track of the white man through the lands of primitive peoples, all over the world. There can be no doubt that the old life of the Pacific—feasting, fighting, making love, and making murder : dressing in a bunch of leaves, and living almost as completely without thought for the morrow as the twittering parrakeets in the mango trees—suited the constitution of the islander better than the life of to-day.

It may have been bad for his spiritual development, and it certainly was bad for any wandering white men who came, by necessity or choice, to visit his far-away fastnesses. But he lived and flourished in those bad days, whereas now he quietly and unostentatiously, and quite without any rancour or regret, dies.

Why? Old island residents will tell you that, even if every disease brought by the white man were rooted out to-morrow, the native would still diminish in numbers. He has done so in islands where the effects of European diseases were comparatively slight. He does so in New Zealand, where the Maori (the supposed ancestor of most of the island peoples) is petted, cherished, and doctored to an amazing extent by the ruling race, and yet persists in dying out, although he is not affected by consumption or other evils to any serious extent. There are undoubtedly other causes, and perhaps among them not the least is the fact that, for most Pacific races, life, with the coming of civilisation, has greatly lost its savour.

It used to be amazingly lively in Tahiti, in the wild old days. Then, the Tahitian did not know of white men's luxuries—of tea and sugar and tinned stuffs, lamps and kerosene, hideous calico shirts and gaudy ties, muslin gowns and frilled petticoats for the women, "bits" to make patchwork quilts with, and beds to put the quilts on, and matchwood bungalows to put the beds in, and quart bottles of fiery gin to drink, and coloured silk handkerchiefs to put away on a shelf, and creaking shoes to lame oneself with on Sundays. Then, he did not let or sell his land to some one in order to get cash to buy these desirable things; nor did his womenkind, for the same reason, adopt, almost as a national profession, a mode of life to which the conventionalities forbid me to give a name. Nor did the distractions of unlimited church-going turn away his mind from the main business of life, which was undoubtedly that of enjoyment. He had no money, and no goods, and did not want either. He had no religion (to speak of) and desired that still less. All he had to do was to secure a good time, and get up a fight now and then when things in general began to turn slow.

It must be said that the existence of the "Areoi," a certain secret society of old Tahiti, went far to minimise the risk of dullness. The members formed a species of heathen "Hell-Fire Club," and they cultivated every crime known to civilisation, and a few which civilisation has happily forgotten. Murder, theft, human sacrifices, cannibalism, were among their usual practices, and the domestic relationships of the Society (which was large and influential, and included both sexes) are said to have been open to some criticism. They were popular, however, for they studied music and the dance as fine arts, and gave free entertainments to every one who cared to come. They travelled from village to village, island to island, giving "shows" wherever they went, and winning welcome and favour everywhere by the brilliance and originality of their improprieties. They were as wicked as they knew how, and as amusing, and as devilish, and as dazzling. . . . How the young Tahitian lad, not yet tattooed, and considered of no importance, must have reverenced and envied them! how he must have imitated their pranks in the seclusion of the cocoanut groves, and hummed over their songs, and longed for the time when he himself should be big enough to run away from home, and go off with the delightful, demoniacal, fascinating Areois!

Then there was always a native king in Tahiti in those days, and a number of big native chiefs, each one of whom had his own little court, with all the exciting surroundings of a court which are never missing in any part of the world, from Saxe-Niemandhausen to Patagonia. And there were tribal fights from time to time, when property changed hands, and war-spears were reddened, and a man might hunt his enemy in the dusk, stealthy, soft-footed, with heart jumping in his breast, along the shadowy borders of the lagoon. . . . Murder and mischief and fighting and greed, pomp of savage courts and stir of savage ambitions, and the other world that nobody knew or cared about, shut off by a barrier of seas still unexplored. . . . It was a life in which a man undoubtedly did live, a life that kept him quick until he was dead. Does the decline of Pacific races look less unaccountable now?

In these days, the Tahitian is undoubtedly improved. He never was a very "bad lot" all round, in spite of the Areois; but Civilisation, of course, had to take him in hand once it was known he was there, for Civilisation will not have loose ends or undusted corners in her house, if she can help it. So the people of Tahiti were discovered, and converted, and clothed, and taught, and they gave up being Areois, and worshipping heathen gods, and going about without shirts and skirts, and they went frequently to church, and supported their white pastors generously, and began to trade with the Europeans, so that the latter made much money.

They are quite happy and uncomplaining, and manage to have a reasonably good time in a quiet way, but they *will* die out, and nobody can prevent them. You see, they are rather bored, and when you are bored, the answer to the question, "Is life worth living?" is, at the least, debatable—to a Pacific Islander.

I have written of this at some length, because,

mutatis mutandis, it applies to nearly all the island races. It is not only the Tahitian who looks back with wistful eyes to the faded sunset of the bad old times, with all their savage gaudiness of scarlet blood and golden licence, and languishes in the chill pale dawn of the white man's civilisation. It is the whole Pacific world, more or less. The Simple Life in the raw original is not, by many a long league, as simple and innocent as it is supposed to be, by those new and noisy apostles of a return to Nature, who have never got nearer to the things of the beginning than a week-end up the Thames—but, unsimple and un-innocent as it is, it suits the coloured man better than anything else. Would one, therefore, wish to put back the clock of time, re-establish heathenism and cannibalism over all the Pacific, and see Honolulu, Fiji, Samoa, with their towns and Government Houses, and shops and roads and plantations, leap back to the condition of the still uncivilised western islands, where no man's life is safe, and the law of might is the only law that is known? Hardly. There is no answer to the problem, and no moral to be drawn from it either. But then, you do not draw morals in the South Seas—they are not plentiful enough.

The Society Islands—which were so named in compliment to the Royal Society—lie between 16° and 18° south latitude, and 148° and 158° west longitude. Tahiti itself is much the largest, the driveway round this island being about ninety miles long. Huaheine, Raiatea Murea, Bora-Bora, and the small islands Taha'a and Maitea, are much less important. The only town of the group is Papeëte.

So much, for the serious-minded reader, already mentioned, who knows most things beforehand, and likes his information cut-and-dried. The commoner and more ignorant reader, I will assume, knows no more about Tahiti than I did before I went, and therefore will be glad of amplification.

Sixteen degrees only from the equator is hot—very hot at times—and does not allow of a really cool season, though the months between April and October are slightly less warm than the others, and at night one may sometimes need a blanket. Everything near the equator is a long way from England, and everything on the south side of the line is a very long way, and anything in the Pacific is so far off that it might almost as well be in another star. Tahiti, therefore, is quite, as the Irish say, "at the back of God-speed."

Perhaps that is where much of its charm lies. There is a fascination in remoteness, hard to define, but not on that account less powerful. "So far away!" is a word-spell that has charmed many a sail across the seas, from the days of the seekers after the Golden Fleece till now.

Papeëte was the first of the island towns that I saw, and it is so typical an example of all, that one description may serve for many.

Imagine, then, a long, one-sided street, always known in every group as "the beach." The reason is apparent —it really is a beach with houses attached, rather than a street with a shore close at hand. The stores—roomy, low, wood-built houses, largely composed of verandah— are strung loosely down the length of the street. Flamboyant trees, as large as English beeches, roof in the greater part of the long roadway with a cool canopy of green, spangled by bunches of magnificent scarlet flowers. Almost every house stands in a tangle of brilliant tropical foliage, and the side streets that run off landwards here and there, are more like Botanic Gardens with a few ornamental cottages let loose among them, than prosaic pieces of a town—so richly does the flood of riotous greenery foam up over low fence tops, and brim into unguarded drains and hollows, so gorgeously do the red and white and golden flowers wreathe tall verandah posts, and carpet ugly tin roofs with a kindly tapestry of leaf and bloom. Foot to foot and hand to hand with Nature stands man, in these islands, let him but relax for a moment, and—there!—she has him over the line! . . . Leave Papeëte alone for a couple of years, and you would need an axe to find it, when you came back.

There are a number of hotels in Papeëte—mostly of an indifferent sort, and none too cheap—and there are several large cafés and restaurants, run on lines entirely Parisian, and a crowd of smaller ones, many owned by Chinese, where the the hard-up white may feed at very small cost, pleasantly enough, if he does not ask too many questions about the origin and preparation of his food. There are three local newspapers, and a military band plays in the afternoons, and there are clubs of all kinds, and not a little society, which—being society—is in its essence bound to be uninteresting and flat, even here in the many-coloured South Seas. But under all this, the native life flows on in its own way, and the Tahitian takes his pleasure after his immemorial fashion, as quietly and as lazily as he is allowed. I have spoken hitherto of only one side of the main street. The other, which gives directly on the sea, belongs to the Tahitian life of Tahiti. Here, a green slope of soft grass stretches down to the greener waters of the sparkling lagoon : delicate palms lean over the still sea-mirror, like beauties smiling into a glass ; flamboyant and frangipani trees drop crimson and creamy blooms upon the grass ; and, among the flowers, facing the sea and the ships and the dreamy green lagoon, lie the natives, old and young. They wear the lightest of cotton clothing, scarlet and rose and buttercup-yellow, and white scented flowers are twisted in their hair. Fruits of many colours, and roots and fish, lie beside them. They eat a good part of the day, and their dogs, sleeping blissfully in the shade at their feet, wake up and eat with them now and then. There is plenty for both—no one ever goes short of food in Tahiti, where the pinch of cold and hunger, and the burden of hard, unremitting, unholidayed work are alike unknown. Sometimes the natives wander away to the river that flows through the town, and take a bath in its cool waters; returning later to lounge, and laze, and suck fruit, and dream, on the shores of the lagoon again. The sound of the surf, droning all day long on the coral reef that bars the inner lake of unruffled green from the outer ocean of windy blue, seems to charm them into a soft half-sleep, through which, with open but unseeing eyes, they watch the far-off creaming of the breakers in the sun, and the flutter of huge velvet butterflies among the flowers, and the brown canoes gliding like water-beetles about the tall-masted schooners in the harbour. With sunset comes a cooling of the heated air, and glow-worm lights begin to twinkle through the translucent red walls of the little native houses scattered here and there. It will soon be dark now : after dark, there will be dancing and singing in the house ; later, the sleeping mats will be laid out, and with the moon and the stars glimmering in through the walls upon their still brown faces, the Tahitians will sleep. . . . So, in the sunset, with

> Dark faces, pale against the rosy flame,
> The mild-eyed melancholy lotus-eaters

wander home.

Only a flash in the long cinematograph of the wonderful track that circles the globe, is Tahiti. I cannot tell of Murea, the marvellous island that lies opposite Papeëte, seven and a half miles away, because, during the few days I spent in Tahiti, no boat was going there, and none could be induced to go. So I had to look at Murea's splintered towers and spiring pinnacles, and wonderful purple goblin palaces, floating high among the clouds, from the tantalising distance of Papeëte harbour. Nor could I join some steamer friends in driving round the ninety-mile roadway, as we had intended—stopping in native towns, and seeing something of the inner life of the island—because no one in the capital had any teams for hire just then, and nobody knew when there would be any. Some of us went up the river to see Pierre Loti's bathing pool, and came back rather disappointed, and others drove out to the tomb of Pomare V., three miles from the town. It was a pile of concrete and stone, modelled after European fashions, and not especially interesting.

One of the ladies of the party wandered off with me down the beach, neither of us being interested in the resting-place of the defunct Pomare—and here we found plenty of food for mind and body both. For was not this a pandanus, or screw-pine, which we had read about, overhanging the lagoon, with the quaintest mops of palmy foliage, set on long broomhandles of boughs, and great fruits like pineapples hanging among the leaves, and yellow and scarlet kernels lying thick on the sand below—the tree itself perched up on tall bare wooden stilts formed by the roots, and looking more like something from a comic scene in a pantomime, than a real live piece of vegetation growing on an actual shore? And were not these cocoanuts that lay all about the beach under the leaning palms—nuts such as we had never seen before, big as a horse's head, and smooth green as to outside, but nuts all the same?

A native slipped silently from among the thick trees beside us—a bronze-skinned youth of eighteen or nineteen, dressed only in a light pareo or kilt of blue and white cotton. He stood with hands lightly crossed on his breast, looking at us with the expression of infinite kindliness and good-nature that is so characteristic of the Tahitian race. We signed to him that we wanted to drink, and he smiled comprehendingly, shook his head at the nuts on the ground, and lightly sprang on to the bole of the palm beside us, which slanted a little towards the sea. Up the trunk of that tree, which inclined so slightly that one would not have thought a squirrel could have kept its footing there, walked our native friend, holding on with his feet and hands, and going as easily as a sailor on a Jacob's ladder. Arrived in the crown some seventy feet above, he threw down two or three nuts, and then descended and husked them for us.

Husking a cocoanut is one of the simplest-looking operations in the world, but I have not yet seen the white man who could do it effectively, though every native is apparently born with the trick. A stick is sharply pointed at both ends, and one end is firmly set in the ground. The nut is now taken in the hands, and struck with a hitting and tearing movement combined, on the point of the stick, so as to split the thick, intensely tough covering of dense coir fibre that protects the nut, and rip the latter out. It comes forth white as ivory, about the same shape and size as the brown old nuts that come by ship to England, but much younger and more brittle, for only the smallest of the old nuts, which are not wanted in the islands for copra-making, are generally exported. A large knife is used to crack the top of the nut all round, like an egg-shell, and the drink is ready, a draught of pure water, slightly sweet and just a little aerated, if the nut has been plucked at the right stage. There is no pleasanter or more refreshing draught in the world, and it has not the least likeness to the "milk" contained in the cocoanuts of commerce. No native would drink old nuts such as the latter, for fear of illness, as they are considered both unpleasant and unwholesome. Only half-grown nuts are used for drinking, and even these will sometimes hold a couple of pints of liquid. The water of the young cocoanut is food and drink in one, having much nourishing matter held in solution. On many a long day of hot and weary travel, during the years that followed, I had cause to bless the refreshing and restoring powers of heaven's best gift to man in the tropics, the never-failing cocoanut.

I will not insult the reader by telling him all the uses to which the tree and its various products are put, because those are among the things we have all learned at our first preparatory school ; how the natives in the cocoanut countries make hats and mats and houses, and silver fish-servers and brocaded dressing-gowns, and glacé kid boots with fourteen buttons (I think the list used to run somewhat after that fashion—it is the spirit if not the letter)—all ·out of the simple cocoanut tree ; a piece of knowledge which, somehow or other, used to make us feel vaguely virtuous and deserving, as if we had done it all ourselves. . . .

But all this time the youth is standing like a smiling bronze statue, holding the great ivory cup in his hands, and waiting for us to drink. We do so in turn, Ganymede carefully supporting the cup in his upcurved hands, and tilting it with a fine regard for our needs, as the water drops down in the nut like the tide on a sandy shore when the moon calls back the sea.

Then we take out purses, and want to pay Ganymede; but he will not be paid, until it becomes plain to him that the greatest politeness lies in yielding. He takes our franc, and disappears among the trees, to return no more. But in a minute, out from the bush comes running the oddest little figure, a very old, grey-bearded man, very gaily dressed in a green shirt and a lilac pareo, and laden very heavily with ripe pineapples. We guess him to be Ganymede's father, and see that our guess was right, when he drops the whole heap of fruit upon the ground at our feet, smiling and bowing and murmuring incomprehensively over it, and then begins to vanish like his son.

"Here—stop!" calls my companion. "We don't want to take your fruit without buying it. Come back, please come back!"

The little old gentleman trots back on his thin bare legs, recalled more by the tone than the words, which he obviously does not understand, and takes a hand of each of us in his own brown fingers. He shakes hands with us gently and firmly, shaking his head negatively at the same time, and then, like the romantic youths of Early Victorian novels, "turns, and is immediately lost to view in the surrounding forest," carrying the honours of war, indubitably, with himself.

"Well, they are real generous!" declares my American companion, as we go back to the tomb. "By the way, Miss G——, I guess you'd better not sit down on that grass to wait for the rest. I wouldn't, if I was you."

"Why not? it's as dry as dust."

"Because the natives say it's somehow or other—they

didn't explain how—infected with leprosy, and I guess they ought to know; there's plenty of it all over the Pacific—— I rather thought that would hit you where you lived."

It did. I got up as quickly as a grasshopper in a hurry. Afterwards, on a leper island thousands of miles away from Tahiti—— But that belongs to another place.

L——, the ever-amiable, our half-caste landlady at the little bungalow hotel, all overgrown with bougainvillea and stephanotis, was grieved because we had seen nothing in the way of "sights," and declared her intention of giving a native dinner for us.

It was not very native, but it was very amusing. It took place in the verandah of the hotel, under a galaxy of Chinese lanterns, with an admiring audience of natives crowding the whole roadway outside, and climbing up the trees to look at us. This was principally because the word had gone forth in Papeëte (which owns the finest gossip-market in the South Seas) that the English and American visitors were going to appear in native dress, and nobody knew quite how far they meant to go—there being two or three sorts of costume which pass under that classification.

The variety which we selected, however, was not very sensational. The ladies borrowed from L——'s inexhaustible store, draped themselves in one or other of her flowing nightdress robes, let loose their hair, and crowned themselves with twisted Tahitian coronets of gardenia and tuberose. A scarlet flower behind each ear completed the dress, and drew forth delighted squeaks from the handmaidens of the hotel, and digs in the ribs from L——, who was nearly out of her mind with excitement and enjoyment. Shoes were retained, contrary to L——'s

A NATIVE DINNER

entreaties, but corsets she would not permit, nor would she allow a hairpin or hair-ribbon among the party. The men guests wore white drill suits with a native pareo, scarlet or yellow, tied round the waist. It was a gay-looking party, on the whole, and the populace of Tahiti seemed to enjoy the sight.

The dinner was served at a table, but most of the dishes were on green leaves instead of plates, and L—— begged us, almost with tears in her eyes, to eat the native dainties with our fingers, as they tasted better that way. Little gold-fish, baked and served with cocoanut sauce, were among the items on the menu : sucking-pig, cooked in a hole in the ground, fat little river crayfish, breadfruit baked and served hot, with (I regret to say) European butter, native puddings made of banana and breadfruit, and the famous raw fish. Some of the guests would not touch the latter, but the rest of us thought it no worse than raw oysters, and sampled it, with much enjoyment. I give the receipt, for the benefit of any one who may care to try it. Take any good white fish, cut it up into pieces about two inches long, and place the latter, raw, in lime-juice squeezed from fresh limes, or lemon-juice, if limes are not to be had. Let the fish steep for half a day, and serve it cold, with cocoanut sauce, the receipt for which is as follows :—Grate down the meat of a large cocoanut, and pour a small cup of sea-water over it. Leave it for three or four hours, and then strain several times through muslin (the fine brown fibre off young cocoanut shoots is a correct material, but the reader may not have a cocoanut in his back garden). The water should at last come out as thick and opaque as cream.

This is the true " milk of the cocoanut " about which one so often hears. It is of immemorial antiquity in the South Seas.

Captain Cook mentions it in his *Voyages*, and describes the cocoanut shells full of it, that were given to every man at a feast, in which to dip his food. When used as a sauce for meat or fish, one or two fresh red peppers from the nearest pepper bush are cut up and put in. Chili pepper, judiciously used, is a fair substitute for the latter. The sauce is also used for many native puddings and sweet dishes, in which case it is made with fresh water and the pepper is left out. As a fish sauce it is unsurpassed, and may be recommended to gourmands as a new sensation. It should be served in bowls of brown cocoanut shell.

Breadfruit some of us tasted for the first time at this dinner. It was universally liked, though a few maintained that it resembled potato more than bread. I found it very like the latter, with a suggestion of floury cracknel biscuit. It is most satisfying and nourishing. One never, in island travels, feels the want of fresh bread when breadfruit is availiable. L—— had cooked it native fashion, peeled and baked on hot stones in a pit in the ground. It is a good-sized fruit in its natural state, about as large as a medium hothouse melon, and bright green in colour. The skin is divided into lizard-like lozenges, and the surface is very rough. Whether it is indigenous to the islands or not, I cannot say, but it was there when Cook came, and it grows wild very freely, providing an immense store of natural food.

Taro we also had, baked native style. It is a plant in use over almost all the Pacific, very easily cultivated and rapidly producing immense bluish-coloured roots, which look like mottled soap when cooked and served. It is extremely dense and heavy, but pleasant to most tastes. The white taro is a less common kind, somewhat lighter.

A TAHITIAN CHEF

The mangoes that were served with the meal (among many other fruits) were of a variety that is generally supposed to be the finest in the world. No mango is so large, so sweet, or so fine in grain, as the mango of Tahiti, and none has less of the turpentine flavour that is so much disliked by newcomers to tropical countries. It is a commonplace of the islands that a mango can only be eaten with comfort in a bath, and many of the guests that evening would not have been sorry for a chance to put the precept into practice, after struggling with one or two mangoes, which were, of course, too solid to be sucked, and much too juicy and sticky not to smear the hands and the face of the consumers disastrously.

L―― gave us many French dishes with our native dinner, to suit all tastes, and gratify her own love of fine cookery, but these would be of little interest to recount. I cannot forget, however, how this true artiste of the kitchen described the menu she had planned, on the morning of the entertainment. She sat down beside me on a sofa to tell the wondrous tale, and, as she recited dish after dish, her voice rose higher and higher, and her great black eyes burned, and she seized me by the arm and almost hugged me in her excitement. When she came to the savouries, tears of genuine emotion rose in her eyes, and at the end of the whole long list, her feelings overcame her like a flood, and, gasping out—" Beignets d'ananas à la Papeëte ; glaces Vénus en Cythère ; fromage――" she cast herself bodily into my arms and sobbed with delight. She was fully fifteen stone, and the weather was exceedingly warm, but I admired her artistic fervour too much to tell her to sit up, and stop crying over my clean muslin (as I should have liked to do), because it seemed to me that L―― was really a true artiste in her own way, and almost worthy to rank, in the history of the kitchen, with Vatel the immortal, who fell upon his sword and died, because the fish was late for the royal dinner.

Of the other evening, when half a dozen guests of mixed nationalities began, through a temptation of the devil, to talk politics at ten o'clock on the verandah—of the fur that, metaphorically speaking, commenced to fly when the American cast the Irish question into the fray, and the Englishman vilified Erin, and the Irishwoman, following the historical precedent, called the Frenchwoman to her aid, and the latter in the prettiest manner in the world, got up and closed her two small hands round the throat of John Bull, and choked him into silence—it would not be necessary to tell, had not the sequel been disastrous to the fair name of our steamship party in Papeëte. For a big banana spider, as big in the body as half a crown, and nearly as hard, came suddenly out from the stephanotis boughs, and, like a famous ancestor, "sat down beside" a lady of the party. This caused the politicians to rush to the aid of the lady, who had of course mounted a chair and begun to scream. The spider proved extremely difficult to kill, and had to be battered with the legs of chairs for some time before he yielded up the ghost—one guest, who found an empty whisky bottle, and flattened the creature out with it, carrying off the honours of the fray. After which excitement, we all felt ready for bed, and went.

"And in the morning, behold" the kindly L—— smiling upon her guests, and remarking : "Dat was a real big drunk you all having on the verandah, after I gone to bed!"

"Good heavens, L——!" exclaims Mrs. New England, pale with horror, "what do you mean?"

"Surely, Mrs. L——, you do not suppose for an

instant any of our party were—I can hardly say it!" expostulates a delicate-looking minister from the Southern States, here for his lungs, who was very prominent last night in arguing Ireland's right to "secede" if she liked.

"That's a good one, I must say," remarks John Bull, rather indignantly.

But L—— only smiles on. She is always smiling.

"Dat don't go, Mr. ——" she says pleasantly. "I couldn't sleep last night, for the way you all kicking up, and the girl, she say you fighting. Madame —— she trying to kill Mr. Bull, all the gentlemen smashing the leg of the chairs, the lady scream—and dis mornin,' I findin' a large whisky bottle, all drunk up."

I am privately choking with laughter in a corner, but I cannot help feeling sorry for Mrs. New England, who really looks as if about to faint.

"*I* don' mind!" declares L—— delightedly. "Why, I been thinking all dis time you haven't been enjoyin' yourself at all. I like every one here they having a real good time. Every one," she smiles—and melts away into the soft gloom of the drawing-room, where she sits down, and begins to play softly thrumming, strangely intoxicating Tahitian dance music on the piano.

"*Elle est impayable!*" says the Frenchwoman, shrugging her shoulders. "From all I hear of Tahiti, my dear friends, I think you shall find yourselves without a chiffon of character to-morrow. . . . But courage! it is a thing here the most superfluous."

Madame was a true prophet, I have reason to know; for many months after, the story of the orgy, held on L——'s verandah by the English and French and American ladies and gentlemen, reached me in a remote corner of the Pacific, as "the latest from Papeëte." What I wanted to know, and what I never shall know, for my boat came in next day, and took me away to Raratonga—was whether the minister from the South eventually died of the shock or not. I do not want to know about the lady from New England, because I am quite certain she did—as certain as I am that I should have, myself, and did not.

Of the prospects in Tahiti for settlers I cannot say much. It was said, while I was in Papeëte, that there was practically no money in the place, and the traders, like the Scilly Island washerfolk of well-known fame, merely existed by trading with each other. This may have been an exaggeration, or a temporary state of depression. The vanilla trade, owing to a newly invented chemical substitute, was not doing well, but judging by what I saw next year in Fiji, the market must have recovered. The climate of Tahiti is matchless for vanilla growing, and land is not very difficult to get.

Quite a number of small schooners seemed to be engaged in the pearling trade with the Paumotus—a group of islands covering over a thousand miles of sea, and including some of the richest pearl beds in the world—(French property). I never coveted anything more than I coveted those dainty little vessels. Built in San Francisco, where people know how to build schooners, they were finished like yachts, and their snowy spread of cotton-cloth canvas, when they put out to sea, and their graceful bird-like lines, would have delighted the soul of Clarke Russell. One, a thirty-ton vessel, with the neatest little saloon in the world, fitted with shelves for trading; and a captain's cabin like a miniature liner stateroom, and a toy-like galley forward, with a battery of shining saucepans, and a spotless stove—snowy paint on hull and deckhouses, lightened with lines of turquoise blue—splendid spiring masts, varnished till they shone—

AN ISLAND SCHOONER   43

cool white awning over the poop, and sparkling brasses about the compass and the wheel, was so completely a craft after my own heart that I longed to run away with her, or take her off in my trunk to play with—she seemed quite small enough, though her "beat" covered many thousand miles of sea. Poor little *Maid of the Islands*! Her bones are bleaching on a coral reef among the perilous pearl atolls, this two years past, and her captain—the cheerful, trim, good-natured X——, who could squeeze more knots an hour out of his little craft than any other master in the port save one, and could tell more lies about the Pacific in half an hour, than any one from Chili to New Guinea—of his bones are coral made, down where the giant clam swings his cruel valves together on wandering fish or streaming weed, or limb of luckless diver, and where the dark tentacles of the great Polynesian devil-fish

> Winnow with giant arms the slumbering green.

The pitcher that goes to the well, and the schooner that goes to the pearl islands, are apt to meet with the same fate, in time. Nevertheless, tales about the Paumotus are many, and interesting enough to attract adventurers from far, if they were known. How the rumour of a big pearl gets out; how a schooner sets forth to run down the game, pursues it through shifting report after report, from native exaggeration to native denial, perhaps for months; how it is found at last, and triumphantly secured for a price not a tenth its worth; how one shipload of shell, bought on speculation, will have a fortune in the first handful, and the next will yield no more than the value of the shell itself—this, and much else, make good hearing.

"Look at that pearl," said a schooner captain to me

one day, showing me a little globe of light the size of a pea, and as round as a marble. "I hunted that for a year, off and on. The native that had it lived way off from anywhere, but he knew a thing or two, and he wouldn't part. I offered him goods, I offered him gin, I offered him twenty pounds cash, but it was all no go. How d'you think I got it at last? Well, I'll tell you. I went up to his island with the twenty pounds in a sack, all in small silver, and when I came into his house, I poured it all out in a heap on the mats. "Ai, ai, ai!" he says, and drops down on his knees in front of it—it looked like a fortune to him. "Will you sell now?" says I, and by Jove, he did, and I carried it off with me. Worth? Can't say yet, but it'll run well into three figures."

The pearling in the French islands is strictly preserved, and the terms on which it is obtainable are not known to me. Poaching is a crime not by any means unheard of. A glance at the map, and the extent of the Paumotu group, will explain better than words why the policing of the pearl bed must necessarily be incomplete.

The steamer came in in due course, and carried me away to the Cook Islands. Huaheine and Raiatea, in the Society group, were called at on the way, but Bora-Bora was left out, as it is not a regular port of call. I am glad I did not land on Bora-Bora, and I never shall, if I can help it. No place in the world could be so like a fairy dream as Bora-Bora looked in the distance. It was literally a castle in the air; battlements and turrets, built of vaporous blue clouds, springing steep and impregnable from the diamond-dusted sea to the violet vault of heaven. Fairy princesses lived there, one could not but know; dragons lurked in the dark caves low down on the shore, and "magic casements, opening on the foam of perilous seas," looked down from those far blue pinnacles.

Perhaps there is a village on Bora-Bora, with a dozen traders, and an ugly concrete house or two, tin-roofed, defacing the beauty of the palm-woven native homes, and a whitewashed church with European windows, and a school where the pretty native girls are taught to plait back their flowing hair, and lay aside their scented wreaths of jessamine and orange-blossom.

But if all these things are there, at least I do not know it, and Bora-Bora can still remain to me my island of Tir-na'n-Oge—the fabled country which the mariners of ancient Ireland sought through long ages of wandering, and only saw upon the far horizon, never, through all the years, setting foot upon the strand that they knew to be the fairest in the world. If they had ever indeed landed there. . . . But it is best for all of us to see our Tir-na'n-Oge only in the far away.

> Le seul rêve, intéresse,
> Vivre sans rêve, qu'est'ce ?
> Moi, J'aime la Princesse
> Lointaine.

CHAPTER III

Is It the Loveliest?—How they deal with the Beachcomber—Cockroaches and Local Colour—The Robinson Crusoe Steamer—Emigrating to the South Seas—The Lands of Plenty—How to get an Island.

EVERY ONE has seen Raratonga, though few travellers have looked on it with their own mortal eyes.

Close your eyelids, and picture to yourself a South Sea Island, of the kind that you used to imagine on holiday afternoons long ago, when you wandered off down to the shore alone, to sit in a cave and look seaward, and fancy yourself Crusoe or Selkirk, and think the "long, long thoughts" of youth. Dagger-shaped peaks, of splendid purple and gorgeous green, set in a sky of flaming sapphire—sheer grey precipices, veiled with dropping wreaths of flowery vine and creeper—gossamer shreds of cloud, garlanding untrodden heights, high above an ocean of stainless blue—shadowy gorges, sweeping shoreward from the unseen heart of the hills—white foam breaking upon white sand on the beach, and sparkling sails afloat in the bay—is not this the picture that wanders ever among

> The gleams and glooms that dart
> Across the schoolboy's brain?

It is not very like the average South Sea Island on the whole—but it is a faithful portrait of Raratonga, the jewel of the Southern Seas.

JUST ADMINISTRATION 47

Nothing is more hotly disputed than the claims of the many beautiful islands among the numberless groups of the Pacific to the crown of supremest loveliness. Tahiti is awarded the apple of Paris by many, Honolulu by a few, Samoa by all who have been there and nowhere else. The few who have seen the quaint loveliness of Manahiki, or Humphrey Island, uphold its claims among the highest, and for myself, I have never been quite certain whether the low atoll islands are not more lovely than all else, because of their matchless colouring. But, if one pins one's faith to the high islands, the accepted type of Pacific loveliness, there is nothing more beautiful between 'Frisco and Sydney, Yokohama and Cape Horn, than Raratonga, chief island of the Cook archipelago.

These islands lie some sixteen hundred miles northeast of New Zealand, and about six hundred miles to the westward of Tahiti. They are eight in number, seven inhabited, and one uninhabited, and cover about a hundred and sixty miles of sea. The largest, Atiu, is about thirty miles round, Raratonga, which is the principal island, containing the seat of government and the only "white" town, is twenty miles in circumference.

The whole group, as well as a number of outlying islands as much as six and seven hundred miles away, is under the guardianship of the Resident Commissioner appointed by New Zealand, to which colony the islands were annexed in 1900. The government, as administered by Colonel Gudgeon, a soldier who won much distinction in the days of the New Zealand Maori wars, is all that could be desired. The beachcomber element, which is so unpleasantly in evidence in other groups, has been sternly discouraged in the Cook Islands, the Commissioner having the right to deport any one whose presence seems undesirable to the cause of the general good. It is a right not infrequently used. During my stay in the island, two doubtful characters, recently come, were suspected of having committed a robbery that took place in the town. There was practically no one else on the island who could have done the deed, or would—but direct evidence connecting the strangers with the crime was not to be had. Under these circumstances, the Commissioner simply deported the men by the next steamer, giving no reason beyond the fact that they were without means of support. There were no more thefts. The colonel might, in the same manner, have ordered myself away by the next steamer, and compelled it to carry me to New Zealand, if he had had reason to suppose that I was likely to disturb the peace of the island in any way, or incite it to violence or crime. The doctor—also a Government official—was empowered to regulate the amount of liquor consumed by any resident, if it appeared to exceed the permitted amount—two bottles of spirits a week. Under these circumstances, one would expect Raratonga to be a little Arcadia of innocence and virtue. If it was not quite that, it was, and is, a credit to British Colonial rule, in all things essential.

Before the annexation, the government was chiefly in the hands of the Protestant missionaries, who, with the best intentions in the world, carried things decidedly too far in the way of grandmotherly laws. Even white men were forbidden to be out of doors after eight o'clock in the evening, on pain of a heavy fine, and the offences for which the natives were fined would be incredible, were they not recorded in the Governmental reports of New Zealand. In Raratonga of the older days (not yet ten years past) a native who walked at dusk along the road with his sweetheart, his arm round her waist after the manner of sweethearts all the world over, was obliged to carry a burning torch in his hand, and was fined if he let it go out. If he was found weeping over the grave of a woman to whom he was not related (surely the strangest crime in the world) he was again brought up and fined. These are only samples of the vagaries of irresponsible missionary rule, but they go far to prove that spiritual and temporal legislation are better kept apart.

A Government accommodation house had been planned, but not built, when I visited Raratonga, so I arranged, on landing, to take an unused house by the week, and "do for" myself, as there seemed no other way of living. Scarcely had I taken possession of my quarters, however, when the residents came down to call, and invite me to stay in their house. I did not know any of them, and they did not know me, but that did not matter—we were not in chilly England, where a whole country-side must discuss your personal history, family connections, probable income, and religious views, for a good six months, before deciding whether you are likely to be an acquisition or not, and calling accordingly. I began to understand, now, the meaning of the term "colonial hospitality," which had formerly fallen on uncomprehending ears. And when I was settled down that evening in the most delightful of bungalow houses, with a charming host and hostess, and a pretty daughter, all doing their best to make me feel at home, I realised that I was about to see something of the true island life at last.

It began rather sooner than I could have wished. When my new friends had gone to bed, and left me sitting up alone in the hall to write letters for the morning's mail, the local colour commenced to lay itself on somewhat more rapidly and thickly than I desired. I am not particularly nervous about insects, but it is trying, when one is quite new to the tropics, to see a horde of cockroaches as large as mice, with fearsome waving horns, suddenly appear from nowhere, and proceed to overrun the walls and floor, with a hideous ticking noise. And when one has steeled oneself to endure this horrid spectacle, it is still more trying to be shocked by the silent irruption of dozens of brown hairy hunting-spiders, each big enough to straddle over a saucer, which dart about the walls on their eight agile legs, and slay and eat the beetles, crunching audibly in the silence of the night. . . . Truly, it was like a waking nightmare.

Those cockroaches! What I suffered from them, during the year or two of island travel that followed! How they spoiled my tea, and ate my dresses (or parts of them), and flew into my hair of moonlight nights, and climbed into my berth on shipboard! It was on a liner that shall be nameless, very early in the course of my wanderings, that I first discovered the tendency of the cockroach to share the voyager's couch unasked, and never again did I know unvexed and trustful sleep aboard a tropic ship. It was a moonlight night, and I was lying looking peacefully at the brilliantly silvered circle of my port, when suddenly a horrid head, with waving feelers, lifted itself over the edge of my berth and stared me coldly in the face. I hit out, like the virtuous hero in a novel, and struck it straight between the eyes, and it dropped to the floor with a dull, sickening thud, and lay there very still. I thought gloatingly of how the blood would trickle out under my door in the morning in a slow hideous stream, and how the stewardess, bringing my early tea, would start and stop, and say in an awestruck tone that one that night had met his doom—and so thinking, I fell asleep.

I woke, with one cockroach in my hair, chewing a plait, and another nibbling my heel. I got up and looked round. It was then that I wished I had never come away from home, and that, since I had come, my sex forbade me to go and berth in the hold. I was convinced that, if I could have done so, I should have had a quiet night, because the hold is the part of a ship where the cockroaches come from, and they had all *come*—they were on the floor of my cabin, and sitting about the quilt.

The hideous battle raged all night, and in the morning I asked one of the mates for an axe, to help me through the coming renewal of hostilities. He recommended boracic acid instead, and I may record, for the benefit of other travellers, that I really found it of some use.

To find out, as far as possible, what were the prospects for settlers in some of the principal Pacific groups, was the main object of my journey to the Islands. It had always seemed to me that the practical side of Pacific life received singularly little attention, in most books of travel. One could never find out how a living was to be made in the island world, what the cost of housekeeping might be, what sort of society might be expected, whether the climates were healthy, and so forth—matters prosaic enough, but often of more interest to readers than the scenic descriptions and historical essays that run naturally from the pen of any South Sea traveller.

Certainly, the romantic and picturesque side of the islands is so obvious that it takes some determination, and a good deal of actual hard work, to obtain any other impressions whatever. But white human beings, even in the islands, cannot live on romance alone, and many people, in Britain and elsewhere, are always anxious to know how the delightful dream of living in the South Seas may be realised. Practical details about island life, therefore, will take up the most of the present chapter, and readers who prefer the lighter and more romantic vein, must turn the pages a little further on.

The number of those who wish to settle in the Pacific is by no means small.

The Pacific Ocean has always had a special interest for the English, from the days of Drake's daring circumnavigation, through the times of Captain Cook and the somewhat misunderstood Bligh, of the *Bounty*, down to the dawn of the twentieth century. The very name of the South Seas reeks of adventure and romance. Every boy at school has dreams of coral islands and rakish schooners, sharks and pearls ; most men retain a shamefaced fancy for stories of peril and adventure in that magical South Sea world, of whose charm and beauty every one has heard, although very few are fortunate enough to see it with their own bodily eyes. For the Pacific Islands are, both in point of time and distance, about the remotest spots on the surface of the globe, and they are also among the most costly for the ordinary traveller to reach. Thus, for the most part, the South Sea dream, which so many hot-blooded young Saxons cherish, remains a dream only. The youth who has a fancy for Canadian farming life, or for stock-raising in Australasia, may gratify his desire with the full approval of parents and guardians in private life, and of Empire-builders in high places. But the British possessions in the South Seas—and what extensive possessions they are let Colonial maps prove—may cry out for settlers from the rainy season to the dry, and round again to the rainy

THE CALL FOR SETTLERS 53

season once more, without attracting a single colonist of the right kind.

What is the reason of this? Where is the broken link? The British Pacific Islands need settlers; young Britons at home are only too ready to adventure themselves. Why do they not? There are several reasons. The first, perhaps, is that neither party can hear the other. In England few possess any information about the South Sea Islands. In the Pacific the white residents (almost all New Zealand traders and Government officials) are possessed with an idea that only wastrels of the worst kind drift out from England to the South Seas, and that nothing better is to be looked for. The result is that at the present date young Englishmen by the hundred are losing their small capital as "pupils" on Canadian farms, or are starving on the roads in South Africa, while all the time the South Sea Islands hold out hands of peace and plenty, begging humbly for a respectable white population. The brown races are dying out with fearful rapidity; at their best they never touched the limitless capacities of the golden Pacific soil. Its richness has always seemed to the original inhabitants an excellent reason for abstaining from cultivation. When the earth produced of itself everything that was necessary for comfort, why trouble to work it? Now, however, when so many groups of fertile islands have fallen into the hands of more progressive nations, things are changed. The white man can live happily and healthily in the Pacific; he can obtain a good return for a small capital at the best, and at the worst cannot possibly suffer from either cold or hunger, since neither exists in the South Seas. He can lease or buy land from the natives at slight cost, work it with small labour, and sell the product to a sure market. Honesty, sobriety, and industry repay their possessor as almost nowhere else in the world. Yet, with all this, the white settler in the Pacific Islands is generally of a more or less undesirable kind.

The " beachcomber " white, without friends, means, or character ; the " remittance man," paid to keep as far away from home as possible ; the travelling ne'er-do-well, with a taste for novelties in dissipation, and a fancy for being outside the limit of Press and post—all these are familiar figures in the Pacific. Kipling's Lost Legion musters there by the score ; the living ghosts of men whose memorial tablets are blinking white on the walls of English country churches, walk by daylight along the coral beaches. Only the steady man, the young energetic man with a future and without a past, the man who can get on without a three-weekly spree of the most torrid kind, commonly keep away. And these are just the men that the " Islands " want. Local trading interest, religious and otherwise, often does its best to keep them from coming, through a natural, if scarcely praiseworthy, desire to retain personal hold of everything worth holding. The Governmental party of every group desires the respectable settler with a little capital, and expresses its desire, as a rule, in gentle wails delivered through Governmental reports—a method about as effective as putting one's head into a cupboard to hail a 'bus in the street. The Press does not recognise the existence of any habitable land in the Pacific, outside Honolulu and Samoa. So the dead lock continues.

I can see the Left Behind in the office raise his head at this, and look through the muddy panes of the counting-house window, or across the piles of summer goods on the shop counters, out beyond the clanging street, and right through the whole round world to the far-away Pacific lands. He wants to get away so very badly, that poor

IDLERS NEED NOT APPLY

Left Behind, and he does not quite see his way to do it, because every one discourages him if he hints at the subject, and he does not know how one could make a living, out in those fairy lands that he wishes so much to see. Well, I am on his side in this matter. If it is a crime to long for a glimpse of the wonderful island world, to ache for a life spent under the free winds of heaven, and a chance of the danger, adventure, and excitement, which are as strong wine to the heart of almost every young Englishman—then it is a crime shared by the best that the nation has ever known, and one which has done more to build up the empire than all the parochial virtues ever owned by a million Young Men's Improvement Societies put together.

The Islands are not the place for the ne'er-do-well, and I would also warn the exasperating young man, who never did a square day's work in his life, never got into trouble with his employers or his superiors, but always found himself misunderstood, unappreciated, and incomprehensibly "sacked," with an excellent character, at the first hint of slacking business—that the islands will not suit him either. If he comes out, he will not starve or go to the workhouse, because you cannot die of hunger where there is always enough vegetable food to keep the laziest alive, and you do not need workhouses, under the same happy conditions—but he will "go native," and there are some who would say he had better starve, a good deal. There are men who have "gone native" in most of the Pacific groups, living in the palm-leaf huts with the villagers—but a white man in a waist-cloth and a bush of long hair, sleeping on a mat and living on wild fruit and scraps given by the generous natives, drunk half the time and infinitely lower, in his soberest hours, than the coloured folk who unwisely put up with him, is not a happy spectacle.

The Cook Islands, which may be taken as a sample of many other groups, are small to look at on the map, and not over large, when one counts up the number of square miles. But one cannot fairly estimate the value of island land by its extent. Much of it is so rich that every foot has its worth, and that is by no means despicable. And, in any case, there is plenty available for the small cultivator—the man who has only a few hundred pounds, and cannot afford to do things on the colossal scale that makes big fortunes.

Among the productions of the group are pineapples, custard apples, coffee, tobacco, pepper, mammee-apple or paw-paw, granadilla, cocoa, cotton, vanilla, limes, lemons, oranges, bananas, castor-oil, and many other useful plants, besides a number of excellent vegetables, not known to most Europeans. Many of the fruits above mentioned grow practically wild. Bananas come to bearing in fifteen months, cocoanuts in seven years, limes in four or five. The water supply is good all round, and there is a monthly steamer from Auckland.

The land in all the islands belongs to the natives, and cannot usually be bought outright. Leases of any length can, however, be secured at very low rates, with the New Zealand Government laws, administered through the Resident, to back up the titles, so that a man who plants cocoanuts—the safest of island products—may be sure that his children and grandchildren will enjoy the fruits of his labour.

In most of the outer islands the natives cannot use more than a small fraction of the land, and are quite willing to let large sections at a shilling or two an acre. In Raratonga, the chief island, there has been more demand for land, and prices are consequently higher; also, the chiefs are not always ready to let, even though

SMALL CAPITAL NECESSARY 57

they do not use what they have. It may be said, however, of the group as a whole, that there is land, and a prospect of a good return for capital, ready for any reasonable number of settlers, if they bring habits of industry and a determination to succeed along with them.

There are two classes of possible settlers to be considered—the man with capital, and the man without.

How much does it take to start a man as a planter, and what return can he expect?

Taking the Cook Islands as a general example (but by no means suggesting that the resources of the Pacific begin and end there) the young Englishman wishing to seek his fortune as a planter should have at least £500 to start on, exclusive of passage-money. He can do excellently with a few hundreds more, but it is as well to put things as low as possible. Copra—the dried kernel of the cocoanut—is the usual, and the safest, investment. It it is always saleable, and the demand increases year by year—so much so, that the large soapmaking firms, who are the chief users of the product, are of late planting out islands for themselves. The cost of clearing and planting the land is about £5 an acre. The rent, in the outer islands, should not exceed a couple of shillings an acre. In about seven years, the returns begin to come in, and in ten years' time the land should be bringing in £5 net profit for every acre of trees. This is, of course, a long time to wait, but bananas can grow on the same land meantime, and will generally yield a quick return. Once the cocoanuts start bearing, they go on for sixty years or more, so that a copra plantation is one of the best investments for a man who has others to come after him.

Banana growing may be managed with less capital, but the profits are not so sure, since fruit is perishable, and cannot wait for the steamer as copra can. Coffee has been grown, but is not of late years doing well, because of something like a "ring" formed in New Zealand to lower the prices. Cotton used to do excellently, and I have never heard any satisfactory reason against its being taken up afresh. It is running wild in a good many parts of the group. The plants above mentioned, however, by no means exhaust the resources of the islands, which are suitable for growing anything that will live in the tropics, and are fortunately not subject to the destructive hurricanes that from time to time do so much damage in Tahiti and the Fijis. Hurricanes are not absolutely unknown, but they are very rare, and not of the worst kind.

The cost of living is not very serious, but it must not be supposed that the settlers can live decently and like white men, on nothing a year. A house costs something to put up, and furniture to a certain small amount is necessary, clothes do not grow on the cocoanut tree, nor do lamps and kerosene, or tools and nails, or fishing lines, or flour and bacon and tea and tinned butter, and the few groceries that the settler may need. Still, with care, a single man can live quite respectably on fifty pounds a year, and enjoy, in all probability, better health than he has had at home.

What the time of waiting will cost the copra planter, each one must work out for himself. He will do best to spend his capital gradually, planting as he can afford. The returns will come in only by degrees, but he will be saved the mortification of seeing a promising plantation leave his possession for a third of its value, simply because he cannot afford to wait until the profits begin.

Copra, the chief article of commerce of the Pacific, is very easily prepared. The cocoanuts, when ripe, are husked, and emptied, and the kernels, as a rule, left to dry in the sun, though some few planters use artificial heat. Bagging is the only other operation necessary.

Bananas are often shipped clumsily and carelessly, in unprotected bunches. It would be much better to pack them in leaves and crate them, as is done in the Canary Islands, where the banana trade is the principal support of the country. Oranges are usually shipped in crates. They grow wild all over the Cook group, and are not attended to in any way, but in spite of this, the orange trade with New Zealand is by no means despicable.

Vanilla is not cultivated for market in these islands, but it would probably repay the experimenter. It does well in most of the Pacific groups, and the returns begin in three years from planting.

Island planters, as a race, seem to be the most conservative of men, and very shy of trying anything new and unproved. There are, of course, good reasons for this, but there are also excellent arguments in favour of exploiting fresh fields. The following brief hints may prove fruitful to enterprising minds.

Only one kind of banana—the sort familiar at home—is usually grown for trade. There are many varieties, however, and some of the very best travel quite as well as the commonplace "China" sort. The large red banana, sometimes called the Aitutaki banana, sometimes the peach banana, on account of its delicate peach-like flavour, is a fruit that would become the fashion at once, if it could be put on the market. One or two planters have gone so far as to send consignments down to New Zealand, but, finding that these did not sell on account of the unusual colour of the fruit, they never made another attempt. At the time of my visit, in 1904, the red banana was practically unobtainable in

New Zealand or Australia. A little intelligent co-operation on the part of the buyers would probably get over the difficulty.

The same may be said of limes, a fruit which grows wild very freely. The lime is like a small, round-shaped lemon, and is not an attractive fruit in appearance. It also suffers under the disadvantage of being very badly represented as to flavour by the bottled "shop" lime-juice, with which the taste of the fresh lime has hardly anything in common. Where it can be obtained fresh, however, no one ever thinks of using lemon as a flavouring in food or drink. The lime is incomparably more delicate and refreshing than the best lemon ever grown. For some unknown reason, however, it is not used in New Zealand, or in the cities of Australia, to which it could be easily and profitably exported from many of the Pacific groups. Instead, the juice of limes is squeezed out by a very rough process, the fruit being run through a wooden hand-press, and is shipped away in casks. The lime trade would certainly rival the orange trade, if worked up.

Dried bananas have money in them, and the industry is especially adapted to some of the lesser Cook Islands, where steamer calls are at present irregular. The dried and pressed banana is better than the fig, and is considered a great delicacy by the few people in the colonies who have tried it. The Cook Islanders peel the fruit, and leave it to dry in the sun. When it is shrunk, dark, and sticky with its own sugar, they compress it into neat little packets covered with dried banana leaf, and tied with banana fibre. These will keep good for many months. Up to the present, the trade is extremely small, but there is no reason why it should not be increased.

POSSIBILITIES

One of the chief troubles of the settler is the guava bush, which runs wild all over the islands, and is extremely hard to destroy. It bears quantities of excellent fruit, but guavas do not pay for exporting, so no one, apparently, has thought of making the island pest profitable. And yet, when I went down to New Zealand, which is in direct communication with the Cook Islands and less than a week away, I found the price of guava jelly in the shops was higher than it is at home. Asked why no one in the islands sent jelly for sale, the grocers said it was because jampots were not made in New Zealand, and had to be imported if wanted. Since most jams in the colonies are sold in tins, this did not appear to me an unanswerable argument. Tins are made in the colonies, and the process of tinning jam or jelly should not be beyond amateur powers. Moreover, common tumblers (which are also made in New Zealand) are a good and profitable way of putting up jellies; purchasers are always willing to pay extra for the advantage of getting something useful along with the dainty itself.

Another item: Dried peppers bring a good price per ounce, and fine Chili pepper grows wild everywhere. So far, trade is nil.

Another: One of the commonest plants in the Southern Pacific, a weed bearing a bright red flower almost exactly like the pine-cone in shape, contains, in the flower, a quantity of white watery liquid, which is declared by the natives, and by many of the whites, to be an exceptionally fine hair tonic. No one, so far as I know, has tried to make anything out of this, or out of the wild castor oil, which is said to be of good quality.

If the settler cannot find some useful hint among these, he may be able to discover a few on the spot for himself.

The second class of settler—the man without capital, or with only a little—is a pariah everywhere. No colony wants him, agents warn him away, friends write to him begging him to stay where he is, and not tempt fortune by going out unprovided with plenty of cash. No doubt there is reason on the side of the discouragers; but there is not a colony in the world, all the same, where you shall not find the man who came out without capital, who endured a few years of hard work and short commons, began to get on, began to save, went on getting on and saving, and by-and-by became one of the most successful men in the place. Whereupon as a rule he becomes an adviser in his turn, and solemnly counsels young men of every kind against the imprudence of tempting fortune with an empty purse.

For all that, and all that, young Britons will continue to do what they are advised not to, and ships will carry out many a man to the far wild countries whose only gold is the gold of youth and health and a brave heart. "Sink or swim" is the motto of this kind of colonist, and if he often goes under, he very often floats on the top, and comes in on the flood-tide of good luck. "Fortune favours the brave"—a proverb none the less true, because of its age.

To have an island of one's own, in the beautiful South Seas, to live remote from strain and worry, and out of the clash and roar of twentieth-century civilisation—to pass one's days in a land of perpetual summer; work, but own no master, possess a country (small though it may be) yet know none of the troubles of sovereignty—this is an ambition of which no one need be ashamed, even though it appear contemptible and even reprehensible to " Samuel Budgett, the Successful Merchant." The planter with a fair amount of capital can realise the dream almost any

THE MAN WITHOUT MEANS 63

day, for every big group in the Pacific has many small unoccupied islands which can be rented for a song, and if the newcomer is made of stuff that can stand being totally deprived of theatres, clubs, music halls, daily posts and papers, and a good many other charms (or burdens) of city life, he has only to pick and choose, secure a good title to his island, decide what he means to grow on it, get his house built, and settle down at once.

But people who have very little money cherish the same ambition, often enough. There are thousands of men in the United Kingdom to whom a South Sea Island of their own would be heaven—only they see no way of getting it. The desire comes, without doubt, of generations of insular ancestors. It is the "Englishman's house is his castle" idea carried a step further than usual, that is all; and the boy that never wholly dies in the heart of every Briton is always ready to wake up and rejoice at the thought.

What is the moneyless man to do?

Well, first of all, he must get out to Sydney or Auckland, each being a port from which island vessels constantly sail, and with which island trade is closely concerned. It will not cost him so much as he thinks. If he goes by Auckland, he can get a third-class ticket from London for fifteen pounds, and Sydney is little more. Arrived, he will make use of the information he has, of course, obtained in London, from the offices of the Agent-General for New Zealand (or Australia, as the case may be) and try and get a job to keep him on his feet while he looks about. If he can do any kind of manual labour, he will not be at a loss—and if he cannot, or will not, he had much better stay at home on an office stool within sound of Bow Bells, and leave the far countries to men of tougher material.

In Sydney or Auckland he will find a good many firms connected with island trading interests, many of whom own trading stores dotted about the whole Pacific. It is often possible to obtain a job from one of these, if the newcomer is capable and steady. In this case, the way of getting up to the islands is clear, and the work of copra trading, keeping store for native customers, fruit-buying and shipping on the spot, is the best possible training for an independent position. If this proves a vain hope (it need not, in the case of a good man, if one may judge by the wretched incapables who occupy the trader's post in many islands) our adventurer must try to raise the cost of a passage as best he can, and see what he can get to do among the white people of the group he has selected, when he arrives. There are so many useless wastrels in most of the islands, that character and capability are to a certain extent capital in themselves. Some one is generally in want of a plantation overseer to replace a drunken employee—some one else would be glad of a handy man to help with house-building of the simple island kind—and in many islands, board and lodging, and a little over, would be easily obtainable by any educated man, who would undertake to teach the children of the white settlers. There are groups in which no one is allowed to land who does not possess a certain minimum of cash, but it is not in any case that I know of more than ten pounds, and most islands have no such regulation.

Once so far on his journey, the would-be island owner must think out the rest for himself. There is sure to be a small island or two for rent, and there will probably be means of making money by slow degrees in the group itself. Where the will is, the way will be found.

The popular dream of finding and taking possession

of an unoccupied island somewhere or other, and "squatting" there unopposed, is a dream and nothing more. The great European nations have long since parcelled out among themselves all the groups worth having, and rent or purchase is the only way to acquire land. Far-away separate islands, remote from everywhere, are still to be had for nothing in a few instances, but they are not desirable possessions, unless the owner can afford a private sailing vessel, and in any case what has not been picked up is little worth picking in these days.

So much for the how and where of acquiring islands. I shall have one or two definite instances to give in another chapter.

CHAPTER IV

Where are the Six Thousand?—Calling on the Queen—A Victoria of the Pacific—The Prince sleeps softly—The Mystical Power of the Mana—How Islanders can die—A Depressing Palace—Round the Wonderful Roadway—The Home of Queen Tinomana—A Princess's Love Story—Once on Board the Schooner!—The Incredible Crabs—Depravity of a Mor Kiri-kiri.

A HUNDRED years ago, Raratonga had six thousand native inhabitants, and was a very flourishing heathen country, where cannibalism was all the fashion, murder of shipwrecked sailors a common custom, and raids upon neighbouring islands the chief diversion. There is no doubt that the Raratongan of those days compared none too well with the Tahitian, who at the worst never was an habitual cannibal, and was almost always friendly to strangers. Williams was the first missionary to arrive in the earlier part of the last century, and the complete conversion of the island was rapid; the Raratongan in a few years was no longer cannibal, no longer warlike, had become hospitable and friendly to travellers, had learned to wear clothes (a good deal more than he wanted or should have had, but the missionary of the early days really did not know what a fatal thing he was doing, when he enforced the wearing of white man's raiment on the unclothed native, and thereby taught him to catch cold, and die of chest diseases). The island had (and has) a large school for the training of mission teachers, and a church and mission house not to be matched in the Pacific for magnificence, and was on the whole a model

AN UNSOLVED PROBLEM   67

of most of the virtues, compared with what it once had been.

There were, and are, drawbacks to the missionary rule, but these have been discussed so freely in almost every book of Pacific travel ever written, that I do not feel it necessary to say over again what has so often been said before. The missionaries certainly civilised the islands, and made them safe to live in. Concurrently with this desirable result, others not so desirable took place, the fruit, in some cases, of irresponsible authority exercised by semi-educated men; in others, of the inevitable fate that follows the introduction of civilisation to primitive races. The Raratongan, like all the other brown folk of the islands, was asked to leap, almost at once, the gulf between utter savagery and comparative civilisation, that had taken his instructors all the time between the Roman Conquest and the end of the Dark Ages to overpass. With the docility of the true Polynesian, he did his best to comply. It was not his fault—and not, one must fairly say, the fault of the missionary either, save in a minor degree—that the effort meant death to him.

There are not nineteen hundred Raratongans living now in the fertile little country that used to support six thousand of their ancestors. There are not enough babies in the island to carry on the population at half its present level, in the future. Not one of the "chief" families, of whom there are a dozen or so, has any living children at all. Consumption is common, and on the increase; more serious diseases are commoner still. A Raratongan seldom lives to be very old, and he almost always dies without resistance or regret. The islanders are happy and sunny in their own quiet way, but the backbone of life has been broken for them, and in the promise of the future, grey or golden, they have no share. To-day is theirs, but they have no to-morrow.

The Arikis, or chiefs, to whom the principal power once belonged, and who still retain much importance, regret this state of affairs in an amiable, fatalistic way, but do not trouble themselves very much over it. They are for the most part of the opinion of Sir Boyle Roche about the claims of posterity; and anyhow, they have their fruit trading to think about, and the next public dancing and singing party, and the last illegal beer-brewing up in the hills—so the decadence of their country sits lightly on their minds.

These Arikis are one and all inferior to the ruling sovereign, Queen Makea, who still contrives to retain a great deal of quiet power in her shapely old hands, in spite of the fact that she is nominally deposed, and her country owned by New Zealand. I had not been in Raratonga more than a day or two, when my hosts took me to call upon the queen, intimating that she would feel hurt if the newcomer was not presented to her.

We walked through the blazing sun of the tropic afternoon, down the palm-shaded main street of Avarua town, to the great grassy enclosure that surrounds the palace of the queen. One enters through a neat white gate; inside are one or two small houses, a number of palms and flowering bushes, and at the far end, a stately two-storeyed building constructed of whitewashed concrete, with big railed-in verandahs, and handsome arched windows. This is Makea's palace, but her visitors do not go there to look for her. In true South Sea Islander fashion, she keeps a house for show and one for use. The islander, though he aspires when "civilised," to own a big concrete house, "all same papalangi" (white man), does not really like living in a building that shuts out the air. He discovered the fresh-air system long before it was thought of by the folk who discovered him, and his own houses are always made of small poles or saplings, set without any filling, so that the whole building is as airy as a birdcage, and almost as transparent. In this he lives, while the big concrete house, with its Auckland made tables, chairs, and beds, and the red and blue table-cloths, and horrible gilt lamps fringed with cut glass lustres, and shrieking oleograph of King Edward in his coronation robes, is kept strictly for show, and perhaps for an occasional festival, such as a wedding party. It is an odd custom, but sensible, on the whole.

Makea's favourite house is a pretty little reed and thatch villa several miles out in the country. When she is in town, she makes some concession to state by living in a small one-storeyed cottage, with a thatch and a verandah, and not much else, close beside her big palace. We found her at the cottage when we called, sitting on the verandah upon an ironwood couch, and petting a little turtle of which she is very fond. It seems a curious sort of creature to adore, but an elderly lady must have her little pet of some kind. In other climes, it is a pug, a parrot, or a cat. Here, the little turtle is considered chic, so the queen has one, the turtle having been always considered a perquisite of royalty in the old days, when the chiefs had the best of everything, even down to the choicest tit-bits of the roasted enemy, while the commonalty had to put up with what they could get.

I was introduced to the queen, who shook hands politely, and sent one of her handmaids for chairs. These being brought, my hostess and I sat down, and the latter conversed with Makea in Raratongan, translating a few conventional politenesses from myself, and conveying others to me in return. The queen wanted to know how I liked the island, if I had really come all the way from England, as she had heard, whether I was not afraid to travel so far alone, how long I hoped to stay, and so forth. All the time, as we talked, her keen black eyes were scanning me silently, rapidly, comprehensively, and making their own judgment, quite independently of the conversation and its inevitable formalities. And I, on my side, was gazing, I fear with some rudeness, at the very remarkable figure before me.

Makea, since the death of her husband, Prince Ngamaru, a few years ago, has laid aside all vanities of dress, and wears only the simplest of black robes, made loose and flowing from the neck in island fashion. She is supposed to be at least seventy years of age, and she is extremely stout, even for her height, which is well over six feet. Yet a more impressive figure than this aged, deposed, uncrowned sovereign, in her robe of shabby black, I have never seen. Wisdom, kindliness, and dignity are written large on her fine old face, which has more than a touch of resemblance to the late Queen Victoria. And oh, the shrewdness, the ability, the keen judgment of men and things, that look out from those brown, deep-set eyes, handsome enough, even in old age, to hint at the queen-like beauty that once belonged to this island queen!

Makea was always known as a wise, just, and very powerful sovereign. She ruled over the whole Cook group, and her word was law everywhere, even to the Prince Consort, the warlike Ngamaru, who to the very last retained some traces of his heathen upbringing, and used to be seen, in the island councils of only a few years ago, making the horrible cannibal gesture which signifies

A MYSTIC POWER

in unmistakable pantomime, "I will tear the meat from your bones with my teeth!" at any other council member who presumed to disagree with him. Their married life was a happy one, in spite of the prince's violent character, and when he died, the widowed queen took all her splendid robes of velvet, silk, and satin, gorgeously trimmed with gold, tore them in fragments, and cast them into his grave, so that he might lie soft, as befitted the prince who had been loved so well by such a queen.

Makea holds much of the real power in her hands to-day, for all that the islands are the property of the British Crown, and administered by a Commissioner. The Raratongan is submissive to chiefs by nature, and the queen, though uncrowned, is still reverenced and feared almost as much as of old. It is firmly believed that she possesses the mystic power known as "mana" among the Maori races, and this, as it gives the owner power to slay at will, is greatly feared. The word is almost untranslatable, meaning, perhaps, something like "prestige," "kudos," or the old English "glamour." It includes, among other gifts, second sight to a certain extent, the power to bring good or evil luck, and the ability already mentioned to deal death at will.

This last may sound like fiction. It is nothing of the sort, it is plain, bald fact, as any one who has ever lived in the islands can testify. There is nothing more commonly known in the South Seas than the weird power possessed by kings and heroes to slay with a word, and instances of its exercise could be found in every group.

Makea does not use it now, so they say. She is old: like aged folks in other places, she wants to "make her soul," and it can readily be imagined that the mission authorities do not approve of such heathen proceedings. Still, there is not a native in Raratonga who does not believe that she could strike him dead with a wish, any day in the week, if she chose : and there are not a few who can tell you that in the days long ago, she exercised the power.

"Makea, she never rude, because she great chief," said a relation of the royal family to me one day. "She never say to any one, 'You go die!' I think. She only saying, some time, 'I wish I never seeing you again!' and then the people he go away, very sorry, and by-n'-by he die—some day, some week, I don' know—but he dyin' all right, very quick, you bet!"

The power to die at will seems to be a heritage of the island races, though the power to live, when a chief bids them set sail on the dark seas of the unknown, is not theirs. Suicide, carried out without the aid of weapons or poisons of any kind, is not at all uncommon. A man or woman who is tired of life, or bitterly offended with any one, will often lie down on the mats, turn his face, like David of old, to the wall, and simply flicker out like a torch extinguished by the wind. There was once a white schooner captain, who had quarrelled with his native crew ; and the crew, to pay him out, lay down and declared they would die to spite him. . . . But this is about Makea the Queen, not about the godless brutal captain, and the measures he took to prevent his men from taking passage in a body across the Styx. They didn't go after all, and they were sore and sorry men when they made the island port, and the captain, who was a very ill-educated person, boasted far and wide for many a day after that, that he would exceedingly well learn any exceedingly objectionable nigger who offered to go and die on him again—and that is all that I must say about it, for more reasons than one.

The queen, after a little conversation, punctuated by intervals of fanning and smiling (and a more charming smile than Makea's, you might search the whole South Seas to find), sent a girl up a tree for cocoanuts, and offered us the inevitable cocoanut water and bananas, without which no island call is complete. Afterwards, when we rose to go, she sent a handmaid with us to take us over the palace, of which she is, naturally, very proud, though she never enters it except on the rare occasion of some great festival.

The palace proved to be as uninteresting as the queen herself was interesting and attractive. It had a stuffy, shut-up smell, and it was furnished in the worst of European taste, with crude ugly sofas and chairs, tables covered with cheap-jack Manchester trinkets, and staring mirrors and pictures—partly sacred art, of a kind remarkably well calculated to promote the cause of heathenism, and partly portraits, nearly as bad as those one sees in the spring exhibitions at home. There were two or three saloons or drawing-rooms, all much alike, on the lower storey. Upstairs (it is only a very palatial island house that owns an upstairs) there were several bedrooms, furnished with large costly bedsteads of mahogany and other handsome woods, and big massive wardrobes and tables—all unused, and likely to remain so. The place was depressing on the whole, and I was glad to get out of it into the cheerful sun, although the heat at this hour of the afternoon was really outrageous.

Another afternoon, I drove out to see Queen Tinomana, a potentate only second to Makea in influence. Tinomana, like Makea, is a dynastic name, and is always borne by the high chief, man or woman, who is hereditary sovereign of a certain district. The present holder of the title is a woman, and therefore queen.

What a drive it was! The roadway round the island is celebrated all over the Pacific, and with justice, for nothing more lovely than this twenty-mile ribbon of tropic splendour is to be found beneath the Southern Cross. One drives in a buggy of colonial pattern, light, easy-running, and fast, and the rough little island horse makes short work of the miles of dazzling white sandy road that circle the shores of the bright lagoon. On one side rises the forest, green and rich and gorgeous beyond all that the dwellers of the dark North could possibly imagine, and opening now and then to display picture after picture, in a long gallery of magnificent mountain views—mountains blue as the sea, mountains purple as amethyst, mountains sharp like spear-heads, towered and buttressed like grand cathedrals, scarped into grey precipices where a bat could scarcely cling, and cloven into green gorges bright with falling streams. On the other, the palms and thick undergrowth hardly veil the vivid gleam of the emerald lagoon lying within the white-toothed barrier reef, where all day long the surf of the great Pacific creams and froths and pours. By the verge of the coral beach that burns like white fire in the merciless sun, the exquisite ironwood tree trails its delicate tresses above the sand, so that, if you leave the carriage to follow on the road, and walk down by the beach, you shall catch the green glow of the water, and the pearly sparkle of the reef, through a drooping veil of leafage fine as a mermaid's hair. Sometimes the buggy runs for a mile or two through thick woods of this lovely tree, where the road is carpeted thickly with the fallen needles of foliage, so that the wheels run without sound, and you may catch the Eolian harp-song of the leaves, sighing ceaselessly and sadly

> Of old, unhappy, far-off things,

when the evening wind gets up and the sun drops low on the lagoon.

The myths of the Pacific are marvellous in their way, but they pass over unnoticed much that could not have escaped the net of folk-lore and poetry in Northern lands. That the lovely ironwood, a tree with leaves like mermaid's locks, and the voice of a mermaid's song in its whispering boughs, should stand bare of legend or romance on the shores of a sea that is itself the very home of wonder, strikes the Northern mind with a sense of strange incongruity. But the soul of the islands is not the soul of the continents, and the poet of the Pacific is still to be born.

Sometimes, again, the little buggy rattles over white coral sand and gravel, on a stretch of road that is fairly buried in the forest. The sun is cut off overhead, and only a soft green glow sifts through. The palm-tree stems sweep upward, tall and white, the gigantic "maupei" rears aloft its hollow buttressed stems, carved out into caverns that would delight the soul of a modern Crusoe, and drops big chestnuts, floury and sweet, upon the road as we pass. The "utu," or Barringtonia Speciosa, one of the most beautiful of island trees, towers a hundred feet into the warm glow above, its brilliant varnished leaves, nearly a foot long, and its strange rose and white flowers, shaped like feather-dusters, marking it out unmistakably from the general tangle of interlacing boughs, and crowding trunks, and long liana ropes, green and brown, that run from tree to tree. If you were lost in the bush, and thirsty, one of those lianas would provide you with waters, were you learned enough in wood lore to slash it with your knife, and let the pure refreshing juice trickle forth. You might gather wild fruit of many kinds, too, and wild roots, mealy and nourishing, or dainty and sweet. And at night, you might creep into your hollow tree, or lie down on the warm sand of the shore, with nothing worse to fear than a mosquito or two.

There are no wild beasts in any of the Pacific Islands, save an occasional boar, which always lives remote from men in the hills, and is much readier to run away than to annoy. There are no poisonous snakes, either, tarantulas, or deadly centipedes and scorpions. I cannot honestly say that the two latter creatures do not exist, but they very seldom bite or sting any one who does not go barefooted, and their venom is not deadly, though painful.

On almost every tree, as we rattle along through the forest, my hostess and I can see the beautiful bird's-nest fern, looking like a hanging basket of greenery. We have not time to stop to-day, but we shall have to go out some other afternoon and cut down a few of the smaller ones for table decoration, for there is a dinner-party coming off, and we are short of pot plants for the rooms. Young palms, most graceful of all green things, shoot up like little fountains in the clearings, some of the smaller ones still root-bound by the large brown nut from which they have sprung. One would never think these dainty ball-room palms were related in any way to the stately white columns spiring high above them, for the full-grown palm is all stem and scarcely any top, in comparison, while the young palm, a mass of magnificent spreading fronds, rises from a short bulb-like trunk that suggests nothing less than further growth.

The drive is six good miles, but it seems only too

short. In a very little while, we have reached Queen Tinomana's village—a picturesque little grassy town, with brown thatched huts, and white concrete cottages washed with coral lime, and gay red and yellow leaved ti trees standing before almost every door—and the queen's own palace, a handsome two-storeyed house, quite as fine as Makea's, stands up in front of us.

Passing by this piece of European splendour, we go to draw a more likely covert, and ere long flush our quarry in a little creeper-wreathed cottage, hidden behind bushes of deliciously scented frangipani and blazing red hibiscus. The queen is on the verandah, seated, like Makea, on an ironwood sofa of state. She sits here most of the day, having very little in the way of government to do, and no desire to trouble her amiable head with the white woman's labourious methods of killing time. Sometimes she plaits a hat to amuse herself, being accomplished in this favourite Raratongan art—a sailor hat with a hard crown and stiff brim, and a good deal of neat but lacy fancywork in the twisting of the plait. Sometimes she receives friends, and hears gossip. Sometimes, she sleeps on the sofa, and wakes up to suck oranges and fall asleep again. The strenuous life is not the life beloved of Tinomana, nor (one may hint in the smallest of whispers) would her much more strenuous sister queen encourage any developments in that direction. It is well, under the circumstances, that both are suited by their respective rôles, otherwise the somewhat difficult lot of the Resident Commissioner might be rendered even more trying than it is.

Tinomana is not young, and she is not lovely now, though one can see that she has been beautiful, as so many of the soft-eyed island women are, long ago. She has had her romance, however, and as we sit on her verandah, drinking and eating the cocoanut and banana of ceremony, the grey-haired white man who is husband of the queen tells the story to me of her love and his, just as it happened, once upon a time.

In 1874 the Cook Islands were an independent group, governed by their own chiefs, or Arikis. The Arikis had much more power in those days than they are now allowed to exercise. They could order the execution of any subject for any cause; they could make war and end it : and no ship dared to call at the islands without their permission. They owned, as they still own, all the land, and their wealth of various kinds made them, in the eyes of the natives, millionaires as well as sovereigns.

"Women's rights" were a novelty to England thirty years ago, but in the Cook Islands they were fully recognised, even at that early period. The most powerful of the Arikis was Makea—then a girl, now an elderly woman, but always every inch a queen, and always keeping a firm hand on the sceptre of Raratonga. Any Cook Islands postage-stamp will show Makea as she was some ten years ago. In 1874 Makea and her consort, Ngamaru, were making plans for the marrying of Tinomana, a young Raratongan princess closely related to Makea. Tinomana would shortly become an Ariki, or queen, herself, and her matrimonial affairs were, in consequence, of considerable importance.

What the plans of Raratonga's rulers for Tinomana may have been matters little. Tinomana was pretty, with splendid long black hair, large soft brown eyes, an excellent profile, and a complexion little darker than a Spaniard's. She was also self-willed, and could keep a secret as close as wax when she so desired. She had a secret at that time, and it concerned no South Sea

Islander, but a certain good-looking young Anglo-American named John Salmon (grandson of a Ramsgate sea-captain, Thomas Dunnett), who had lately landed at Raratonga from the trading schooner *Venus*, and had been enjoying a good deal of the pretty princess's society, unknown to the gossips of the island. It was a case of love at first sight; for the two had not been more than a few days acquainted when they came privately to James Chalmers, the famous missionary, then resident in Raratonga, and begged for a secret marriage.

James Chalmers refused promptly to have anything to do with the matter, and furthermore told Tinomana that he would never marry her to any white man, no matter who it might be. In his opinion such a marriage would be certain to cause endless trouble with the other Arikis—apart from the fact that Queen Makea was against it. So the lovers went away disconsolate. Raratonga was keeping holiday at the time, because a great war-canoe was to be launched immediately, and a dance and feast were in preparation. But Tinomana and her lover were out of tune with the festivities, and no woman in the island prepared her stephanotis and hibiscus garlands for the feast, or plaited baskets of green palm leaves to carry contributions of baked sucking-pig and pineapples, with as heavy a heart as the little princess.

On the day of the feast an idea came to Salmon. There were two schooners lying in Avarua harbour. One, the *Coronet*, had for captain a man named Rose, who was as much opposed to Salmon's marriage as Chalmers himself. The *Humboldt* schooner, on the other hand, had a friend of Salmon's in command. From him some help might be expected. Salmon visited him secretly, found that he was willing to assist, and arranged for an elopement that very night. Tinomana was willing; nobody suspected; and the feast would furnish a capital opportunity.

There was no moon that evening, happily for the lovers, for the smallest sign would have awaked the suspicions of the watching *Coronet*. When the feast had begun, and all Raratonga was making merry with pig and baked banana, raw fish and pineapple beer, Tinomana contrived to slip away and get back to her house. Womanlike, she would not go without her "things"; and she took so long collecting and packing her treasures—her silk and muslin dresses, her feather crowns, her fans and bits of cherished European finery from far-away Auckland—that the suspicions of a prying girl were aroused. Out she came, accompanied by two others—all handmaidens to Tinomana—and charged the princess with an intention to elope. Tinomana acknowledged the truth, and ordered the girls to hold their tongues, offering them liberal rewards. This was not enough, however; the three girls demanded that Tinomana, in addition to buying their silence, should shield them from the possible wrath of the great Makea by taking them with her. She was forced to consent; and so, when the impatient lover, lurking in the darkness near the harbour, saw his lady coming at last, she came with three attendants, and almost enough luggage to rival Marie Antoinette's encumbered flight to Varennes.

Eventually, however, the party put off in a canoe, the girls lying flat in the bottom, with Tinomana crouching beside them and Salmon holding a lighted torch, which he waved in the air as they went. For the boat had to pass close by the *Coronet*, and Captain

Rose, somehow or other, had become suspicious, and young Salmon knew he would think nothing of stopping any boat that could not give an account of itself. So Salmon took the torch, to look like a fishing-boat going out with spears and torches to the reef, and, paddling with one hand while he held the light aloft with the other, he passed the *Coronet* safely, knowing well that his face would be unrecognisable at a distance of fifty yards or so in the wavering shadow of the flame.

Beyond the reef lay the *Humboldt* waiting. Tinomana and her maids and her luggage were swung up the side with small ceremony; Salmon hurried after, and a small but welcome breeze enabled the schooner to slip out to sea unnoticed in the dark. She made for Mangaia, another of the Cook Islands, some hundred and fifty miles away, and reached it in a couple of days. But the *Humboldt* had hardly made the land when the dreaded *Coronet* appeared on the horizon, carrying every stitch of sail, and with her decks, her "Jacob's-ladder," and her very yardarms crowded by furious Raratongans. The fugitives were caught!

At first they had not been missed. The islanders were feasting and drinking, the Arikis were unsuspicious, and the *Coronet* had seen only a fishing-canoe with a solitary man on board gliding out to the reef. But with the morning light came the knowledge that Tinomana was absent from her palace, that Salmon had not come home, and that the *Humboldt* was gone. Raratonga was enraged, and all the more so because pursuit appeared for the moment to be impossible. They knew that the *Humboldt* had probably made for Mangaia; but the breeze had died away, and the *Coronet*, her sails flapping idly against her rakish masts, lay helpless in harbour. Some brilliant spirit, however, proposed that the schooner should be towed out, in the hope of catching a breeze beyond the reef; and half a dozen great whaleboats, manned by powerful arms, were harnessed to the *Coronet's* bows. Out she came through the opening in the foaming coral reef, with screaming and splashing and tugging at oars, into the blue, open sea, and beyond the shelter of the peaky, purple hills. The breeze was met at last, the boats cast off and dropped astern, and the *Coronet*, carrying half Raratonga on board, set sail for Mangaia.

Once within the range of the *Humboldt* the *Coronet* lowered a boatful of armed men, and the latter made for the schooner lying-to under the shelter of the Mangaian hills. Captain Harris, of the *Humboldt*, however, ordered his crew to shoot down the first man who attempted to board, and the attacking boat thought better of it. Beaten by force they tried diplomacy, in which they were more successful. They told Captain Harris that all his cargo of valuable cotton, lying on the wharf at Raratonga ready for shipment, would be destroyed unless he gave the princess back. This meant absolute ruin, and the captain had to submit. Salmon told Tinomana that it was best to give in for the present, as they were caught; but that the parting would be only for a time. And back to Raratonga went the disconsolate princess, bereft of her lover and her stolen wedding, and with the anticipation of a good scolding to come from the indignant Arikis.

For some months after this disaster Salmon wandered about from island to island, living now in Raiatea, now in Flint Island, now in Mauke—always restless and always impatient. At last he judged the time had come to make a second attempt, and tried to obtain a passage to Raratonga. Schooner after schooner refused

THE QUEEN INTERVENES

to take him, but finally a little vessel called the *Atalanta* braved the wrath of the Arikis and brought him back. During his absence time had worked in his favour, and the opposition to the marriage was now much weaker. The Arikis received him coolly and fined him twenty pounds' worth of needles, thread, and tobacco for his late excursion, but they no longer refused to let him see Tinomana. The missionary, however, still objected to the marriage, and as he was the only clergyman available for the ceremony it seemed as if things, on the whole, were " getting no forrader."

At this juncture the great Makea stepped in, and with the charming variability common to her sex, took the part of the lovers against all Raratonga as strongly as she had before opposed their union. She was not then in Raratonga, but in another of the Cook Islands, Atiu. From thence she sent the schooner *Venus* to Raratonga, ordering the captain to fetch Tinomana and Salmon to Atiu, where the local missionary would marry them, or Makea would know the reason why.

Raratonga—obstinate Raratonga!—still refused to give its princess to a foreign adventurer, though it trembled at the thought of defying the Elizabethan Makea. A band of warriors came down to the harbour to see that Salmon did not get on board the ship. As for Tinomana, they did not dare to oppose her departure, when the head of the house had actually summoned her. But the princess had no notion whatever of going alone. Salmon was smuggled on board in the dusk and hidden under a bunk. A pile of mats and native "pareos," or kilts, was placed over him, and there, in the heat of the tropic night, he lay and sweltered, while the *Venus* swung to her cable and the warriors hunted the ship and found nothing. When they went off, baffled, the schooner put to sea. A Raratongan vessel, still suspicious, chased her to Atiu, but Makea informed the pursuing crew that it would be bad for their health to land on her property unasked; and, as this great Pacific Queen had, and has, the reputation of keeping her word when it is passed, the Raratongans did not dare to set foot on shore. This time it was they who went home disconsolate.

And so the young couple were married " and lived happily ever after." Tinomana and her consort now reside at Arorangi, Raratonga, in their long, low house, set among frangipani trees and oranges, and covered with flowering tropical creepers, and seldom or never occupy their palace. Tinomana's five children are dead; she herself is growing old, but the memory of those long-past years of adventure and romance is still with her. Her life glides quietly and dreamily by, within the sound of the humming ocean surf, under the shadow of the purple Raratongan hills. She has had her day, and there remain the quiet sunset and the softened twilight, before the time of dark.

The queen had little to say to us, for she does not speak English, nor is she shrewdly curious about men and things outside of sleepy Raratonga, like her sister sovereign, Makea. She smiled a good deal, and said some polite things about my dress, which illustrated a new fashion, and seemed to interest her more than anything else connected with the call. I had brought a gift with me for Tinomana, a silk scarf of a peculiarly screaming blue, and I presented it before I took my leave with some politenesses that the royal consort rapidly translated for me. The queen was much pleased with the gift, and began trying its effect on several different hats at once. Then we had some more cocoanut water, and said good-bye, and drove home again in the yellow sunset.

The crabs were getting noisy as we passed along a soft bit of sandy road close by the shore. They are fairly active all day, and at night seem to wake up a little more completely than before. One can hear them rattling and scratching loudly all over the stones and rubbish about the shore; the ground is riddled with their holes—as we pass, they dart in at their front doors as swiftly as spiders, and stand looking cautiously round a corner till the threatening apparition is gone. They are not nice things, these crabs—they are tall and spindly and insect-like in build, with a scrawny body set on eight spider-like legs, and ugly, sharp, thin claws. They live on the land, but haunt the beach a good deal, because of the débris to be found there, and they are such nasty feeders that not even the natives will eat them, which is saying a good deal.

They have an uncanny fancy for coming into houses. If your residence is not raised up on a good verandah, which they cannot surmount, you may be alarmed some night by a ghostly tapping and ticking on the floor, like nothing you have ever heard or dreamed of before, and while you are wondering fearfully what the sound may be, you will suddenly become aware of something clumsy and noisy scrambling among the mosquito curtains of your bed. At this, if you are of common human mould, you will arise hastily, tangling yourself up in the curtains as you do so, and call loudly for a light. And when one is brought, behold the offender scuttling hastily away on eight long thin legs into the outer dark, without stopping to make an explanation or an apology. You are so annoyed that you put on a dressing-gown and follow him out on the verandah, a stick in your hand and murder in your heart; but just as you reach the steps, there is a loud "flump" on the floor, and a centipede as big as a sausage, with a writhing black body and horrible red legs and antennæ, flashes past the edge of your sweeping draperies. At this you give it up, and get back to your mosquito curtains. You are just falling asleep, when—— Good Heavens! what is it?

Surely nothing but a burglar could have made that fearful noise in the outer kitchen!—a burglar, or a madman, or both in one. It sounds as if some one were beating somebody else with an iron bucket. Perhaps it may be only a native dog chasing a cat. Up go the curtains once more, letting half the mosquitoes in the island in, and off the wretched traveller sets for the kitchen, accompanied by a brave but pallid hostess, who says she is extremely sorry her husband *would* choose this week for going away from home.

There he is! there is the author of the noise—a black, bristly, incredibly hideous hermit crab as big as a biscuit—out of his shell, and fighting like grim death in an empty kerosene tin, with another crab nearly as big, and quite as vicious. Number one has got too big for the second-hand univalve shell he lived in, and is touring the country trying to replace it. Number two, also outgrowing his clothes, has got half a broken sardine box in the kerosene tin (which acts as ash-bucket to the house), and he thinks it is the loveliest new shell he has ever seen. So, unluckily, does the other crab, and they are in the act of putting it to ordeal by combat, when we invade the scene of the battle, and rudely shake the crabs and the shells and the sardine tin all off the end of the verandah together.

"What on earth brings crabs into people's houses?" you ask amazedly, as you go back to bed again. It seems an insane action for any sensible crab, considering that we are half a mile from the sea.

"Pure cussedness," says my friend wrathfully. "They even climb up the verandah posts, and sit among the flowers. What for? Spite, I think; there isn't anything more ill-natured in the world than a hermit crab."

If it is not a moonlight night, now, we get to sleep at last, but if it is, and the oranges are ripe——

Well, that is the time the "mor kiri-kiris" choose to perform their orisons; and when they are playing the devil with the holy peace and calm of midnight on the roof, not even a fourth mate newly come off his watch, could sleep below.

"Here, you blank, blank, blank, unspeakable, etcetera, let go that orange!"

"I shan't, blank your double-blank limbs and wings! I got it first!"

"Then just look out, you mangy, fox-faced, clumsy-winged beast, for I'll rip the inside out of your rotten carcase with my claws."

"Like to see you!" (somewhat muffled with stolen orange).

"You will!"

Shriek, shriek, yell, howl, scream.

"You've bitten my toe off, you trebly-blanked vermin!"

"Meant to!"

"Clear off!"

"Won't!"

"Come on again, then!"

"Pax! pax! here's the great pig with fur on its head that lives in the house, coming out with a gun. I'm off."

"So am I, but we'll go back again the moment it goes in."

That is the way one sleeps in the orange season, in a place that happens to be popular with the "mor kiri-kiri," or flying-fox—a bat with a furry body as big as a cat's, long sharp white teeth, a head exactly like a fox, and the crustiest disposition of anything living on the island.

CHAPTER V

Feasting and Fun on Steamer Day—The Brown People of Raratonga—Who sent back the Teeth?—Divorce made easy—Climbing a Tropical Mountain—A Hot-water Swim—Out on the Rainbow Coral Reef—Necklaces for No One.

STEAMER day in Raratonga, as in all the islands that rejoice in the privilege of a regular steamer service, is beyond comparison the event of the month. Almost before dawn on the day which is expected to see the boat arrive, the traders are up and about, seeing to the carting of their fruit and copra, and making ready the shelves of the stores for the new goods coming in from Auckland. All the residents, men and women, white and brown, are getting out the cleanest of muslins and drill suits, and looking up the shoe-whitening box, which perhaps has not been much in demand since the steamer called on her way back from Tahiti last month. The daughters of the white community are making tinned-peach pies, and dressing fowls, in case of callers—these are the inevitable " company " dishes of the Pacific—and the native women are bringing out their newly made straw hats, and ironing their gayest of pink or yellow or scarlet cotton, squatting cross-legged on the floor as they work. Cocoanuts for drinking are being husked by the men of the village, and laid in neat piles under the verandahs, out of the sun ; and in most of the little birdcage houses, the children are impounded to grate cocoanut meat for cream ; while the dying yells of pigs make day hideous from the groves beyond the town.

When the tiny trail of smoke, for which every one is looking, first rises out of the empty sea, it may be on the day expected, or it may be later—there is little time in the Great South Seas—the whole island is agape with excitement. The natives shriek with delight, and make haste to gather flowers for wreaths and necklaces: the clean suits and frocks are put on by brown and white alike, and the populace begins to hover about the wharf like a swarm of excited butterflies. The great whaleboats are ready to rush out at racing speed to the steamer, long before she comes to a stop in the bay—she dares not come into the harbour, which is only fit for small craft—passengers from Auckland come ashore, anxious to see the island curiosities, and find to their embarrassment that they are unmistakably regarded in that light themselves; and, as soon as may be, the mail comes after them. Upon which event, the whole population makes for the Government buildings, and flings itself in one seething breaker against the door of the Post Office, demanding its mails. While the letters are being sorted by a handful of officials locked and barred out of reach within, it rattles at the doors and windows, and as soon as the bolts are withdrawn, the mighty host, breathless and ruthless, bursts in like a besieging army. But when all are in, nobody has patience to wait and open papers, in order to know what has been going on in the outer world all these weeks. Purser, passengers, and even sailors are seized upon, and compelled to stand and deliver news about "the war," and other burning questions, before any one thinks of opening the envelopes and wrappers in their hands

Minds being satisfied, bodies now assert their claim. Steamer day is feast day—beef day, ice day, day for enjoying all the eatables that cannot be had in the island itself. There is mutton in Raratonga, but not much at the best of times, and of beef there is none at all. So all the white folk order beef to come up monthly in the ship's cold storage, and for two happy days—the meat will keep no longer—they enjoy a feast that might perhaps more fairly be called a "feed." About noon on steamer day, a savoury smell, to which the island has long been a stranger, begins to diffuse itself throughout Avarua. Every one, with true island hospitality, is asking every one else to lunch and dinner, to-day and to-morrow, so that Mrs. A. and her family may have a taste of Mr. B.'s sirloin, and Mr. B. get a bit of the C.'s consignment of steak, and the A.'s and B.'s and E.'s enjoy a little bit of Colonel Z.'s roast ribs. A sensuous, almost unctuous, happiness shines like a halo about every face, and after dusk white dinner coats flit up and down the perfumed avenues, thick as night-moths among the orange bloom overhead. To-morrow there will be great doings in the pretty bungalow on the top of the hill, for the Resident Commissioner has got a big lump of ice as a present from the captain of the steamer, and is hoarding it up in blankets to give a dinner-party in its honour. The white man who could consume a lump of ice all by himself, in the island world, would be considered capable of any crime, and the hospitable Commissioner is the last person to shirk his obligations in such a matter.

Once the steamer has come and gone, a dreamy peace settles down upon the island. There is seldom much certainty as to clock time, since every one goes by his own time-piece, and all vary largely, nor does any one heed the day of the month overmuch. This pleasant disregard of time is the true secret of the fascination of island life—or perhaps one of the secrets, since no one has ever really succeeded in defining the unspeakable charm of these lotus lands. Imagine a civilised community, where people dine out in evening dress, leave cards and have "At Home" days, yet where there is no post except the monthly ship mail, there are no telegrams, trains, trams, times, appointments, or engagements of any kind! Picture the peace that comes of knowing certainly that, for all the time of the steamer's absence there can be no disturbance of the even current of life; no great events at home or abroad, no haste, or worry, or responsibility! People keep young long in Raratonga; faces are free from weariness and strain; the white man with the "burden" laughs as merrily and as often as the brown man who carries nought but his flowery necklace and his pareo. Nobody is rich—rich men do not come down to the islands to run small plantations, or trading stores, or to take up little appointments under a little Government—but every one has enough, and extravagance is impossible, since luxuries are unpurchasable on the island. There are no social distinctions, save that between white and brown—all the seventy or eighty white residents knowing one another on a footing of common equality, although in England, or even New Zealand, they would certainly be split up into half a score of mutually contemptuous sets.

As for the natives—the jolly, laughing, brown-skinned, handsome men and women of the island—their life is one long day of peace and leisure and plenty. The lands of the six thousand who once inhabited Raratonga are now for the most part in the hands of the nineteen hundred survivors, and every native has therefore a good deal more than he wants. Breadfruit, bananas of many kinds, oranges, mammee-apples, and countless other fruits, grow altogether, or almost, without cultivation ; taro, yam, and sweet potatoes need little, and cocoanuts are always to be had. A native house can be put up in a day or two, furniture is superfluous, and clothes consist of a few yards of cotton print. The Raratongan, therefore, owes no tale of labour to Nature or Society for his existence in quiet comfort, if he does not choose to work. But in many cases he does choose, for he wants a buggy and a horse, and a bicycle or two, and a sewing machine for his wife ; shoes with squeaking soles for festive wear—deliberately made up with "squeakers" for island trade, these—bottles of coarse strong scent, tins of meat and salmon as an occasional treat, and, if he is ambitious, one of those concrete, iron-roofed houses of which I have already spoken, to enhance his social position, and make the neighbours envious, what time he continues to live peaceably and comfortably in his palm hut outside—not being quite such a fool in this matter as he looks.

Sometimes the Raratongan will go so far as to get his front teeth stopped with gold by a travelling dentist, purely for style, since he is gifted by nature with grinders that will smash any fruit stone, and incisors that will actually tear the close tough husk off a huge cocoanut without trouble. It is related of one of the wealthier Raratongans that, being stricken in years and short of teeth, he purchased a set of false ones from a visiting dentist, and that the latter, when he next returned to the island, was astonished to find the set thrown on his hands as no good, on the grounds that they would not husk cocoanuts !

In order to secure all these more or less desirable luxuries, the Raratongan trades in fruit and copra. That is to say, he cuts up and dries (strictly at his leisure, and when he feels like it) a few thousand cocoanuts, or nails up some hundreds of oranges, and scores of banana bunches, from his overflowing acres, in wooden crates, to send down to Auckland. This labour, repeated a few times, brings him in good British gold by the handful. Copra, sold to the traders in the town, fetches about seven pounds a ton, and a family working for a few days can prepare as much as that. Other produce is hardly less profitable, to a cultivator who has more land than he wants, provides his own labour, and need spend nothing on seeds or plants. There is, at most, only light work, and that seldom, so that the Raratongan can, and often does, spend the greater part of his time singing in choruses on the verandahs of the houses, dancing to the thrilling beat of a native drum under the cocoanut trees, or fishing lazily off the reef.

The Raratongans are all, to a man, good Christians—good Protestants of the Dissenting variety, good Catholics, and, in a few cases, enthusiastic Seventh Day Adventists—being readily enough inclined to adhere to a cult that makes it sinful to work on the seventh day of the week, and impossible to work on the first. It is said that Mormon missionaries have visited the group, but failed to make converts. Without going into details that might disturb the sensitive mind, one feels obliged to remark, in this connection, that the failure was probably on all fours, as to cause, with the ill-success of the merchant who attempted to sell coals to Newcastle.

And—still concerning this matter—" one word more, and I have done." Some weeks after my arrival, I was going round the group in company with the Resident

Commissioner and a few more officials, who were holding courts and administering justice in the various islands. The Commissioner was late getting back to the ship one afternoon, and the captain asked him if he had been detained.

"Only a little while," replied the guardian angel of the group, cheerfully rattling his pockets, which gave forth a pleasant chinking sound. "Another dozen of divorces. We'll have a new road round the island next year." And he went to dinner.

Divorce in the Cook Islands is not an expensive luxury. If memory serves me right, it costs under thirty shillings, and there is a sixpence somewhere in the price —I am unable to say why. But I remember very well indeed, after the officials had gone home, when I was travelling round about other islands with a captain, who had just taken over the ship and did not know the Cook group, that dignitary came to me one day and said :

"I can't make out these hands of mine. They're a very decent lot for niggers, and don't give no trouble, but one and another, now that we're going round the islands, keeps coming to me and asking me for an advance on their wages, because, says they, they've been a long time from home, and they wants it—and every blessed one of them he wants the same advance !"

"Was it so-and-so?" I asked, mentioning a certain small sum with a sixpence in it.

"How on earth did you know?" was the reply.

"Price of a divorce from the Commissioner," I explained.

"Well !" said the captain, who was a hard-shelled old whaler, with a strong religious cast. And again— "Well !"

"That's what I think myself," I explained. "But it certainly fills the exchequer. I hear the score runs up to ten or twelve apiece, often enough."

"Disgustin'," said the captain, spitting over the rail.

"Certainly," I agreed.

But the incident has its own significance, so I have recorded it.

I linger long over the life and ways of Raratonga, for I spent many very happy weeks there—studying native customs, and taking notes? Well, perhaps—a little, at all events. Raratonga is not quite so lazy a place as Tahiti, and the climate is less trying. Still—still——

How impossible it is to explain to the reader who has never spent a hot season in the tropics! I think I shall not try. There were missed opportunities—there were things I ought to have studied, and did not, and things I should have seen, and didn't see. It is of no use to say why. Those who have passed between the magic line of Cancer and Capricorn will not need to be told, and the others could not understand.

I did something to satisfy my conscience, however, when I climbed the highest mountain in Raratonga— a peak something over three thousand feet high, so the residents said. It was reported that the Admiralty survey did not agree by a hundred feet or so, with the local estimate. I know myself that both were wrong; that peak is ten thousand, or perhaps a little more. Did it not take myself and two or three others from seven a.m. until nine p.m., to get up and down, working as hard as white ants (there is nothing in the islands really busy except the ants) all the time?

We went the wrong way—several wrong ways—we lost our food and our water, and got so thirsty that we licked the leaves of the trees, and so hungry that it was agony to know ourselves above the zone of the orange and banana all day, and see the food we could not reach till night hanging in clusters far below. We did most of our climbing by the heroic method of swarming up perpendicular rock faces on the ladders of the creepers, and a good deal of it by scrambling along in the tops of small trees, like monkeys. When we got to the top there was just room for the whole party to stand and cheer, and we cheered ourselves vigorously. People do not climb mountains—much—in the islands of the Pacific, and the peak we were on had been trodden by only one or two white men, and no white women.

"There used to be natives up here often enough, some years ago, shooting wild fowl," said one of our guides, letting the smoke of his pipe curl out over "half a duchy," lying blue and green, and far, far down, under his elbow. "But they stopped coming. Several of 'em got killed, and the others didn't think it good enough."

"How did they get killed?" I ask, listening to the wild cocks crowing in the sea of green down below, like a farm-yard gone astray.

"Oh, climbing!"

When we had finished admiring the view of the island, we started down again. And now, what with our hunger, and our fatigue, and the wild adventures in impossible places we had had coming up, we all became rather tired, and more than rather reckless. Over and over again, slithering down steep descents, we let ourselves go, and tobogganed, sitting, we did not care where. The lianas crashed, the red-flowered rata snapped and fell on us, the lace-like tree ferns got in our way with their damp black trunks, and banged us as we tumbled past. Every one knew that if we did not get off the precipice slopes before dark, we should have to halt wherever we might be, and wait till morning, holding tight to the trunk of a tree to keep from falling down into depths unknown. But no one said anything about it.

And in the end, we got back safe—sore and tired and hungry; not thirsty however, for we had found a stream in the interminable dark of the valley, and had all put our heads into it like brutes, the moment our feet felt the welcome hollow and splashed into the water. The ladies of the party had not a whole gown among them, and not very much else, so shrewdly had the thorns and creepers of the close-knitted forest squeezed and torn us. Still, we had got up where no white women had been before, and we were all very proud, though we had to slink homeward in the dark, avoiding the lights of the houses, and each slip in unobserved at the back doors of our respective homes. But we had done the climb, and—— "That was something," as Hans Andersen would have said.

Picnics we had in plenty, while I stayed. Sometimes they were bathing picnics, when the ladies of half a dozen houses went off to spend the day down on the shore, and swim in the lagoon. The water, not more than five feet deep in any place, was the colour of green grass when the sun shines through, and it was as warm as an ordinary hot bath. One could spend hour after hour amusing oneself with swimming tricks, coming out now and then to roast for a little on the hot, snow-white coral sand, where bits and branches of coral pretty enough for a museum lay scattered everywhere, and exquisite flowering creepers spread their long green tails of leafage—often thirty or forty feet in length, and all starred with pink or yellow blossoms—right across the broad expanse of the beach. Coming out finally, it was customary to find a big rock, and stand with one's back against it till the wet bathing dress was half dried with the blistering heat of the stone. This was supposed to prevent chills. I think myself that one would have to hunt a chill very hard indeed in the hot season in Raratonga, before catching it. It is not a place where one hears of "chill" troubles, and there is no fever of any kind. When you find a draught there, you tell every one else in the house about it, and they come and sit in it with you. When you give tea, to callers, it is correct to serve cold water on the tray to temper the beverage, and put a spoon instead of a butter knife, in the butter dish.

Nor does it cool down overmuch at night, in the hot months, though in the "cold" ones, you may want a blanket now and then. The temperature being so equable all round, chills are, naturally, not to be looked for and feared at every turn, as in the great tropic continents, where there is no surrounding sea to prevent rapid radiation of heat, and sudden changes of temperature are frequent and deadly. On the whole, there is much to be said in favour of the climate of the Southern Pacific, and little against it. It enjoys a long cool season of at least six months, when the heat is not at all oppressive. Three months of the year are very hot and damp, and three neither hot nor cool. At worst, the thermometer seldom goes above ninety in the shade. White children can be brought up in the islands without injury to health, and many of the older residents have spent the best part of a long life in the South Seas, and attained to a venerable age, without ever suffering from illness. The Government doctor in Raratonga leads an easy life on the whole, and in the other islands of the Cook Group the entire absence of medical advice seems to trouble no one.

A reefing picnic was among the many pleasant entertainments to which I was invited during my stay. "Reefing" is such a favourite entertainment in the islands that nearly every white woman has a reefing skirt and shoes in her wardrobe—the former short, like a hockey skirt, the latter stout and old. Buggies are gathered together in the town, and the picnickers drive to a suitable spot some distance away, where the horses are taken out and tethered, and the "reefers" secure a canoe to bring them to their destination—the coral barrier reef, lying between the lagoon and the sea.

Paddled by some of the native guests (for there are generally a few Raratongans included in the party) the canoes glide easily over the shallow water towards the reef, flights of the exquisite little sapphire-coloured fish that haunt the coral rocks, scattering beneath the keel like startled butterflies. Now the water is of the most vivid and burning emerald, shooting green lightnings to the sun, now, as we near the reef, it begins to change in colour, and——

Oh!

Why, the canoe is floating on a liquid rainbow—on a casket of jewels melted down and poured into the burning sea—on glancing shades of rose, and quivering gleams of violet, and gold and blue and amethyst and chrysophrase, all trembling and melting one into another in marvels of colouring that leave all language far behind. Under the keel, as we shoot forward, rise and sink wonderful water-bouquets of purple, pink, and pearl; great lacy fans of ivory; frilled and fluted fairy shells, streamers of brilliant weed, and under and through all these wonders glint, from far below, the dark blue depths of unplumed caverns beneath. It is the coral reef, and we are going to land upon a spot exposed by

ON A CORAL REEF

the tide, and see what we can see of these wonders, by-and-by. If we were bent on fishing, we might spend a pleasant hour or two catching some of these peacock and parrot-coloured fish that flutter through these wonderful water-gardens. But reefing proper is more amusing, after all.

At a point where the coral juts out above the sea, we leave the canoe, and start to walk about. It is very like trying to walk on a gigantic petrified hair-brush. The coral is peaked and pointed, and wrought into honeycombed sponges of stone, and there is nowhere for the foot to rest in security. Besides, the reef is covered with sea urchins possessing spines as long and sharp as a big slate-pencil, and these things pierce through any but the stoutest shoes. The colours of the sea-urchins are fascinating, and we pick up a good many, in spite of difficulties. Then there are tiger shells, shiny and spotted, in hues of orange and brown, and beautiful scarlet and pinky and lilac and chequered shells, and the daintiest of goffered clam shells, pearl white within, ivory white without, as large as a pea-pod, or as large as a vegetable dish—you may take your choice. And, if you are lucky, there is a varnished brown snail shell that you would not think worth picking up, if you did not happen to know that it has a "peacock-eye" gem, good to set in brooches, inside its plain little front door—like the homely brown toad of fable, that carried a jewel in its head. Much other spoil there is to put in your basket, and many things that you have no desire to possess at all—among them the huge hanks of slimy black string, which are alive, and wrigglesome, and not at all pleasant to put your hand on—and the wicked-faced great eels that look suddenly out of holes, and vanish, bubbling; and the revolting, leprous-spotted fish with the spiny back, that one may chance to see lurking at the bottom of a pool, every spine charged full of deadly poison for whoever touches it with unwary foot or hand. Indeed, the friends who are with you will warn you not to put your fingers into any pool, but to hook out shells and other spoil with a stick, if you want to be really careful, for there are as many stinging and biting things among the beauties of the coral reef, as there are thorns in a bed of roses.

I have secured a good many shells, and a Reckitt's blue starfish as big as a dinner-plate, and one or two other curiosities, and now I want, above everything else, one of those miraculous coral bouquets that bloom so temptingly just beneath the surface at this point. One of my friends asks me which I will have—with a smile, that, somehow or other, seems to amuse the rest. I select a pinky-violet one, and with some dragging and pounding, it is detached, and held up in the sun.

"Oh!" I exclaim disappointedly, and every one laughs. The beautiful bunch of coral flowers is a dirty liver-colour, and the magical hues are gone.

"It's the water that gives the colours," explains the coral-gatherer. "Every one is awfully disappointed about it."

"Are there no colours at all, then?"

"Oh yes, a little shade of pinkiness, and a touch of green, and that purply-brown. But you should see the corals when they are cleaned and dried. You'd better have these, you won't know them when they're bleached; they're like spider's webs and lace furbelow things, all in white."

"Is there none of the real red stuff?" I ask somewhat ruefully, balancing myself with difficulty upon a sort of ornamental sponge-basket of spiky coral.

"Not here. All these volcanic islands have a ring of coral reef right round, but the coral is always the white kind. There's a very little red coral in Samoa, and about Penrhyn, I believe. But, speaking generally, it's all white in the Pacific."

I think of the dreams of my childhood, and the delightful pictures of palmy islands circled round with a chevaux-de-frise of high spiky red coral, which used to flit before my fancy on holiday afternoons. It is true that the cold practicalities of the *Voyage of the Challenger*, which somebody gave me in my "flapper" days, once and for all, to my bitter disappointment, knocked the bottom out of those cherished schemes of going away to live on something like a glorified coral necklace, some day. But I wonder, as I get into the canoe again, and glide shorewards and teawards, paddled by the swift brown arms of native girls, how many grown-up people still hold to that delightful fancy, not knowing that it is as impossible to realise as a dream of rambling in the moon?

Tea is preparing on the shore when we get back, very wet and dirty, but very well pleased. The native girls among the guests immediately offer us spare dresses. It is the mode among Raratongans to take two or three dresses to a picnic, and retire every now and then into the bush to change one smart muslin or cotton "Mother Hubbard" for another—just for pure style. So there are plenty of clothes to spare, and in a minute or two the damp, seaweedy "reefers" are fitted out with flowing garments of clean cambric and silk, of a mode certainly better adapted to the climate than the fitted garments of the "papalangi."

This question of dress is a burning one among island ladies. The native loose robe, hung straight down from a yoke, is very much cooler, and the doctors say, healthier, than belted and corseted dresses such as European women wear. But there is nevertheless a strong feeling against it, because it is supposed to mean a tendency to "go native," and the distinguishing customs of race acquire, in the island world, a significance quite out of proportion to their surface importance, because of the greatness of the thing they represent. Therefore, the white woman, unless she is suffering from bad health, and needs every possible help to withstand the heat of the climate, sticks to her blouses and corsets, as a rule, and sometimes "says things" about people who do not. For all that, and all that, the native woman is in the right, and if the other would agree to adopt the pretty, womanly, and essentially graceful robe of the native, no one would be the loser, and half of island humanity would be greatly the gainer.

Later, when the dusk is coming down, and the magic moon of the Islands is creeping, big and round and yellow-gold, out of a purple sea, we drive home again through the scented gloom of the forest, the endless song of the reef accompanying the voices of the native women, as they chant strange island melodies of long ago, that no one in these days, not even the singers themselves, can fully translate or understand. The moon climbs quickly up as we drive, and the road is as light as day, when our wheels roll into the sleeping town.

CHAPTER VI

The Simple Life in the South Seas—Servant Problems again—Foods and Fruits of the Country—The Tree that digests—Home-made Vanilla—The Invaluable Lime—How to cook a Turtle—In an Island Bungalow—The Little House on the Coral Shore—Humours of Island Life—Burying a Cycle—A Network of Names—Mr. Zebedee-Thunderstorm-Tin-Roof—The Night-dress that went to Church—The Extraordinary Wedding—South Sea Musicians—A Conductor's Paradise—Society Journalism in Song.

HOUSEKEEPING in the South Sea Islands demands a section to itself. All who are uninterested in such matters may, and doubtless will, begin to skip at this point.

Nothing helps the white house-mistress more than the simple standard of living set in most of the islands. It is true that if you are the wife of an important official in the Government House entourage of Fiji, or if you live in civilised, Americanised Honolulu, you will have to " do things " much as they are done at home. But, with these two exceptions, life in that enormous section of the globe known as the South Seas (much of it, by the way, is north of the Line) is simple and unpretentious. In describing the home life of the white settlers in Raratonga, I describe what is, with small local variations, the life of settlers in almost every group of the Pacific, certainly, the life of all in the eight different groups I visited myself, during the years I spent in the South Seas. All over the island world, people dine in the middle of the day, except when entertaining friends, keep few servants or none, and dress and feed simply, because nothing else is possible. The trade cottons in the stores form the material of every lady's dresses, and as for the making, common consent, not to speak of climatic conditions, votes the simplest style the best. Where every stitch of sewing in dress or blouse must be done by the person who is to wear the garment, it is astonishing how soon one grows to regard elaborate tuckings, flouncings, inlayings, with hostility, and how satisfied the eye becomes with the simpler and less "fatigued" lines of the garments fashioned by women who cannot hire a dressmaker for love or money. Evening dress is almost always of the "blouse" description, and in a climate which works universal mischief with delicate white skins, no matter how they are protected, this is no matter for regret. Men buy their drill suits ready-made from the trading stores at a few shillings apiece, and, with a white dinner-jacket and black cummerbund, any one is ready for the gayest of evening entertainments.

The great dress question—being thus resolved into the simple elements of a few cotton frocks for every day, and a muslin or two for best, behold! half the worry of modern life is lifted at a blow. "One must look like other people"—the goad of the toiling townswoman—becomes in the islands, "One looks like other people because one must," and the words are a lullaby of rest.

After dress, come servants, in the list of small worries that turn a woman's fair locks grey, and swell the takings of the fashionable hairdressers. Well, it cannot be said that there is no servant trouble in the islands. White servants simply do not exist; they are far too much in demand in America and Australasia to desert either of these domestic paradises for the hotter and lonelier islands. Native girls cannot be had either, since they marry at thirteen or thereabouts. Native boys and men are the only resource. They come to work by the day, and are fed in the house; their wages are generally about five shillings weekly, in the case of a boy, and ten shillings for a man. So far as they go, they are satisfactory enough; they work hard, and are extremely honest, and they are amiability and good-nature itself. But their scope is decidedly limited. They can garden, under direction; they can sweep, fetch wood and water, clean the cooking-stove, husk and open the cocoanuts, wash, peel and boil the vegetables, scrub the verandah floor, clean the knives, wash up dishes, and whiten the shoes. That is about all. The mistress of the house and her daughters, if she is lucky enough to have any, must do all the serious cooking, make the beds, dust, tidy, and lay the table for meals.

One cannot say, however, that health suffers from the necessity of doing a certain amount of housework every day. On the contrary, the white women of the islands are strong and handsome, and do not seem to suffer from the heat nearly so much as the semi-invalid ladies who have come to be regarded as the type of white womanhood in India, that paradise of excellent service and servants.

Otherwise, the islands help out the housekeeper considerably. She can grow as much excellent coffee as the family are likely to want, on a few bushes in the back yard, and peppers only have to be pulled off the nearest wild chili tree. Taro, yam, sweet potato, can be bought from the natives for a trifle, or grown with very little trouble. There will probably be enough breadfruit, mango, orange, lime, and mammee-apple in the grounds of the house, to supply all the family needs, and if any one likes chestnuts, they can be picked up under the huge maupei trees along any road. The mammee-apple or paw-paw, mentioned above, is one of the most characteristic fruits of the islands. In Raratonga, it grows with extraordinary fertility, springing up of itself wherever scrub is cleared away, and coming to maturity in a few months. It is a slender palm-like tree, from ten to thirty feet high, with a quaintly scaled trunk, very like the skin of some great serpent, and a crown of pointed, pinnated leaves, raying out fanwise from the cluster of heavy green and yellow fruit that hangs in the centre. The fruit itself is rather like a small melon, though wider at one end than the other. It looks like a melon, too, when cut open, and is both refreshing and satisfying, with a sweetish, musky flavour. The small, soft black seeds in the centre are a sovereign cure for dyspepsia, as is also the fruit itself in a lesser degree. The whole of this wonderful tree, indeed, seems to be possessed of digestive powers, for the toughest fowl or piece of salt beef will become tender in a few hours, if wrapped in its leaves. When boiled in the green stage the fruit is undistinguishable from vegetable marrow, and if cooked ripe, with a little lime juice, it can be made into a mock apple pie, much appreciated by settlers in a land where the typical British fruit cannot be grown.

Cooking bananas are much used, and grow wild on the lands of the natives, who sell them for a trifle. Every house has its own patch of eating bananas of many kinds, and orange-trees are almost sure to be there as well. There is always a huge bunch of bananas, and two or three great palm-leaf baskets of oranges, on the verandah of every house, and the inmates consume them both in uncounted numbers all day. Pineapples are easily raised in the little bit of garden, or they can be bought for a

FRUIT AND VEGETABLES

penny a piece. A vanilla vine will probably spread its beautiful thick leaves over the fence, and hang out, in due season, a store of pods for flavouring use in the kitchen. Arrowroot may be grown or bought—a big basket sells for sixpence, and it has no more to do with the arrowroot of the grocer's shop at home, than a real seal mantle worth three figures has to do with a two guinea "electric." Limes grow wild everywhere, and the island housewife makes full use of them. They clean her floors, her tables, her enamelled ware, stained table linen, or marked clothing; they wash her hair delightfully, and take the sunburn off her face and hands; they make the best of "long drinks," and the daintiest of cake flavouring, they are squeezed into every fruit salad, and over every stew; they take the place of vinegar, if the island stores run low; in truth, they are used for almost every purpose of domestic cooking, cleaning, or chemistry.

Cabbage of an excellent kind grows wild in a few islands. Tomatoes, small but excellent in flavour, are found on the borders of the seashore, in many. Nearly all English vegetables are grown by the white settlers with extremely little trouble. The egg-plant, known in England as a greenhouse ornament, here thrives splendidly in gardens, and instead of the little plum-like fruit of the British plant, produces a great purple globe as big as a fine marrow, which resembles fried eggs very closely, if sliced and cooked in a pan. But in truth there is no limit to the richness and generosity of the island soil. Were it not for the troublesome item of butcher's meat, housekeeping in the Pacific would be marvellously cheap and easy. That, however, is the housekeeper's bugbear. Outside of Samoa, Fiji, Tonga, Tahiti, the Marquesas, and Honolulu, fresh beef is not to be had at all, and fresh mutton not often. In very many islands tinned meat and fowls are the only resource ; and the lady of the house must tax her ingenuity to the utmost to find ways of disguising the inevitable "tin." Curry, stew, pie, mince; mince, pie, stew, curry—so runs the monotonous programme in most houses ; and disguise it as one may, the trail of the tin is over it all.

It is a great day in the islands when turtle are caught. They are not common in the groups frequented by white people, since they prefer the lonely, barren atolls where the soil is dry and infertile ; but now and then a "school" is found, and a big catch made. Then there is rejoicing in the land, and cooking in every house of an uncommonly liberal and elaborate kind. The South Sea turtle are enormous, often weighing as much as seven or eight hundred pounds, and occasionally touching the thousand. Such a monster as this would easily feed a large household for a week—but alas, in tropical climates fresh meat, even when scalded, will not keep more than three days ; so a good deal is usually wasted. The famous turtle soup is made from the flippers, which are full of gelatine ; and it may safely be assumed that no London aldermen fed on dying creatures carried half across the world has ever tasted soup so good as that made from a fine healthy turtle just out of the sea. The grass-green fat of the upper shell is used to put in the soup, and to fry the thick steaks of turtle beef, also to baste the big roast of turtle meat that is generally a feature of a turtle dinner. The eggs (of which there will probably be a large bucketful at least) are fried in green fat, and eaten as they are, shell-less, crisp and golden, tasting rather like roast chestnut. The tripe is cooked like ordinary tripe ; the liver is fried. An excellent dinner, but surely an

ARCHITECTURE

indigestible one ? By no means. It is a curious property of this turtle meat that a much larger quantity of it can be eaten than of any ordinary butcher's meat, without any sense of repletion or after ill effects. This is the great dainty of the South Sea islands, and if to a turtle dinner be added bisque soup made from mountain river crayfish, a real island fruit salad, with lime juice and cocoanut cream, a freshly plucked pineapple, a dish of mangoes, granadillas, and a cup of island-grown coffee, not the Carlton or the Savoy could do better for a travelling prince.

All South Sea Island "white" houses are more or less alike, being built of coral concrete (occasionally of wood) and fitted with imported windows and doors. The verandah is the great feature of the building; for there the family will probably spend most of their time, reading, smoking, receiving callers, or simply lounging in long chairs and listening to the monotonous singing of the natives in the thatched reed houses near at hand. Splendid climbing plants wreathe the pillars and sloping roofs of these verandahs—stephanotis, Bougainvillea, and countless gay tropical flowers whose ugly Latin names only an accomplished botanist could remember. Gardenias, gorgeous white trumpet lilies, tall bushes of begonia; pink, yellow and scarlet hibiscus, crimson poinsettia, delicate eucharis lilies, run riot about the grounds, and orange and lemon flowers fill the air with an exquisite perfume.

Within, the high-pitched, deep, church-like roof rises above a range of partition walls separating the different rooms, but giving a common air supply to all, since the dividing walls are not more than ten or twelve feet high. There are no secrets in an island house; what any one says at one end can be heard at the other, and a light burning late in anybody's bedroom keeps all the rest awake. In the older houses the roof is of " rau " or plaited pandanus thatch, of a soft brown tone, delightfully cool and exceedingly picturesque. The rafters, in such a house, will be almost black with age, and beautifully latticed and patterned with finely plaited " sinnet " (cocoanut fibre). More modern houses have corrugated iron roofs, generally painted red. The water supply from these roofs is of some importance, and they are less expense and trouble than the thatch ; but the latter is incomparably the more picturesque, and a good deal the cooler as well.

The floor is always covered with native matting (pandanus leaf, split and plaited). This is of a pleasant tan colour in tone, and very cool and clean. The furniture is generally basket and bamboo, with a native " tappa " cloth (of which I shall have more to say later on) on the table. There are sure to be groups of old native weapons on the walls—lances and spears and clubs and arrows—and a few island fans, arranged in trophies, and garlanded with chains of shells. On the steps of the verandah one usually finds a fern or two, planted in big white clam-shells off the reef, and there may be others in the drawing-room. A piano is a great luxury ; the island climate is not kind to pianos. Harmoniums are more common.

The bedrooms may have ordinary beds imported from Auckland, or they may have (what is quite as good) native bedsteads made of ironwood, laced across with sinnet, and covered with soft pandanus leaf mats, over which the under sheet is laid. Unless it is the cool season there will not be a blanket. Mosquito curtains, of course, protect each bed. All windows and doors are wide open, day or night, hot season or cool.

The South Sea housekeeper has a few insect plagues

to fight against, but not nearly so many as her sister in India or Jamaica. The ants eat everything that is not hung or covered up. Enormous hornets, in the cool season, lurk about ceilings, bookcases and cupboards, sleepy, cross, and ready to dart a fearful sting, if accidentally touched. Cockroaches are destructive at all times. Fleas do not trouble much, and flies are only annoying in a few islands. Mosquitoes are troublesome in the hot season, but give little annoyance at other times. Centipedes and scorpions exist, but are not common. They do come into houses occasionally, and (being very poisonous, though not deadly) frighten the inmates quite as much as the inmates undoubtedly frighten them. It is the rarest possible thing, however, to hear of a European being bitten.

Education is not an unsolvable problem in the islands, since quite a large number of groups possess convent schools, where even such extras as music, languages, and fancy needlework can be taught. I give a picture of one such school in Raratonga, attended by natives and white children alike, and extremely successful with its pupils.

On the whole, the difficulties of housekeeping are somewhat less than at home, and the cost certainly much smaller. It is true that a good many tinned stuffs are used, and tinned food is always dear; but the cheapness of everything that the soil produces makes up that difference, and the simple standard of living swings the balance still further to the right side. I am of opinion myself that white families would benefit both in comfort and in pocket by adopting the native style of house, which is, as already mentioned, a structure of small neat sticks or poles set very closely and strongly, but not filled in. The roof is always thatched. In such a house, the air circulates freely without any draught, and there is a pleasant, diffused light during the daytime. At night, when native houses are more or less transparent, the privacy-loving white can draw thin cotton curtains across his walls until the lights are put out. I give a picture of one such house, built for and used by white people, and conspicuous for the simple beauty of the design. The interior was very plainly furnished with a few bamboo tables and chairs, and a light stretcher bed or two. Its curtains were of printed muslin from the stores, and its floor was nothing but white coral sand brought from the beach. The house stood sheltered by tall palms, and the sea was so near that all day one could watch the soft sparkle of the creaming surf through the half-transparent walls, and all night long one slept to the matchless lullaby of the humming reef.

(*Windows blurred with beating mud, grey London roaring by in the rain; haggard faces, and murky summer, and the snake of custom clipping stranglingly about the free man's throat—O Island wanderer, back in the weary North, does your sea-bird's heart fly swift from these to those, and sicken for the lands where you must go no more?*)

* * * * *

Raratonga is full of funny things, if one knows where to look for them. One would not suppose that the tombs of the natives were a likely spot. Yet I would defy the most serious of graveyard moralisers to count over the list of things that the Raratongan buries in the tombs of his departed relatives, without feeling his seriousness badly shaken. Little household ornaments belonging to the deceased are pathetic, certainly: so, in a lesser degree, are the Sunday clothes that often accompany their wearer on the long journey. But what is one to say of bicycles, Japanned bedsteads, and even pianos? All these things have been buried by Raratongans in the big concreted tombs that crop up sociably along the edges of the public road every here and there. The piano, I must add, was dug up again, by order of an indignant missionary, who gave the disconsolate mourners a good lecture on heathenistic practices, and the necessity of drawing the line somewhere.

Native names are sometimes exceedingly funny to the perverted white mind, although to the owners they may be dignified, poetic, and even beautiful. One young coffee-coloured lady of my acquaintance had been named (in Raratongan) "Cup-of-Tea." Another was "Box-with-a-Hole-in-It"—another "Tin-of-Meat." I should suppose, from my knowledge of their religious training, that each of these ladies possessed a godly scripture name of her own, properly bestowed on her at her proper baptism. But in the Cook Islands, the name a native is christened by, and the name he or she goes by, are almost always distinct, which is certainly confusing. Worse confusion still is caused by the odd habit of changing these commonly accepted names on any great occasion that seems to need special commemoration. The natives themselves never seem to become puzzled over all these name-changes, but so much can hardly be said of the whites. It is, at the least, perplexing to employ a gardener called Zebedee by the missionaries, Thunderstorm by his friends, and Tin Roof by his relatives—like the notable character in *The Hunting of the Snark*,

> Whose intimate friends called him Candle-Ends,
> And his enemies Toasted Cheese.

But it is even worse to be informed—some day, when you go to look after Zebedee-Thunderstorm-Tin-Roof down in the village, and ask why he has not turned up to weed your pineapples—that his name isn't any of the three, but "Barbed Wire," because he has just finished putting up a fence of barbed wire round the grave of his boy who died last year, and has resolved to call himself, henceforth, "Barbed Wire," in memory of his son!

Native notions about European clothes often provide a feast of fun for the whites, who set the copies in dress. When a lace-trimmed garment of mine, usually reserved for private wear under the shades of night and the shelter of a quilt and sheet, went to Sunday morning church as a best dress in full daylight, on the person of the laundress who had been entrusted with my clothes for the wash, the funny side of the affair was so much the more conspicuous, that the borrower never got the reproof she certainly ought to have had. And when a certain flower toque, made of poppies (a blossom unknown to the Pacific) first drove the women of the island half-distracted with excitement, and then led to thirty-six native ladies appearing simultaneously at a dance in Makea's grounds, wearing most excellent copies of my Paris model, done in double scarlet hibiscus from the bush, the natural outrage to my feelings (which every woman who has ever owned a "model" will understand) was quite swallowed up in the intense amusement that the incident caused to everybody on the grounds.

I was unfortunate enough to be away on the island schooner when a great wedding took place—the nuptials of one of the queen's nieces—and so missed the finest display of native dress and custom that had occurred during the whole year. The bride, I heard, wore fourteen silk dresses—not all at once, but one after the other, changing her dress again and again during the reception that followed the wedding ceremony in the mission church, until she almost made the white spectators giddy.

The presents were "numerous and costly" from the guests to the bride, and from the bride to the guests, for it is Raratongan custom to give presents to the people who

WEDDING PRESENTS

come to your wedding ; a fashion that would considerably alleviate the lot of the weary wedding guest, if only it could be introduced over here. The gifts for the bride were carried in by the givers, and flung down in a heap one by one, each being duly announced by the person making the present, who showed no false modesty in describing his contribution. "Here's twenty yards of the most beautiful print for Mata (the bride), from Erri Puno!" "Here's three baskets of arrowroot, the best you ever saw, for Mata, from Taoua." "Here's eighteen-pence for Mata and Tamueli, from Ruru," flinging the coins loudly into a china plate. So the procession went on, until the gifts were all bestowed, the bride meanwhile standing behind a kind of counter, and rapidly handing out rolls of stuff, tins of food, ribbons, gimcracks of various kinds, to her guests as they passed by. When all is added up, the amusement seems to be about all that any one really clears out of the whole proceeding.

The Cook Islanders are among the most musical of Pacific races. They have no musical instruments, unless " trade " mouth-organs, accordions, and jew's harps may be classed as such, but they need none, in their choral singing, which is indescribably grand and impressive. Here as elsewhere in the islands, one traces distinctly the influence of the two dominant sounds of the island world—the low droning of the reef, and the high soft murmur of the trade wind in the palms. The boom of the breakers finds a marvellously close echo in the splendid volume of the men's voices, which are bass for the most part, and very much more powerful and sonorous than anything one hears in the country of the "superior" race. The women's voices are somewhat shrill, but they sound well enough as one usually hears them, wandering wildly in and out of the massive harmonies of the basses.

just as well, when oratorios of this kind are to be heard every evening among the " rau " roofed huts—

> " Big-Nose who lives in the white house has got a new suit of clothes."
>
> *Chorus.* "A new suit of clothes, a new suit, suit, suit of clothes !"
>
> " Big-Nose cannot fasten the coat, he is so fat, ai ! ai, fat like a pig fit for killing !"
>
> *Chorus.* "Ai, Ai ! a pig for killing, like a pig for killing, Big-Nose is like a pig fit for killing !"
>
> " Big-Nose had a quarrel with his wife to-day, a quarrel, a great quarrel, Big-Nose drank wisiki, much wisiki."
>
> (All together, excitedly.) "A quarrel, a great quarrel, much wisiki Big-Nose drank, Big-Nose !"
>
> " The wife of Big-Nose of the white house has long hair, though she is very old, long hair that came to her in a box by the sitima (steamer) !"
>
> *Chorus.* " Long hair, long hair, long hair, in a box on the steamer. A box on the steamer, on the steamer, long hair for the wife of Big-Nose who lives in the white house."

A resident who really understood the natives and their music once or twice translated choruses for me that were quite as personal as the above. I have never since then wondered, as I used to wonder, where on earth the merry peasants of opera, with their extraordinary knowledge of the principals' affairs, and their tireless energy in singing about them, were originally sketched.

(Scholars will probably trace a resemblance to the Greek chorus here. I leave it to them to work out the wherefore, which makes me giddy even to think of, considering the geographical elements involved in the problem.)

But now enough of Raratonga, for the schooner *Duchess* is waiting to carry me away to the other islands of the group, and, after many thousands of miles travelled by steamer upon " all the seas of all the world," I am at last to learn what going to sea really is.

CHAPTER VII

The Schooner at last—White Wings *versus* Black Funnels—Not according to Clark Russell—The Marvellous White Woman—The Song of the Surf—Why not?—Delightful Aitutaki—Into an Atoll—A Night in the House of a Chieftainess—The Scarlet Devil—Nothing to wear—How to tickle a Shark—The Fairy Islets—A Chance for Robinson Crusoe.

THE schooner *Duchess* was in at last.
We were almost growing anxious about her in Raratonga—almost, not quite; for after all, she was only a fortnight overdue, and that is not much for an island schooner, even when she is run by white officers. When the easy-going native runs her, no one ever knows when she will leave any port, and no one would venture to predict that she will ever arrive at all. There are generally a good many native-owned schooners about the South-Eastern Pacific, but, though all the numbers keep up, the identity varies, and if you return after a few years and ask for the ships you used to know, the answer will be,

Of their bones are coral made.

I have not space to tell you here of the native schooner that started from one of the Cook Islands, not so very long ago, to visit another island less than two hundred miles away, but, because of the wild and weird navigation of her owners, went instead to somewhere over a thousand miles off; toured half the Pacific; stayed away six months; and finally came back to her own little island by a happy chance, without ever having reached the place she set out for after all. But it has a good deal of local colour in it.

The *Duchess*, however, was not a native schooner, being owned by whites, and run by a British captain, mate, and boatswain, assisted by eight island seamen. There was, therefore, a reasonable prospect of getting somewhere, sometime, if I travelled in her ; so I took my passage, and, for the first time, literally " sailed away "— to see the outer islands of the Cook Group, and later on, solitary Savage Island, Penrhyn, Malden, Rakahanga, and Manahiki.

For more than four months afterwards, with a single break, the little *Duchess* of 175 tons was my home. Little she seemed at first, but before long she assumed the proportions of quite a majestic vessel. There was no schooner in those waters that could touch her, either for speed, size, or (alas !) for pitching and rolling, in any and every weather. Her ninety-five foot masts made a brave show, when clothed with shining canvas ; her white hull, with its scarlet encircling band, and the sun-coloured copper glimmering at the water-line, stood out splendidly on the blazing blue of the great Pacific. " A three-masted topsail schooner " was her official designation. The unofficial names she was called in a calm, when the great Pacific swell brought out her full rolling powers, are best left unreported.

I cannot honestly advise the elderly round-the-world-tourist, doing the Pacific in orthodox style, to desert steam for sail, and try the experience of voyaging " off the track " among the islands never visited by liners. But the true traveller, who wanders for the joy of wandering, and is not afraid or unwilling to " rough it " a good deal, will find a sailing trip in the Pacific among the most fascinating of experiences. Beyond the radius of the belching funnel a great peace reigns ; an absence of time, a pleasant carelessness about all the weighty and tiresome things that may be happening outside the magic circle of still blue ocean. There is no "let-her-slide" spirit in the whole world to compare with that which blossoms spontaneously on the sun-white decks of a Pacific schooner. Looking back upon all the island boats that I have known, I may say that there was not so much discipline among the lot as would have run a single cross-channel boat at home, that every one was satisfied if the officers refrained from "jamborees" between ports ; if some one was sometimes at the wheel, and if the native crew knew enough of the ropes to work the ship reasonably well, in the intervals of line-fishing and chorus-singing. And in one and all, whatever might happen to passengers, cargo, ship, or crew, "take things as they come," was the grand general rule.

. . . . .

"This is your cabin," said the cheerful little pirate of a captain. He was celebrated as the "hardest case" in the South Pacific, and looked not quite unworthy of his reputation, though he was dressed as if for Bond Street in the afternoon, and mannered (on that occasion) as if for an evening party.

What I wanted to say, was "Good God ! " What I did say was : "Oh, really ! very nice indeed." For I saw at once that I must lie, and it seemed as well to obtain the fullest possible advantage from the sin. There was no use mincing words, or morals, in such a case.

The cabin had a floor exactly the size of my smallest flat box, which filled it so neatly that I had to stand on the lid all the time I was in my room. It had a bunk about as large as a tight fit in coffins, and a small parrot-perch at one side, which was not meant for parrots, but for me, to perch on, if I wanted to lace my boots without committing suicide when the ship was rolling. On the perch stood a tin basin, to do duty as a washstand. There was a biscuit-tin full of water underneath.

This was all that the cabin contained, except smells. The latter, however, crowded it to its fullest capacity. It had some mysterious communication with the hold, which perfumed it strongly with the oppressive, oily stench of ancient copra, and it had also a small door leading into the companion that went down to the engine-hole (one could not call it a room), in which lived the tiny oil engine that was supposed to start instantaneously, and work us out of danger, in case of any sudden need. (I say supposed, because—— But that comes after.)

This engine-hole had a smell of its own, a good deal stronger than the engine (but that is not saying much)—compounded of dirt, bilge-water, and benzolene. The smell joined in a sort of chorus with the copra odour of the hold, and both were picked out and accentuated by a sharp note of cockroach. It was the most symphonic odour that I had ever encountered. As for the port, that, I saw, would be screwed down most of the time owing to the position of the cabin, low down on the main deck.

"Very nice," I repeated, smiling a smile of which I am proud to this day. "Such a dear little cabin!"

"I'm glad you like it," said the captain, evidently relieved. "You see, there's four Government officials coming round this trip, and that takes our only other cabin. I chucked the bo'sun out of this; he's sleeping anywhere. Anything else you'd like?" he continued, looking at the biscuit-tin and the shiny basin with so much satisfaction that I guessed at once they were a startling novelty—the bo'sun having probably performed his toilet on deck. "We don't have lady passengers on these trips, as we aren't a Union liner exactly, but we're always ready to do what we can to please every one."

"I want first of all a new mattress, and sheets that haven't been washed in salt water, and then I want some air and light, and thirty or forty cubic feet more space, and I think, a new cabin, and I'm almost sure, another ship," I said to myself. Aloud I added: "Nothing whatever, thank you; it is charming," and then I went in and shut the door, and sat down on my bunk, and said things, that would not have passed muster in a Sunday-School, for quite ten minutes.

What I had expected I don't know. Something in the Clark Russell line, I fear—a sparkling little sea-parlour, smelling of rope and brine, looking out on a deck "as white as a peeled almond," and fitted with stern windows that overhung half the horizon. It was borne in upon me, as I sat there among the smells and ants and beetles, that I was in for something as un-Clark-Russelly as possible. "Well," I thought, "it will at least be all the newer. And there is certainly no getting out of it."

So we spread our white wings, and fluttered away like a great sea-butterfly, from underneath the green and purple peaks of Raratonga, far out on the wide Pacific. And thereupon, because the rollers rolled, and the ship was small, I went into my cabin, and for two days, like the heroine of an Early Victorian romance, "closed my eyes, and knew no more."

On the third day I was better, and in the afternoon Mitiaro, one of the outer Cook Islands, rose on the horizon. By three o'clock our boat had landed us—

the official party, the captain, and myself—on a beach of foam-white coral sand, crowded with laughing, excited natives, all intensely eager to see the "wahiné papa," or foreign woman. White men — traders, missionaries, the Resident Commissioner of the group—had visited the island now and again, but never a white woman before ; and though many had been away and seen such wonders, more had not.

The officials went away to hold a court of justice ; the captain and myself, before we had walked half across the beach, being captured by an excited band of jolly brown men and women, all in their Sunday best shirts and pareos, and long trailing gowns. They seized us by our elbows, and literally ran us up to the house of the principal chief, singing triumphantly. Along the neatest of coral sand paths we went, among groves of palm and banana, up to a real native house, built with a high "rau" roof, and airy birdcage walls. About half the island was collected here, drinking cocoanuts, eating bananas, staring, talking, laughing. In spite of their excitement, however, they were exceedingly courteous, offering me the best seat in the house—a real European chair, used as a sort of throne by the chief himself—fanning myself and my guide industriously as we sat, pressing everything eatable in the house on us, and doing their best, bare-footed brown savages as they were, to make us enjoy our visit.

All islanders are not courteous and considerate, but the huge majority certainly are. You shall look many a day and many a week among the sea-countries of the Pacific, before you meet with as much rudeness, selfishness, or unkindness, as you may meet any day without looking at all, on any railway platform of any town of civilised white England. And not from one end of the South Seas to the other, shall you hear anything like the harsh, loud, unmusical voice of the dominant race, in a native mouth. Soft and gentle always is the island speech, musical and kind—the speech of a race that knows neither hurry nor greed, and for whom the days are long and sweet, and "always afternoon."

When we went out to see the island, it was at the head of a gay procession of men, women, and children, singing ceaselessly, in loud metallic chants and choruses. Shy of the strange white apparition at first, the women grew bolder by degrees, and hung long necklaces of flowers and leaves and scented berries round my neck. They took my hat away, and returned it covered with feathery reva-reva plumes, made from the inner crown of the palm-tree. They produced a native dancing kilt, like a little crinoline, made of arrowroot fibre, dyed pink, and tied it round my waist, over my tailor skirt, explaining the while (through the captain, who interpreted), that the knot of the girdle was fastened in such a way as to cast a spell on me, and that I should inevitably be obliged to return to the island. (It is perhaps worthy of note that I did, though at the time of my first visit there seemed no chance of the ship calling again.) Decked out after this fashion, I had a *succès fou* on my return to the schooner, and was greeted with howls of delight on the part of my fellow-passengers, who had managed to escape adornment, being less of a novelty. It was of course impossible to remove the ornaments without offending the givers.

More houses, and more hosts, standing like Lewis Carroll's crocodile on their thresholds, to welcome me in "with gently smiling jaws." We visited till we were tired of visiting, and then strolled about the town. Cool, fresh, and clean are the houses of little

Mitiaro, dotted about its three miles' length. Their high deep-gabled roofs of plaited pandanus leaf keep out the heat of the staring sun: through their walls of smoothed and fitted canes the sea-wind blows and the green lagoon gleams dimly: the snowy coral pebbles that carpet all the floor reflect a softly pleasant light into the dusk, unwindowed dwelling. Outside, the palm-trees rustle endlessly, and the surf sings on the reef the long, low, perilous sweet song of the dreamy South Sea world—the song that has lured so many away into these lonely coral lands, to remember their Northern loves and homes no more—the song that, once heard, will whisper through the inmost chambers of the heart, across the years, and across the world till death.

Yet—why not?

Why not? The thought followed me as ceaselessly as the trampling of the surf (now, in the open, loud and triumphant, like the galloping of a victorious army) while I wandered over the little island, up and down the coral sand paths that led through groves of feathery ironwood, through quaintly regular, low, rich green shrubberies, starred with pale pink blossoms; among wild grey pinnacles of fantastic rock, clothed in trailing vines —always towards the open sky and the limitless blue sea. Why not? In England, even yet,

> We are not cotton-spinners all,

nor are we all old, blood-chilled by the frost of conventionality, dyed ingrain with the conviction that there is nothing but vagabondage and ne'er-do-well-ism away from the ring of the professions, or an office desk in the E.C. district. For the young and adventurous, the South Seas hold as fair prospects as any other semi-civilised portion of the globe. For those who have seen and have lived, and are wearied to death of the life and cities and competition, the island world offers remoteness, beauty, rest, and peace, unmatched in the round of the swinging earth. And to all alike it offers that most savoury morsel of life's banquet—freedom. Freedom and a biscuit taste better to many a young Anglo-Saxon than stalled ox seasoned with the bitter herbs of dependence; but the one is always at hand, and the other very far away.

Well, the gulf can be spanned; but he who cannot do the spanning, and must long and dream unsatisfied all his life, had best take comfort: it had not been for his good. The Islands are for the man of resource; again, of resource; and once more, of resource. Look among the lowest huts of the lowest quarters that cling to towns in the big islands, and there, gone native, and lost to his race, you shall find the man who was an excellent fellow—once—but who in emergency or difficulty, " didn't know what to do."

If there is a lesson in the above, he who needs it will find it.

Mitiaro is the island, already referred to, where dried bananas are prepared. The natives make up their fruit in this way for market, because steamers never call, and sailing vessels only come at long and irregular intervals. A very small quantity goes down in this way to Auckland, and I heard, in a general way, that there were supposed to be one or two other islands here and there about the Pacific, where the same trade was carried on. One cannot, however, buy preserved bananas in the colonies, unless by a special chance, so the purchasing public knows nothing of them, and is unaware what it misses. In the opinion of most who have tried them, the fruit, dried and compressed in the Mitiaro way, is superior to dried figs. It is not only a substitute for fresh bananas, but a dainty in itself. The whaling shops pick up an occasional consignment in out-of-the-way places, and are therefore familiar with them, but one never sees them on a steamer. There may be useful hints, for intending settlers, in these stray facts.

We lay over-night at Mitiaro, and got off in the morning. Aitutaki was our next place of call, and we reached it in about a day. It is, next to Raratonga, the most important island in the group, possessing a large mission station, a Government agent, and a post-office. It enjoys a call once a month from the Union steamer, and is therefore a much more sophisticated place than Mitiaro. In size, it is inferior to Raratonga and Atiu, being only seven square miles in extent. Its population is officially returned as 1,170. These are almost all natives, the white population including only the Government agent, two or three missionaries, and a couple of traders.

It is bright morning when we make Aitutaki, and the sea is so vividly blue, as we push off in the boat, that I wonder my fingers do not come out sapphire-coloured when I dip them in. And I think, as the eight brown arms pull us vigorously shoreward, that no one in the temperate climes knows, or ever can know, what these sea-colours of the tropics are like, because the North has no words that express them. How, indeed, should it have?

We are rowing, as fast as we can go, towards a great white ruffle of foam ruled like a line across the blue, blue sea. Inside this line there lies, to all appearance, an immense raised plain of green jade or aquamarine, with a palmy, plumy island, cinctured by a pearly beach, far away in the middle. Other islands, smaller and farther away, stand out upon the surface of this strange green circle here and there, all enclosed within the magic ring of tumbling foam, more than five miles across, that sets them apart from the wide blue sea. It is only a lagoon of atoll formation, but it looks like a piece of enamelled jewel-work, done by the hand of some ocean giant, so great that the huge sea-serpent itself should be only a bracelet for his arm. The raised appearance of the lagoon is one of the strangest things I have yet seen, though it is merely an optical delusion, created by contrast in colour.

We are fortunate, too, in seeing what every one does not see—a distinct green shade in the few white clouds that overhang the surface of the lagoon. Here in Aitutaki, a great part of the sky is sometimes coloured green by the reflections from the water, and it is a sight worth witnessing.

Through an opening in the reef we enter—the boatmen pulling hard against the outward rush of the tide, which runs here like a cataract at times—and glide easily across the mile or so of shallow water that lies between us and the shore. One or two splendid whale-boats pass us, manned by native crews, and the other passengers tell me that these boats are all made by the Aitutakians themselves, who are excellent builders.

There is a very decent little wharf to land on, and of course, the usual excited, decorated crowd to receive us, and follow us about. I am getting quite used now to going round at the head of a continual procession, to being hung over with chains of flowers and berries, and ceaselessly fed with bananas and cocoanuts, so the crowd does not interfere with my enjoyment of the new island. We are going to stop a day or two here, and there will be time to see everything.

When you sleep as a rule in a bunk possessing every attribute of a coffin (except the restfulness which one is led to expect in a bed of that nature), you do not require much pressing to accept an invitation to "dine and sleep" on shore. Tau Ariki (which means Chieftainess, or Countess, or Duchess, Tau) lives in Aitutaki, and she had met me in Raratonga, so she sent me a hearty invitation to spend the night at her house, and I accepted it.

Tau is not by any means as great a personage as Makea, or even as great as Tinomana, the lesser queen. She is an Ariki all the same, however, and owns a good deal of land in Aitutaki. Also, she is gloriously married to a white ex-schooner mate, who can teach even the Aitutakians something about boat-building, and she is travelled and finished, having been a trip to Auckland—the ambition of every Cook Islander. So Tau Ariki is a person of importance in her own small circle, and was allowed by the natives of the town to have the undoubted first right to entertain the white woman.

Tau's house, in the middle of the rambling, jungly, green street of the little town, proved to be a wooden bungalow with a verandah and a tin roof, very ugly, but very fine to native eyes. There were tables and chairs in the "parlour"; and the inevitable boiled fowl that takes the place of the fatted calf, in Pacific cookery, was served up on a china plate. A rich woman, Tau, and one who knew how the "tangata papa" (white folk) should be entertained!

She gave me a bedroom all to myself, with a smile that showed complete understanding of the foolish fads of the "wahiné papa." It had a large "imported" glass window, giving on the main street of the town, and offering, through its lack of blinds, such a fine, free show for the interested populace, that I was obliged to go to bed in the dark. There was a real bed in the room, covered with a patchwork quilt of a unique and striking design, representing a very realistic scarlet devil some four feet long. It seemed to me the kind of quilt that would need a good conscience and a blameless record, on the part of the sleeper reposing under it. To wake in the middle of the night unexpectedly, with the moonlight streaming in, forget for the moment where you were, and, looking round to find a landmark, drop your startled eyes upon that scarlet fiend, sprawling all over your chest—— Well, I had a good conscience, or none —I do not know which—so I felt the red devil would not disturb my slumbers, and he did not.

There was nothing else in the room, except a new, gold-laced, steamship officer's cap, whereto there seemed neither history nor owner, reposing on the pillow. If there was any mystery about the cap, I never knew it. I put it out on the windowsill, and a hen laid an egg in it next morning, and no doubt the hen lived happily ever after, and I hope the officer did, and that is all. It seems pathetic, but I do not know why.

There was nothing to wash in, but Tau knew her manners, and was quite aware that I might have a prejudice against sitting in a washing tub on either the front or the back verandah, to have buckets emptied on my head in the morning. So she made haste to leave a kerosine tin full of water, before going to her camphorwood chest, and extracting a pink silk dress trimmed with yellow lace, for me to sleep in.

"I'm afraid that won't do; it's too—too good to sleep in," I remarked.

"Nothing too good for you, you too much good self!" was the amiable reply.

"But I could not sleep in it, Tau. There's—there's too much of it," I objected, not knowing how to word my refusal without impoliteness.

"All right," commented my hostess, throwing a glance at the purple gloom of the torrid hot-season night outside. "He plenty hot. I get you pareo, all same mine." And she disinterred a brief cotton kilt of red and yellow, considerably smaller than a Highlander's.

"That's too little," objected the exacting guest, rather to poor Tau's perplexity. How was one to please such a visitor? At last, however, after refusing a figured muslin robe that was as transparent as a dancing-robe of classic Ionia (there are other analogies between those robes, if one might go into the subject; but I fear the British public must not be told about them), and a pink shirt belonging to the white husband, a neat cotton day gown was discovered, offered, and accepted, and peace reigned once more in the exceedingly public guest-chamber of Tau Ariki's house.

Concerning quilts, by the way, one may here add a short note. Patchwork is the delight of the Cook Island women, and has been so, ever since that absorbing pastime was first introduced to them by the missionaries' wives. They are extremely clever at it, and often invent their own patterns. Sometimes, however, they copy any startling device that they may chance to see—the more original, the better. A really good patchwork quilt is considered a possession of great value, and (one is sorry to say) often preferred to the fine, beautifully hand-woven mats in which the islanders used to excel. They still make mats in large numbers, but the patchwork quilt has spoilt their taste for the finer mats, and these

FISHING FOR SHARKS

latter are getting scarce. One of the quilts I photographed in Mitiaro, and here present its portrait.

In the morning, shark-catching was the order of the day. Aitutaki is celebrated for this sport all over Australasia, and I was very glad to get a chance of joining in it. One does not catch sharks, in Aitutaki, after the usual island fashion, which is much like the way familiar to all sea-faring folk—hook and line, and a lump of bad pork, and tow the monster to the shore when you have got him. No, there is something more exciting in store for the visitor who goes a-fishing in Aitutaki lagoon. The water is very shallow for the most part, and heats up quickly with the sun, especially when the day is dead calm, and there is not a ripple to break the force of the rays. By noon, the lagoon is unbearably warm in all the shallow parts, and the sharks which inhabit it in large numbers, begin to feel uncomfortable. Some of them make for the opening in the reef, and get out into the cooler sea beyond. Others, one will suppose, are lazy, and do not want to be troubled to swim so far. So they head for the coral patches here and there, and lie on the sand in the shelter of the rocks, their bodies thrust as far into the clefts and crannies of the coral as they can manage to get. This is the Aitutakian's opportunity. He is perfectly fearless in the water, and he knows that the shark is, after all, a stupid brute. So he arms himself with a knife, takes a strong rope, noosed in a slip-knot at one end, in his hand, and dives from his whale-boat into the warm green water, where he has marked the latter end of a shark sticking out from a patch of coral, some three or four fathoms underneath the surface.

The shark, being head in, does not see anything, but by-and-by he becomes aware of a delicate tickling all along his massive ribs, and as he rather likes this, he stays quite still, and enjoys it. It is the Aitutakian, tickling him as boys tickle a trout in a stream at home, and for exactly the same reason. He has got the noose in his left hand, and his aim is to slip it over the shark's tail, while he distracts the brute's attention by pleasantly tickling with the other hand. Perhaps he manages this at the first attempt—perhaps he is obliged to rise to the surface, and take a breath of air, going down again to have a second try. But, in any case, he is pretty sure to get the noose on before the shark suspects anything. Once that is accomplished, he rises to the surface like a shooting air-bubble, swings himself into the boat, and gives the order to "haul in!"

The men in the boat lay hold of the rope, tighten with a sharp jerk, and tail on. Now the shark begins to realise that something has happened ; and realises it still more fully in another minute or two, when he finds himself fighting for his life on the gunwale of a rocking boat, against half a dozen islanders armed with knives and axes. The battle is short ; the great brute is soon disabled by a smashing blow on the tail, and in another hour or two the village is feeding fat on his meat, and his fins are drying in the sun, to be sold to the trader by-and-by, for export to China. No dinner-party in China is complete without a dish of daintily dressed shark's fins, and a good proportion of the supply comes from the Pacific.

This is shark-fishing, as practised in Aitutaki. But I was not destined to see it at its best, for the day turned out breezy, and there was such a ripple upon the water that the natives declared the sharks would be extremely difficult to see or capture. Nevertheless, the captain and I decided to go, as there was a chance, though a faint one. We hired a boat, and took with us, as well as the rowers, Oki, a diver of renown. If Oki could not raise a shark for us, it was certain that no one could.

The captain of the missionary steamer *John Williams* had told me about the fishing some weeks before, and added that he had seen a shark caught himself, and tried to photograph it, but the photo was not a success, because, as he put it, " the shark moved ! "

This story wandered about in my mind as we shot across the lagoon to the fishing grounds, and the boat began to look uncomfortably small. " What does the shark do when you get it into the boat ? " I inquired rather anxiously.

" Makes the devil of a row, and the devil of a mess," said our own captain cheerfully. " But don't you mind him. Let sharks alone, and they'll let you alone ; that's always been my experience."

Conscious that I was never unkind to animals, not even tigers or sharks, I tried to feel at ease. But I did not quite succeed, until we got to the coral beds, and Oki put everything else out of my head by going head first overboard, and starting out among the rocks below (it was calmer here, and we could see him pretty plainly) to look for a shark.

His thin brown body showed up shadowy and wavering, upon the sands at the bottom, as he glided like a fish all along the patch of reef, inspecting every cave or crack where a shark might hide. He did not seem to be incommoded in the least by the three or four fathoms of water above him, but moved about as quietly and easily as if he had been swimming on the surface. I felt sure he must be at the point of death, as the seconds flew by, and he still glided in and out of the rocks, with nothing but the gleam of his white pareo to show his whereabouts, whenever he slipped into the shadow of one of the many clefts in which a shark might lie hidden. But Oki knew very well what he was about, and he did not seem at all exhausted when he shot to the surface again, after rather more than two minutes' absence, and told us gloomily that " No shark stop ! "

We tried again, and again. Oki took the slip knot down with him every time and every time he brought it up in his hand, unused. Melancholy, deep and silent, settled upon the boat. But at last the luck changed ; our diver came up, and announced with a smile, that there was a shark down there, very far into the coral, and if he could only reach the animal's tail, it would be all right.

One of the boatmen at this went to help him, and together they swam down to the bottom, and began fumbling interminably in the shadow. It was clear that they were making every effort to tempt the shark out, for one could see Oki straining wildly with his arm in the cleft, " tickling " industriously, while the other hovered head downwards outside, trailing the noose like a loop of seaweed in his hand. But all proved vain. Exhausted, the men rose at last, and gave it up. The shark was too far in, they said, and the noose could not be got on. If we remembered, they had told us it was not a good day, and they hoped we thought enough had been done. As for themselves, they were very tired doing our pleasure, and their lungs were sore, but they thought some plug tobacco—the black sticky kind, and a good deal of it—would set them all right again.

This was outside the letter of the agreement, which had included a good price for the boat and nothing else ; but we promised some tobacco, when the stores should be reached, and asked for some more particulars about the fishing.

"Do you ever find the shark head out, instead of tail out?" I queried.

"Yes, sometime he come head out," said Oki, reversing a green cocoanut on his nose, and swallowing in great gulps.

I waited till he had finished before I asked:

"What happens then?"

"Shark he fight, and we fight too," said Oki simply.

"And which wins?"

"All the time the Aitutaki boy he win, but sometime the shark he win too," was the cryptic reply.

. . . . .

Shark fins, I was told, sell for about six shillings a pound. Some of the traders in the islands further north, where sharks are abundant, make a good deal of money taking the fish on a hook and line, and drying the fins for sale. It should be a fairly profitable industry, as the fins of a medium shark appear to weigh a good deal—not less than three or four pounds, at a guess.

It was on my second visit to Aitutaki that I went out to the lesser islands of the lagoon; but the tale of that expedition may well come here.

These islets are of various sizes, from a mere rock with a couple of palms on it, to a fertile piece of land over a mile long, richly grown and wooded. They all lie within the great lagoon, and are therefore sheltered by a natural breakwater of the reef from the violence of the storms that occur in the rainy season. The nearest is about three miles from the mainland. All are quite uninhabited, and no particular value is set on them by anybody. They belong to the various chief families of the big island, but any one who wished to rent one in perpetuity (the New Zealand Government laws, which rule here, do not permit outright sale) could probably secure it for a very few pounds a year.

I was anxious to see them, for it seemed to me that islands suited to the realisation of Robinson Crusoe dreams could hardly be found the wide Pacific over. A desolate isle five hundred miles from anywhere, sounds well in a story, but the romance of such a spot is apt to wear very thin indeed after a few months, if one may believe the experiences of those who have tried it. Practical details are seldom considered by would-be Crusoes; they have, however, a knack of thrusting themselves into the foreground just when retreat is impossible. If you elect to live on a remote island, how are you going to keep up communication with the outer world? You will want at least a few commodities of civilisation from time to time, and they cannot swim across half the great South Seas, from Auckland or 'Frisco, up to your front verandah unaided. You will want mails, newspapers, and letters, unless haply you are a criminal flying from the near neighbourhood of the black cap and the drop—and how are these to come? Trading schooners will not call at your island unless you have plenty of cargo for them, and even then, you may not see them twice a year. Steamers, of course, you must not expect. If you keep a small vessel of your own, you must be thoroughly sea-trained to run and navigate her, and you will need to bring a few island men to your kingdom as crew, and they will want to go home again, and make trouble, and finally run off with your ship some dark night, and maroon you there for good. No, the "desert" island idea is best left to the shelves of the school library.

But at Aitutaki, and in some similar collections of atoll islands Robinson Crusoe's way is made easy and pleasant—or so it seemed to me, crossing the lagoon that afternoon on my way to the islets that were lying waste and uninhabited out on its broad expanse. From three to five miles away from the mainland, these islets are sufficiently isolated for any one who has not quarrelled with the whole human race. There is a steamer once a month, at the little pier near the settlement. There are one or two stores on the main island, where common provisions, cotton stuffs, spades, and knives, and such simple things, can be purchased. The lagoon is usually so calm that a native canoe would serve all ordinary needs of communication, for any one living on an islet. A house could be built in a few days, of the native type: and a good concrete bungalow could be put up with native help, in a very few weeks. Why should any one want to live in such a spot? Well, it is not necessary to argue out that question, because I have found by experience that quite a remarkable number of people do. It was for those people that I crossed the lagoon that day, and I know I shall have their thanks.

A whale-boat and a crew were necessary for the trip. I engaged both in the village, and went down to the wharf followed by a " tail " of seven stalwart islanders, dressed in white and crimson pareos, berry necklaces, and a curiously representative collection of steamship caps and jerseys. The Aitutakian is an inveterate traveller, and all these men had been away in a steamer somewhere as deck hands—or else their friends had, and they had begged a steamer cap and jersey or two here and there: it was all the same to them. The P. & O.— the Union S.S. Co. of New Zealand—the Shaw, Savill, and Albion—the Orient—Burns Philp—were all represented (so far as caps and jerseys went) by my boat's crew, and very well pleased with themselves and their poached attire they evidently were.

Provisions had to be purchased, they declared, as we should not be back before afternoon. So into the big store the whole party went to see me victual the ship. I bought biscuits and meat, exactly half what they asked, and they were so uplifted with joy at the amount of the supplies that they sang all the way down to the boat; and, once in it, treated me to an exhibition of rowing, the like of which I never expect to see again. The Aitutaki man is the smartest boatman, and the best hand with an oar, in the Southern Pacific. Never a man-of-war comes round the Cook group that her men do not try conclusions with the Aitutakians, and if report speaks truth, the result is not always flattering to British pride. Nor is this astonishing, to any one who has seen these islanders row. We had six miles of a pull, and every inch was against a strong head wind, and through a decidedly choppy sea. Yet, in spite of these handicaps, the men rowed the whole way at racing pace, oars springing, spray flying, the great whale-boat tearing through the water as though a mortal enemy were in pursuit. The coxswain, in the stern, kept slyly urging the rowers on to let the foreign woman see what they could do, and they pulled "all out"—or what looked extremely like it—from start to finish. I do not think any white crew that ever held an oar could have lived with that splendid six-mile rush. And when we neared the first island, and gradually slacked speed, there was not one among those seven mighty chests that heaved faster than at the start. Truly, I thought, they had earned their picnic.

But the islets! If Raratonga was the realisation of a childish dream, this was the embodiment of a vision of fairyland. There can surely be nothing on earth more lovely than the islet constellation enclosed by Aitutaki reef. The water, shallow, sun-jewelled, and spread out over a bed of spotless coral sand, is coloured with a brilliance that is simply incredible. Emerald and jade and sapphire—yes, one expects these, in the hues of tropic seas. But when it comes to whole tracts of glancing heliotrope and hyacinth, shot with unnamable shades of melted turquoise and silver, and all a-quiver with pulsations of flashing greens, for which there is no name in any language under the pallid northern or burning southern sun—then, the thing becomes indescribable, and one can only say : " There is something in that little corner of earth beyond the touch of words, so you will never know anything about it, unless you too go there, and see it for yourself. And when you have seen, you will come away burning to describe, as I was—but you will not be able."

In the midst of this magical sea, rise the islets themselves—fairyland every one. Their little beaches are sparkling white, as only a coral beach can be ; palm-trees, heavy-headed with their loads of huge green nuts, cluster thick along the shores ; coral-trees drop their blood-red flowers into the glass-like water of the lagoon ; ripe oranges swing their glowing lamps among the darker green of the woods that rise behind. Big white clams with goffered shells, each holding meat enough for one man's dinner, gleam along the edges of the shore ; large, long-legged crabs wander rustling and rattling among the stones. The murmur of the barrier reef is very far away ; its thin white line of foam gleams out a long way off, under a low horizon, sky shot strangely with lilac blue—a lonely, lovely, exquisite place, the like of which one might seek the world all over, and never find again.

We landed on the sand, and I set about exploring, while the men knocked down cocoanuts, and squatted in the shade to drink them, and suck fresh oranges. The island on which we had landed was one of the smaller ones, not more than an acre or two in extent. It rose to a high point in the centre, and was so thickly wooded all over, that I could hardly make my way through. There was no sign of life or habitation, and the ripe fruit was everywhere rotting on the ground.

I pictured the little islet with a high brown roof peeping out among its palms, a neatly kept pathway cut through the bush, and a snug boathouse on the shore, covering a fine whaleboat, while a graceful native canoe lay on the sand, ready for any one to lift down into the water at any minute. I wonder, will the picture ever body itself out in real, for some tired-out soul, weary of cities and competition, or some pair of lovers, who find the world well lost in each other, here among the far islands of the sweet Southern Seas? I shall never know, for the "sea-bird's feather" was in the pillow on which I slept my first baby sleep, and I wander always on. But it may be that these words will be read by some to whom they are, or shall be, a part of life's own history.

We did not get to the other islands that day, partly because I wasted so much time looking for shells, and partly because the largest were still some miles away, and the wind was stronger than ever. One, I heard, had ground enough for a paying plantation, and was already fairly well supplied with cocoanuts. All are perfectly healthy and free from fevers of any kind, and though mosquitoes are present in rather large numbers, careful clearing of their breeding grounds would in time drive them away.

.   .   .   .   .

INQUIRIES

In case author, or publishers, should be inundated with inquiries about South Sea Islands, it may be as well to say that all over the Pacific, the Governors, Commissioners, and Resident Agents of the various groups are always ready to furnish information to honest inquirers.

CHAPTER VIII

Jumping a Coral Reef—The Great Wall of the Makatea—Makaia's Wonderful Staircases—A Clothing Club of the Pacific—Cool Costumes in Atiu—The Lands that lie waste—Mystery of a Vanished Tribe—Fashions in Hair-Dressing—The Sign-Language of the Sex—Invited to a Feast.

MANGAIA, where we next stopped, proved quite an exciting place. You cannot land upon Mangaia in the ordinary way: the reef that surrounds it is unbroken, and girdles the whole island in a fortress moat of its own. The only way to land is to get into one of the numberless native canoes that crowd about the ship, and let the copper-coloured owner take you over the reef in his own way, which is the determined and decisive way of a steeplechaser at a fence. It is most excellent fun and a new thing in sensations. As the little dug-out—made of nothing more elaborate than a hollowed mango log, with an outrigger at one side—rushes shoreward on the crest of a foaming roller, you watch with rather anxious interest the movements of the dusky boatman, who poises his paddle in the air, waits, looks, and strikes the water, always at exactly the right moment—usually when you are just beginning to think of kicking off your shoes.

There is the reef right in front, a pearly shadow in the blue, with up-springing spears of ivory, bared like the teeth of a tiger, when the wave rolls back. Are we going to jump that? We are indeed. The boatman lifts his paddle—we sweep upwards on the sloping blue satin neck of

LANDING ON MANGAIA

a curling wave. No no, that will not do—not this time. He backs water—we hang on the crest of the wave—but we are not going to be drowned, or snapped up by the sharks that haunt the reefs, because the boatman is a born islander, and what he does not know about canoeing over a reef, neither you nor I need attempt to teach him. Another wave, a monster this time, swinging us up into the air as if we were a couple of grasshoppers out paddling in a walnut shell. That will do : here she goes ! The wave roars with us ; the wicked white fangs gleam on either hand : our rough thick keel scrapes agonisingly on the coral, and there is a smother of foam and tumbling blue and bursting green all about the cranky little craft. Bump ! we have struck—we strike again, but it does not seem to matter in the least : over we go, and we are in the smooth, safe, shallow green water inside, and across the reef. And here are a dozen men of Mangaia, splashing about in the lagoon, ready to pick up the visitor in their powerful arms as soon as the canoe grounds in the shallow water, and carry her ashore.

That is how one lands on Mangaia.

This island is of a good size, being some thirty miles in circumference. Its formation is very notable, being indeed rather celebrated among geologists. It is supposed to be of volcanic origin, like most of the " high " islands. From the sea, it looks much like any other place of the same size. But, going inland, one is astonished to find that a mere strip of land close round the coast terminates the ground available for walking on. A high irregular cliff wall, from fifty to a hundred feet in height, encloses the whole interior of the island, which thus resembles in shape a very large cup set on a very small saucer. Within the cup lie all fertile lands, the taro beds, the yam fields, the pineapple patches, the tangled bush, where cotton used to be grown in the days of the American war, the low green shrubberies that produce the finest coffee in the Cook Islands. To reach them, there is only one way—that furnished by a really wonderful rocky staircase, built in prehistoric times by the ancestors of the present natives. If one were to find such a work in any other of the Cook Islands, one might regard it as proof positive of the existence of an older and more industrious race, in the days before the New Zealand Maori took possession of these lands, and grew effeminate and idle in the occupying.

But the people of Mangaia, though identical in descent with incurably indolent and sensual Aitutakians and Raratongans, have been moulded by their environment to a degree that amounts to an actual difference in character. The barrier reef has always prevented the free communication enjoyed by other islands, so that they were able to develop along their own lines of character, without modification from outside. With an island that possessed only a limited amount of fertile land, a matchless fortress in the interior, and a complete barrier about the exterior, it was a foregone conclusion that the Mangaians should become inhospitable, reserved, and hard-working, as compared with the prodigally generous and idle folk of the open and fertile islands. They did so. In the days before the missions, some sixty years ago, the Mangaians were the fiercest cannibals in the group, and determinedly hostile to strangers : nor were they ever as pleasure-loving as the other Cook Islanders. To-day they are harder in character than the folk of the other islands ; kindly to strangers, but hardly gushing in their reception of them, and so much more industrious than the Aitutakians or Raratongans that Mangaian men are sought as servants all over the group.

THE MAKATEA

There is, therefore, no difficulty in understanding how the people of Mangaia found energy and time to construct the staircases that span the great wall of "Makatea," enclosing the inner part of the island. Being obliged day after day to climb with infinite pains the sharp rocky heights of the cliff, in order to get from the fishing grounds to the plantations, they would certainly not be long in devising some means of lessening this inconvenience. The staircases which are the result must have taken many years and much labour in constructing, and it is difficult to understand how a people unacquainted with the use of any mechanical contrivance could have placed so many large blocks of stone in the positions which they occupy. The illustration shows one of the staircases—the outer one—but does not give any idea of the sharp angle at which it ascends. The climb is, indeed, rather a breathless matter to strangers, though the natives run up and down the stairs, laden with heavy burdens, as easily as if they were on a level. In height, the flight is about a hundred feet.

The steps are very high and irregular, and on an extremely torrid afternoon it is not exactly the walk one would choose for pure enjoyment. However, our time in Mangaia was short, so I explained to a native girl that I wanted to see the Makatea, and she at once called up half the village to join the procession.

Attended, therefore, by my young guide and the inevitable following, I went up the mighty stairs, and across the tract of level land lying at the top. It is nearly a mile before one comes upon the cup-like valley in the centre of the island, so it must be allowed that the rim of the cup is a thick one. After a pleasant walk through groves of cocoanut and guava, we came upon the inner side of the wall, and stood on the edge of a great grey circular cliff, spiked, spired, and towered with extraordinary eccentricity, and splendidly garlanded with falling masses of sea-green creeper. At one point, a huge split in the rock had evidently provided a foundation for the second staircase, which was rougher than the first, made of great blocks of stone irregularly laid here and there so as to fill up the split in part, and give a foothold to the climber. Still, it was a big piece of work, and must have taken a good many years—generations, perhaps—to complete. Down in the valley below, which seemed to be two or three miles across, were all the native plantations and gardens, and as we jumped down from block to block, we met hard-faced muscular women toiling upwards with heavy loads of vegetables and fruit. In the taro fields, terraced so as to let a little stream trickle through and create an artificial swamp, the workers seemed to be women only. They dug and scraped in the thick mud under the burning sun, leaving off their tasks long enough to stare and question a little, and then setting stolidly to work again. The men were probably out fishing or pigeon shooting. In spite of Christianity, the island woman always carries the heavy end of the load, where there is one to carry; the man is the hunter, the woman the labourer and beast of burden, as in the cannibal times of long ago.

There are some remarkable caves in the island, and I went into them for a mile or so, in company with the local missionary, who kindly offered to act as guide.

Caves, however—as most people will allow—are much alike in all parts of the earth, and there is nothing to differentiate the long, dark, dripping passages, half-glimpsed halls, gloomy crevasses, and dimly sparkling stalactite candelabra of a South Sea Island cave, from those of a cave near Brighton or the Land's End. There is no need, therefore, to describe the caves of Mangaia further than to say that they were quite up to the usual pattern, and that at all events, they gave a touch of "Swiss Family Robinson" to the island atmosphere that was pleasing to the imagination.

It had, of course, nothing to do with Mangaia, but I wondered as we walked back from the caves towards the top of Makatea, how it was that the interesting shipwrecked people who live in caves as described in fiction, never seem to be troubled with damp? I have, personally, never seen a cave—out of a book—that was not first cousin to a showerbath, and I should be surprised if any one else had. Who ever saw a genuine cave roof that was not covered with stalactites, large or small? and what makes stalactites but endless drip? If I were a shipwrecked person, I should certainly prefer the temporary house the "useful" character always puts up in half an hour with the aid of four growing trees and the ship's mainsail, to the cave that is invariably discovered in the second chapter. I should know for certain that the former was the driest—even when it rained.

I cannot leave the subject of the strange Makatea, without telling yet a little more about it, for it has not often been described or mentioned. Geologists say that it is the product of a double volcanic upheaval. The first convulsion threw up the island itself, and, in the course of ages, the usual encircling reef of coral was built up round it by the busy coral insects, working under the water. Then came a second upheaval, and the island and reef together were cast up two hundred feet. The Makatea is thus the ancient reef that once surrounded the original small island which is represented by a crown of heights in the middle of the cup of the crater, and by the sunk-down valley about it. The narrow strip of land that edges the beach to-day is a later formation.

One cannot mistake the character of the great coral cliff, which is quite unlike any kind of stone, or indeed anything but itself. The passing ages have turned it to rock, but to rock which is hollowed in every direction with caves, small and great, and filled with fossil shells as a pudding is filled with plums. No unprotected foot can tread the surface of these heights, which are simply a mass of serried grey spears, sharp and cruel as the top of a wall protected by broken glass. The natives, if convenience leads them to cross any part of the Makatea other than the staircases, usually protect their feet with thick sandals of woven coir fastened on with cords. One can imagine how much this peculiar protection must have added to the safety of the interior of the island, in the old predatory days.

The caves were often used for burying places in time gone by, and it is only a few years since a "find" of skulls of a type differing in several particulars from those of the present day, was made in one of the largest caves by a schooner captain. Rumour says that he sold them for a good price, but the purchasers were not known.

Another use of the coral caves in the old days (over fifty years ago) was a shelter for fugitives of various kinds. The Mangaians were not a pleasant people, in those times, either to strangers or each other. The outsider was cooked and eaten for the mere offence of presuming to exist. The Mangaian was never sure that some one who had a spite against him would not murder him—probably by poison, in the use of which these people were as expert as the Borgias themselves. Under these circumstances, the caves were never without their occupants, living in secret, and creeping out at night to pick up a little food. Many and romantic are the stories told by the missionaries and traders of these stirring times, if I had space to relate them.

Mangaia is a beautiful island, but that goes without saying, in the exquisite Cook Group. It has about half a dozen white people, and the native population is said to number something under two thousand.

Though a pleasant island and a healthy one, it cannot be recommended to planters, as there is not an inch of land available for rent. The natives themselves are keen traders and bargainers, and export much of their fruit and copra direct to Auckland. Most of what they make is spent in trade-finery, for which they have an uncontrollable passion. On Sundays, the churches are a very flower-garden of frippery, the men turning out in the most brilliant of shirts, ties, and suits, the women decking themselves in long loose robes of muslin, sateen, or cheap silk, coloured in the most screaming hues—pea-green, royal blue, scarlet, and orange being all strong favourites. Their hats, made by themselves out of silky arrowroot fibre, are often trimmed with the costliest ribbons and artificial flowers, and even with ostrich plumes to the value of two or three pounds. It is somewhat puzzling, I was told, to see several entire families got up in the same extraordinary style, unless you know the reason, which is, that these various households have joined together in a club, putting all the money they have made into one purse, and sending it down to Auckland on their own account for a bale of gorgeous clothing, all alike. Thus you will see twenty or thirty women, on a Sunday morning, dressed alike in robes of vermilion satinette, and wearing huge hats, crowned by three ostrich feathers, red, yellow, and blue, arranged after the fashion of the Prince of Wales's crest. This is one of the clubs, and there are sure to be others that vie with them in startling attire. Such are the weaknesses—after all, venial ones indeed—of the sturdy-souled Mangaian.

Atiu was our next stop, and here the reef-jumping process had to be repeated in another form. The ship's whale-boat, steered by our captain, who was the cleverest hand at the big sixteen-foot steer-oar of any white man I have ever seen, approached the edge of the reef, and danced about in front of it, until the passengers found an opportunity of leaping out on to it. Then, rather wet-footed (but no one minded that, in a temperature like the hot room of a Turkish bath) we were picked up by natives waiting on the shallow side, and carried through the lagoon, which was not more than a foot or two deep.

On landing, we found a number of the men standing on the shore ready to receive the Commissioner. They had been fishing, and were clad simply and coolly in a rag and a feather apiece—the latter worn in the hair, over one ear. Their dress, however, did not seem to embarrass them at all, and they came forward and shook hands with every one, quite politely. All the Cook islanders are supposed to be Christianised and civilised, but in some parts of the group the civilisation, at all events, seems to be wearing very thin, and this is notably the case in Atiu, an island rather larger than Raratonga, which has no resident missionary, save a very conceited and upsetting young native teacher. The Atiuans were of old a wilder and fiercer race than even the Mangaians, and such determined cannibals that they used to make raids on the surrounding islands for the simple purpose of filling their cooking ovens, and enjoying a mighty feast. Great war canoes, laden with gory corpses, have many a time been drawn up on the very stretch of sand where we landed, and the grandfathers of the men who greeted us have sung and danced in fierce exultation to see the fat limbs and well-fed bodies of their enemies laid in ghastly heaps upon the snowy beach, ready for the cooking pits that since early morning had been glowing with flame in anticipation of the banquet.

"Meek-faced Atiuans" was the nickname bestowed upon these islanders, in derision, by those who knew their wiliness and treachery. There is not much that is meek-faced about them to-day. They certainly look rougher and less amiable than any others of the Cook Islanders, and they are by no means so amiable and easy-going as the Raratongans, Aitutakians, and people of Mitiaro and Mauke. However, it cannot be said that they are in any way dangerous, and the stray white people who have lived in the island (there was only one at the time of my visit) have always got on well with them. Rough, as I said before, they certainly are. A ring I wore on my hand attracted the attention of one or two of the men, and they crowded round, fingered it, and actually tried to snatch—an attempt very shortly put an end to by the Commissioner, who ordered them off peremptorily. The incident, although small, illustrates a standard of manners that one would certainly not encounter in any other part of the group, or indeed in any one of the Southern or Eastern Pacific groups that I afterwards saw.

There was a good deal of native-manufactured lime-juice to be got away here, and the people (most of them more completely dressed than the party that had received us on the shore) were busy rolling down the casks into the water, where the out-going tide took them, and floated them across the reef to the schooner. It seemed a strange way of taking on cargo, but I learned, afterwards, that it is not uncommon in islands surrounded by a dangerous reef.

The walk up to the settlement proved to be a good three miles, Atiu being one of the very few islands whose natives do not live down on the shore. The scenery was fine—wide rich plains covered with low scrub, or clothed with thick herbage, alternating with heavy forest. There is no better soil in the islands than that of Atiu. Guavas are a common weed; pumpkins run wild, trailing their long green vines and heavy fruit right across the track, mangoes, chestnuts, Pacific cherries, and other fruits, grow without care or cultivation. Any tropical product can be raised, and land is exceedingly cheap. The reef has always been a handicap to the island; but I heard that a part had been blown up to admit of a boat passage, some time after my visit, also that the Union steamers had begun to call for cargoes—an important event in the history of any island, and one likely to do much for its future.

The people are few in number—only nine hundred —and do not attempt to use more than a very small portion of the thirty-two square miles of their territory. Much is available for letting, and every inch of the island is worth cultivating, although to a stranger's eye it is hardly as fertile in appearance as other portions of the Cook Group that are much less valuable. Coffee, copra, oranges, bananas, sweet potatoes, could be profitably grown for export. The climate is good and healthy.

The people have not dwindled down to their present small numbers through natural decay. Like another more famous island, Atiu is "swarming with absentees." In the Society Islands, and here and there in other groups, whole villages full of Atiuans are to-day to be seen, who emigrated from their native country twenty or thirty years ago, owing to difficulties with the missionaries, and went to seek an asylum in lands where strings were drawn somewhat less tightly than they were at home.

They never returned, though the island, when I saw it, had no resident white missionary at all, and in consequence their lands have lain idle ever since. The ill wind has blown good to planters and settlers, however, so one need not quarrel with it.

Like Mangaia, Atiu has a cave—only a much larger one, and it has a mystery connected with the cave, which no one has yet attempted to solve.

Sixty years ago or more (I was told—I do not swear to the truth of this or any other island story that I have not had the opportunity of investigating in person), an invading tribe came to Atiu, and in the course of several battles, defeated and put to rout one of the lesser tribes of the island. The vanquished ones, fearing that they would be killed and eaten, plucked up courage to try a desperate expedient, and hid themselves in the cave, into whose dark recesses no native had ever before ventured, for fear of offending the evil spirits that were said to live therein. After waiting for a day or two, the enemies gave up the contest, and went away again. It was now safe for the hunted tribe to come forth, and the other inhabitants of the island looked to see them return—for after all, it did not seem likely that the evil spirits would destroy so many. They waited in vain. From the unknown depths of the cave—unknown, in its innermost recesses, to the present day—no sign, no message reached them; no living soul ever came forth of the many men, women, and children who had braved the dangers of that dark portal. Lost they were, lost they remained.

What happened to them? No one knows. It is not easy to destroy a whole tribe, and leave no sign. But the one white man who partly explored the cave some years ago, found nothing to hint at the nature of the tragedy. It is true that his candles gave out, and the cord that served him for a guide back among the endless windings of the place, came to an end, so that he never knew quite how far the place went, or how many ramifications it had. Still, it is strange enough that not so much as a single human bone was to be seen. If the tribe had lost their way, and perished of hunger, some traces would certainly have been visible—a spear, a shell ornament, perhaps a skeleton. If they had fallen in a body over some treacherous inner precipice, the dangerous place would have been discoverable. Perhaps some new explorer will unravel the mystery, one of these days. It will not be a steamer passenger, however, for the Union boats on their rare calls do not stay long enough for any one to land, and the cave requires two clear days to reach and see.

As we were not even stopping overnight ourselves, I had no opportunity of making an exploration on my own account. Thus the mystery rests unsolved— unless some one may have come to the island in a stray trading schooner since my visit, and found time enough to explore the unknown parts of the haunted cavern. The natives of Atiu, needless to say, put down the whole thing simply and solely to the revenge of the "local demons."

The people of the settlement, when we reached it, greeted our party with boisterous cheerfulness. The officials went to hold their court, as usual, and I, being as usual quite uninterested in the details of native boundary disputes conducted in an unknown tongue, amused myself with the women of the village. It might be more correct to say that they amused themselves with me. I do not think any white woman had been up to the settlement before I visited it, and the curiosity of the girls was uncontrollable. They crowded round me, they slyly felt my hair to see if the coils were attached to my head in Nature's own way (by which I conclude that the wearing of false hair is not unknown to themselves), they rubbed my dress material in their fingers, they poked me all over to see if I was real, and conducted such searching investigations into the quantity and style of my clothing, that I was obliged to speak to one or two as sharply as I knew how (the tongue was alien, but the tone was understood) and make them desist. Withal, they were not ill-natured, though certainly a little ill-mannered. They did not forget the duties of hospitality, but pressed fruit and cocoanut water on me, and one woman insisted on giving me a bottle full of honey to take away—a gift that was much appreciated by my fellow-passengers on the schooner, later on.

I gratified them extremely by loosening the hair of one or two, and putting it up in the latest fashionable style, which proved so popular that the whole feminine half of the island set to hair-dressing at once, and before I left the island that day, a general and complete revolution in coiffure had taken place. We had a good deal of feminine talk among ourselves, before the men came out again: the fact that I did not know anything of the language, save perhaps half a dozen words, was no bar to a certain amount of thought-interchange. How was it done? Signs, for the most part: scraps, guesses, hints, stray native words made to do double and treble duty. Could I have talked to the husbands and brothers of the women in the same way? No, certainly not. All through my wanderings among the uncivilised folk of the island world, I was constantly interested and amused to see how quick the women were in the language of signs and makeshifts, how very uncomprehending the men. If I wanted to make a request of any kind, on an island where I did not know any of the language, I instinctively sought for a woman to interpret my signs for a boat, a guide, a trader's or missionary's house, and so forth; and found that the women understood, almost as surely as the men, under the same circumstances, did not. Psychologists may make what they like of the fact. Women, who have talked the "sign-language" to each other, many and many a time, over the innocent thick heads of their unsuspecting better-halves, friends, or brothers, will never doubt it. We are not as clever as men—let the equality brigade shriek if they like, "it's as true as turnips is, as true as taxes"—but neither are we as stupid. God forbid!

I had practically the whole day to put in somehow, so, after the delights of hair-dressing had palled, and the afternoon was passing on, I accepted the invitation of a cheerful, though rather rough-looking pair of girls, whom I found crushing limes for lime juice in a very primitive sort of hand press, and followed them in to dinner in one of the native houses.

There was a distinguished guest to be entertained—a woman of Atiu who had been away from the island with her husband for many months, and had now returned in the *Duchess*, quite civilised and chic and modern, with the up-to-dateness of far-away Auckland. This celebrity, regarded as a very Isabella Bird among the island women, scarce any of whom had ever seen the other side of their own reef, was seated on the mats when I entered, her legs folded under her, native fashion; not without evident discomfort, for the heels of very high-heeled, pointed boots are painful under such circumstances, and corsets laced to bursting point are absolutely deadly. Ritia's dark face was ominously empurpled, and perspiration due as much to agony as to the heat (which was undeniable) streamed over her forehead and down her nose, from under the brim of her incredible picture hat. But pride upheld her, for who among the other women of the island owned such magnificent clothes?

The people of the house received me with exultation. Now, the feast was indeed a gorgeous one, and the sea-green envy sure to be the lot of every housewife in settlement with whom I had not dined, shed additional lustre on the triumph. The food was just coming in as I entered and folded myself up on the mats—roast sucking-pig, smelling very good ; a fat boiled fowl; some fish from the lagoon, baked like the pig in a ground oven, and done to a turn ; arrowroot jelly ; young green cocoanuts, with the meat still unset, clinging to the thin shell like transparent blanc-mange ; breadfruit, smoking and floury ; baked pumpkins ; bananas, roasted in their skins ; sweet potatoes ; chestnuts. A large cocoanut, picked at the right stage for drinking, stood at each guest's right hand, and in the middle was a big bowl of milky cocoanut cream, into which each guest was supposed to dip his food as he ate.

Plates there were none, but I have never thought clean, fresh, green leaves, a foot or two across, unpleasant substitutes for delf or china, which is handled and used by hundreds of eaters, and must be washed in greasy hot water at the end of every meal. There is a good deal to be said for the native custom, whether the point of view be that of convenience, cleanliness, or simple beauty.

I, as the principal guest, was offered everything first, which obviated any unpleasantness that might have arisen from the entire absence of knives and forks. There is no hardship in eating with your fingers, if yours are the first to plunge into every dish, and you have your nice fresh leaf to yourself. The little pig I did not touch, because no one who has lived as much as a week in the islands will venture on native pork, good as it looks and smells. When an unfortunate beast is killed by strangulation, and never bled, and when you know that it has lived at its gipsy will, and fed more abominably than a land-crab, you are apt to find you are " not hungry" when its crackling little carcase comes to table in cerements of green leaves, and you ask for the breadfruit and the fish instead.

The feast seemed likely to go on all afternoon, since no native thinks he has eaten enough, on such an occasion, until he is as gorged and as comatose as a stuffed anaconda. There is no obligation to stay longer than one likes, however, so I washed my hands and withdrew, as soon as it seemed good to me to do so.

And by the way, if we of the civilised countries think that we invented fingerbowls, either in form, or in use, we are mistaken. The South Seas invented them, a few hundred years before we found out they were necessary to our own delicate refinement. A bowl full of water is handed round to every diner in a South Sea house. The water is from the river, pure and fresh; the bowl is of a mould more perfect than the most exquisite models of ancient Greece, delicately hued with pale brown in the inner part, and deep sienna brown outside. It is half a cocoanut shell—beautiful, useful, practically unbreakable, yet not of sufficient worth to prevent its being thrown away to-morrow and replaced by a fresh one from the nearest palm. Fresh plates and cups for one's food are a refinement that our refined civilisation has not attained to yet. You must go to savages to look for them.

I thanked my hosts for their entertainment, in good English, when I left. They understood the words and tone almost as clearly as if I had spoken in their own language, and gave me a ringing salutation that followed me down the road. That a number of Atiuan men, coming up from the shore, burst out laughing when they saw me, and held on to each other in convulsions of merriment at the sight of my absurd white face and ridiculous clothes, did not detract from the real kindliness of the reception the island had given me. The manners of the Atiuan would certainly throw a Tahitian or a courtly Samoan into a fit; but for all that, he is not at bottom a bad sort, and could certainly be made something of with training.

One of the Arikis of Atiu—a woman again : there seemed to be very few male chiefs in the islands—was pointed out to me as I went down to the shore, and I photographed her sitting in her chair. She looked dignified, and her long descent was visible in the pose of her small head, and the delicacy of her hands, but she did not possess much claim to beauty.

The *Duchess* was standing off and on outside the reef when I came out on the beach again, and the barrels were merrily floating out, rolled down into the water by the hands of busy brown men and women. It was a pretty scene in the low yellow sunlight of the waning afternoon, and I carried it away with me, long after we had sailed, as a pleasant recollection of Atiu.

CHAPTER IX

Islands and Adventures—What about the Missionary?—The Lotus Eaters—How to hunt the Robber-Crab—The Ship that would not sail—Proper Place of a Passenger—One Way to get wrecked—The Pirate and the Pearls.

MAUKE, Manuwai, and Takutea still remained to be seen, before the *Duchess* could spread her wings for Raratonga again. We sailed from one to another in the course of a few days. There was no hurry, and a day wasted here or there troubled none of us.

Sometimes the "trades," which are very fickle about here, came up and caught our towering canvas in a cool embrace; then the great hollows of the sails hummed with the music that the ocean wanderer loves, and the *Duchess* skimmed the rolling blue hills like a flying-fish. Sometimes the wind fell, and the booms swung and creaked lazily above the burning deck; then we trolled for albacore and bonito, shrieking with savage joy when our bit of long-desired fresh food came flapping and fighting over the rail; or we watched the crew hook devil-faced grey sharks, which "took charge" of the deck when captured, hitting terrible blows with their tails, and snapping stout ropes with their savage teeth; or we got out boats, and rowed them for miles between the double furnaces of the blazing sun and the glowing sea, coming back to the ship scorched into cinders, stiff with exertion, but happy. At night the Southern

Cross burned white in the velvet sky, and the coral rocks about the lagoons showed in shimmering pale blue underneath fifty feet or more of clear, moonlit water. Lying on the poop, like seals on sand, the little knot of passengers, captain, and mate, "yarned" for hour after hour—strange, wild tales of frontier life in new lands; of adventures in unknown seas; of fights, and more fights, and fights yet again—literature in the rough, a very gallery of vivid pictures wasted unseen . . . and yet, what should any man who had the rich reality care about its pale shadow, Story? "Do you care much for reading?" "Well, no," answers the bare-footed officer lying with his head in a coil of rope; "books aren't very interesting, are they?"

I, watching the mizzen truck swing among the stars, look back over the long, long trail—long both in distance and in time—that separates this small heaving deck in the midst of the tropic seas from the rush of the wintry Strand. Nights in islands of ill reputation, when I slept with "one eye open" and one hand within touch of my revolver (for there are incidents of my wanderings that I have not told, and only those who know the Eastern Pacific may guess at them); days when only a fifty-to-one chance kept the little schooner from piling her bones on a spouting coral reef in mid-ocean—rough fare, hard lodging, and long fatigue, sometimes, all to be "eaten as helped," without comment or complaint, for that is the rule of island life—the pungent taste of danger, now and then, gratefully slaking some deep, half-conscious thirst derived from fiercer centuries; the sight of many lands and many peoples—these, and other pictures, painted themselves among the little gold stars swept by the rocking masts, as I lay, remembering. I thought of the pile of untouched "shockers" in my cabin; of grey London and its pyramids of books and armies of writers; of the mirror that they hold up to life, and the "magic web of colours gay" they weave, always looking, like the Lady of Shalott, in the mirror, and seldom joining the merry rout outside, where no one cares a pin for coloured tapestries, and looking-glasses are left to half-grown girls. No, truly; "books are not interesting," when you can have life instead.

Upon which some one proposed "Consequences" in the cabin, and I made haste to climb down.

Another day, gold and blue as are almost all the days of the "winter" season, and another island, burning white and blazing green, and another tumbling reef to jump, with the help of a powerful boat-holder, who stands in the midst of the surf, and drags the dinghy forward at the right moment. This is Mauke: we are getting on with the group, and begin to realise that some time or other, even in these timeless regions, will actually see us back at Raratonga.

Mauke proves to be a pretty little place, some six miles in circumference, "low" in type, but park-like and garden-like and dainty enough to wake covetous desires in the heart of almost any traveller. It has the finest oranges in the group—growing completely wild—and we are greeted on the shore by the usual crowd of flower-wreathed natives, bearing splendid branches of rich yellow fruit, which they present to every one with eager generosity. There are only three hundred and seventy natives in the island, and much of the land lies waste, though it is exceedingly fertile. The Mauke folk take things easy on the whole, and are not keen on trading. They export some oranges, some copra, a few bunches of dried bananas, and they buy a fair amount of cotton cloth, and shirts, and cutlery, from the white trader's store. But no one, so far, has grown fat on what Mauke makes or buys.

There were, at the time of my visit, only one or two whites in the place. The greater portion of the land available for planting lay unused. Probable rents, on long leases, were quoted to me as a shilling or so an acre.

The call at Mauke was short, and I saw little of the island. The natives insisted, however, that I should come up to the village and look at their church, of which they are very proud, so I headed the inevitable procession through the orange and lime and guava groves, to the little group of houses, partly thatch and reed, partly whitewashed concrete, that made up the settlement. The church was, of course, much the least interesting thing in the island. South Sea churches, with one or two happy exceptions, are blots in a world of beauty, monuments of bad taste, extravagance, and folly, that do very little credit to the religions they represent. In the days when most of them were built, the one idea of the missionary was the assimilation of the native to white men's ways and customs, as far as was possible, by any means conceivable—wise, or otherwise. In building churches for the new converts, the pattern followed was that set by Europeans for use in a cold climate, on sites that had a distinct money value per yard. Consequently, while South Sea houses, for coolness, are made almost all window and door, or else built, native fashion, in such a way that the air blows through the walls, South Sea churches are almost without ventilation, and (because the style of architecture selected is that of the whitewashed barn description) quite without beauty of any kind. In most cases, they have cost the islands appalling sums to build, and continue to demand a good deal to keep them in repair. There are happy exceptions here and there. Niué, of which place I have more to say later on, possesses a church built with exquisite taste and perfect regard to convenience, and the Catholic cathedral in Samoa is designed with much consideration as to climate, and appearance as well.

Mauke's church, however, is not one of the exceptions, being exceedingly bald and ugly, and it is furthermore disfigured by the most horrible lapse of taste to be seen in almost any island church—the decoration of the pulpit and communion rails with silver dollars nailed on in rows. I told the crowd of natives, eager to hear the praises of their wonderful church, that I had never seen anything like it in my life—which seemed to afford them much gratification. I did not add what I thought—that I sincerely hoped I might never see anything like it again.

A statement made only once or twice is fairly sure to miss the observation of the average reader, so I make no apology for saying here, as I have said in other parts of this book, that I am not one of those people who are opposed to mission work, or indifferent to religion; neither am I inclined to minimise the effects of the work done by missionaries in converting and civilising the Pacific generally. That the missionaries are infallible and always wise, however, in their methods of dealing with the natives, I do deny—which is only equivalent to saying that they are human, like the people at home. Nor do I think that, in these days, the missionary who takes up work in the Southern and Eastern Pacific has any need to wear the martyr aureole which is so persistently fitted on to the heads of all who go to " labour " in the island world. We are not in the days of Cook: cannibalism, over most of the Pacific, is dead and forgotten,

CRITICISM

violence to white people of any kind is unheard of, the climates are usually excellent, the islands beautiful, fertile, and happy, and the missionary's work is much the same as that of any country clergyman at home, save for the fact that his congregation are infinitely more submissive than whites would be, and incline to regard their teacher as a sovereign, not only spiritual, but temporal. The mission house is always much the finest building on the island, and the best furnished and provided. The missionary's children are usually sent away to be educated at good home or colonial boarding schools, and afterwards return to take up their parents' work, or possibly to settle in the islands in other capacities. The life, though busy, is devoid of all stress and strain, and there is no apparent difficulty in " making both ends meet "—and overlap. In the Southern and Eastern Pacific, the missionaries are conveyed from group to group in a mission steamer that is little inferior to the yacht of a millionaire, for comfort and elegance. They are constantly assisted by gifts of all kinds, and treated with consideration wherever they go, and in most cases enjoy a social position much better than that originally possessed at home. It is hard to see why a profession, which is so pleasant and profitable, should be exalted over the work of thousands of struggling pastors and clergymen at home, who too often know the pinch of actual want, and are in many cases obliged to lead lives of the greyest and narrowest monotony.

What is the moral? That one should not give money to missions? Certainly not. But if I were a millionaire, and had thousands to give in such a cause, I would give them carefully, with inquiry, directed to more sources than one, and would distribute them so that they should be used, if possible, in adding to the numbers of the Christian Church, rather than in teaching geography and English grammar and dressmaking to amiable brown people who are, and have been for generations, a good deal more Christian than ninety in a hundred whites. I believe firmly that most of the older missions in the Pacific could be continued perfectly well with the aid of native teachers, at one-twentieth the present cost—much as the teaching of outlying far-away islands, where residence is unpleasant for white families, is carried on to-day, with the aid of a yearly visit or so. That the present system will ever be modified, however, I do not believe. The reasons for such a conclusion are too obvious to need discussion.

I have wandered a good way from the church at Mauke. But there are many points on this subject of island missions, nevertheless, on which I have not touched.

Some of the men of Mauke were very busy on the shore, when our party passed down again to the boat. They made a bright picture, in their gay pareos of scarlet and yellow, and the snowy coronets of scented island flowers that they had twined about their heads. But the most picturesque thing about them was their occupation, which was neither more nor less than sand-castle building! There they sat, those big grown men, with never a child among them to make excuse for their play, building up churches and houses of the milk-white coral sand, scooping dark windows in the edifices, training green creepers up them, and planting out odd little gardens of branching coral twigs off the reef, in the surrounding pleasances. They had bundles of good things tied up in green leaves, lying somewhere in the shade of the guava bushes, and they had brought a pile of husked cocoanuts down to the shore with them, to drink when they pleased.

A "DESERT" ISLAND

They may have been waiting for a native boat, or they may have been simply making a day of it. In any case, they were sublimely happy.

(*Cold rain on the miry road ; faint gold sunset fading to stormy grey ; wet leaves a-shiver in the dusk—and the long, long way before the tired feet. A day of toil, a comfortless night. A handful of coppers in the pocket ; food and fire that must be bought with silver ; freedom, rest, enjoyment, that cost unattainable gold. The sacred right of labour ; a white man's freedom. O, brown half-naked islanders, playing at sand-castles on your sun-bathed shore, with unbought food lying among the unpurchased fruits beside you, what would you give to be one of the master race ?*)

Takutea we did not call at, since it was uninhabited, but the *Duchess*, under her daring little pirate of a captain, made no bones about running as close to anything, anywhere, as her passengers might desire, so we saw the fascinating place at fairly close quarters. In 1904, when I saw it, it was a real "desolate island," being twelve miles out in the open sea from the nearest land (Atiu), and totally uninhabited. Its extent is four or five hundred acres ; it is thickly wooded with cocoanuts, and has a good spring of water. The beautiful " bo'sun bird, whose long red and white tail feathers have a considerable commercial value, is common on the island. No one had visited it for a long time when we sailed by ; the wide white beach was empty, the cocoanut palms dropped their nuts unheeded into earth that received them gladly, and set them forth again in fountain-like sprays of green. The surf crumbled softly on the irregular fringing reef ; the ripples of the lagoon laid their ridgy footsteps along the empty strand, and no Man Friday came to trample them out with a step of awful significance. I wanted Takutea very badly indeed, all for myself; but I shall not have it now, neither will the reader, for some one else has bought it, and it is to be turned into a cocoanut plantation.

Manuwai, better known as Hervey Island, is not many miles away, but we took a day or more to reach it, partly because the winds were contrary, partly because (with apologies to the Admiralty Surveys) it was wrongly charted, and could not be found, at first, in a slight sea-fog. Manuwai has changed its ownership and its use, of late, but in 1904, it was a penal settlement and a copra plantation combined, being used as a place of punishment for sinful Cook Islanders, who were compulsorily let out as labourers to the Company renting the two islets of which this so-called group is composed.

The islands between them cover about fifteen hundred acres, according to the estimate given me. They have no permanent inhabitants, and when first taken up for planting, were quite desolate of life. A far-away, melancholy little place looked Manuwai, under the rays of the declining sun, as we came up to the reef. The two low islands, with their thick pluming of palms, are enclosed in the same lagoon, sheltered by a reef of oval form. There were a couple of drying-huts on the beach, and some heaps of oily smelling copra, when our boat pulled in. About twenty men, some convicts, some hired labourers, were gathered on the shore, fairly dancing with excitement, and the rest of the population—one white overseer, and one half-caste—were waiting on the very edge of the water, hardly less agitated. No ships ever called except the *Duchess*, and she was long overdue.

I stepped on shore, and was immediately shaken hands with, and congratulated on being the first white woman to set foot on the island. Then we all went for a walk, while the native crew fell into the arms of the labourers, and with cries of joy began exchanging gossip, tobacco, hats, and shirts, bartering oranges from the ship for cocoanut crabs from the island, and eagerly discussing the question of who was going home in the *Duchess*, and who would have to stop over till her next call, perhaps six months hence.

Manuwai is not one of the most beautiful of the islands, but anything in the way of solid ground was welcome after the gymnastics of the too-lively *Duchess*. The cocoanut plantations, and the new clearings, where the bush was being burned away, interested the officials from Raratonga, and the "boulevard" planted by the overseer—a handsome double row of palms, composing an avenue that facetiously began in nothing, and led to nowhere, received due admiration. We heard a good deal about the depredations of the cocoanut crabs, and as these creatures are among the strangest things that ever furnished food for travellers' tales, I shall give their history, as I gathered it, both in Manuwai and other places.

One must not, by the way, believe all that one hears, or even half, among the "sunny isles of Eden." Flowers of the imagination flourish quite as freely as flowers and fruits of the earth, and are much less satisfactory in kind. Also, it is a recognised sport to "spin yarns" to a newcomer, with the pious object of seeing how much he—or she—will swallow; and where so much is strange, bizarre, and almost incredible, among undoubted facts, it is hard to sift out the fictions of the playful resident.

However, the cocoanut crab is an undeniable fact, with which many a planter has had to wrestle, much to his loss. It must be confessed that I had expected something very exciting indeed, when I heard in Tahiti that cocoanut or robber crabs were still to be found in some parts of the Cook Group. One of the most grisly bugbears of my youth had been the descriptions of the terrible cocoanut crab that attacked the "Swiss Family Robinson" on their wonderful island. It was described, if my memory serves me, as "about the size of a turtle" and was dark blue in colour; it descended rapidly backwards down a tree, and immediately went to the attack of a Robinson youth, who repulsed it at the peril of his life. . . . On the whole, I thought it would make things interesting, if it really was in the Cook Group.

I never was more disappointed in my life than when I really saw one. It was dead, and cured in formalin, and only brought down from an island house as a show, but that was not the trouble. It was not more than two and a half feet long, lobster tail and all; it was not in the least like a turtle, and any small boy armed with a good stick could have faced it without fear, at its worst. No, decidedly the terrible crab was not up to the travellers' tales that had been told about it.

Still, it was worth seeing, for it was like nothing on the earth or in the sea that I had ever encountered. It had been excellently preserved, and looked wonderfully alive, when laid on the sand at the foot of a cocoanut palm. Its colour, as in life, was a gay mixture of red and blue. It had a long body like a colossal lobster, and two claws, one slight and thin, the other big enough to crack the ankle-bone of a man. It was an ugly and a wicked-looking thing, and I was not surprised to hear that it fights fiercely, if caught away from its hole, sitting up and threatening man or beast with its formidable claw, and showing no fear whatever.

In the daylight, however, it is very seldom seen abroad. We walked through groves that were riddled with its holes that afternoon, but never even heard the scuffle of a claw. The creature lives in rabbit-like burrows at the foot of palm-trees, and the natives can always tell the size of the inmate by a glance at the diameter of the hole by which it enters its burrow. At night it comes out, climbs the nearest palm, and gets in among the raffle of young and old leaves, fibre, stalks, and nuts, in the crown, there it selects a good nut, nips the stalk in two with its claw, and lets the booty drop with a thump to the earth, seventy or eighty feet below. Then the marauder backs cautiously down the tree, finds the nut, and proceeds to rip and rend the tough husk until the nut as we know it at home is laid bare. A cocoanut shell is no easy thing to crack, as most people know, but the robber crab with its huge claws makes nothing more of it than we should make of an egg, and in a minute the rich oily meat is at the mercy of the thief, and another fraction of a ton of copra is lost to the planter. It goes without saying that any stray nuts lying on the ground have been opened and destroyed, before the crab will trouble itself to climb.

Cocoanut crab is very good eating, and as it is mostly found in barren coral islands where little or nothing will grow but palms, the natives are always keen on hunting the "robber." Sometimes he is secured by thrusting a lighted torch down a hole which possesses two exits—the crab, hurrying out at the unopposed side as soon as the flame invades his dwelling. Sometimes the islanders secure him by the simple process of feeling for him in his burrow, and stabbing him at the end of it with a knife. This is decidedly risky, however, and may result in a smashed hand or wrist for the invader. A favourite plan is the following : Slip out in the dark, barefoot and silent, and hide yourself in a cocoanut grove till you see or hear a crab making his way up a tree. Wait till he is up at the top, and then climb half-way up, and tie a band of grass round the trunk. Now hurry down, and pile a heap of rough coral stones from the beach at the foot of the tree. Slip away into the shadow again, and wait. The crab will start to come down presently, backing carefully, tail first, for he has a bare and unprotected end to his armoured body, and uses it to inform himself of his arrival on the safe ground below. Half-way down the tree he touches your cunning band of grass. "Down so soon?" he remarks to himself, and lets go. Crack! he has shot down forty feet through air, and landed smashingly on the pile of stones that you carefully prepared for his reception. He is badly injured, ten to one, and you will have little trouble in finishing him off with your knife, and carrying home a savoury supper that is well worth the waiting for. That is the native way of hunting robber crabs.

When one lives on a cocoanut plantation, on an island that contains practically nothing else, one comes in time to know everything that is to be known about cocoanuts in general. But even the manager of Manuwai could not solve for me a problem that had been perplexing me ever since I had first seen a cocoanut palm—a problem, indeed, that after several more years of island travel, remains unanswered yet.

Why is no one ever killed by a cocoanut?

The question seems an idle one, if one thinks of cocoanuts as they are seen in British shops—small brown ovals of little weight or size—and if one has never seen them growing, or heard them fall. But when one knows that the smallest nuts alone reach England (since they are sold by number, not by weight) and that the ordinary nut, in its husk and on its native tree, is as

FALLING NUTS

big as one's own head, and as heavy as a solid lump of hard wood—that most trees bear seventy or eighty nuts a year, and that every one of those nuts has the height of a four-storey house to drop before it reaches the ground—that native houses are usually placed in the middle of a palm grove, and that every one in the islands, brown or white, walks underneath hundreds of laden cocoanut trees every day in the year—it then becomes a miracle of the largest kind that no one is ever killed, and very rarely injured, by the fall of the nuts. Nor can the reason be sought in the fact that the nuts cannot hurt. One is sure to see them fall from time to time, and they shoot down from the crown of the palm like flying bomb-shells, making a most portentous thump as they reach the earth. So extremely rare are accidents, however, that in nearly three years I did not hear of any mishap, past or present, save the single case of a man who was struck by a falling nut in the Cook Islands, and knocked insensible for an hour or two. This is certainly not a bad record for a tour extending over so many thousand miles, and including most of the important island groups—every one of which grows cocoanut palms by the thousand, in some cases, by the hundred thousand.

Travellers are often a little nervous at first, when riding or walking all day long through woods of palm, heavily laden with ponderous nuts. But the feeling never lasts more than a few days. One does not know why one is never hit by these cannon-balls of Nature—but one never is, neither is anybody else, so all uneasiness dies out very quickly, and one acquiesces placidly in the universal miracle.

Planters say that most of the nuts fall at night, when the dew has relaxed the fibres of the stalks. This would be an excellent reason, but for the fact that the nuts don't fall any more at night than in the daytime, if one takes the trouble to observe, and that damp, or dew, tightens up fibres of all kind, instead of relaxing them. If one asks the natives, the usual answer is : " It just happens that way " ; and I fancy that is as near as any one is likely to get to a solution.

Manuwai, since I saw it, has been purchased outright by a couple of adventurous young Englishmen, who are working it as a copra plantation. Takutea has, therefore, a neighbour in the Robinson Crusoe business, and is not likely to be quite so solitary as in times past.

The tour of the group was now ended, and the Government officials were conveyed back to Raratonga with all possible despatch—which is not saying very much, after all. There followed a luxurious interval of real beds and real meals, and similar Capuan delights, in the pretty island bungalow where my lot for the time had been cast. Then the *Duchess* began to start again, and peace was over. A sailing vessel does not start in the same way as a steamer. She gives out that she will leave on such a day, at such an hour, quite like the steamer ; but there the resemblance ends. When you pack your cabin trunk, and have it taken down at 11 a.m., you find there is no wind, so you take it back and call again next day. There is a wind now, but from the one quarter that makes it practically impossible to get out of port. You are told you had better leave your trunk, in case of the breeze shifting. You do, and go back for the second time to the hostess from whom you have already parted twice. The verandah (every one lives on verandahs, in the islands) is convulsed to see you come back, and tells you this is the way the ship always does " get off." You spend a quiet evening,

and go to bed. At twelve o'clock, just as you are in
the very heart of your soundest sleep, a native boy
comes running up to the house to say that the captain
has sent for the passenger to come down at once, for
the wind is getting up, and he will sail in a quarter of
an hour! You scramble into your clothes, run down
to the quay, get rowed out to the ship, and finish your
sleep in your cabin to the accompaniment of stamping
feet and the flapping sails; and behold, at eight o'clock,
the bo'sun thunders on your door, and tells you that
breakfast is in, but the breeze is away again, and the
ship still in harbour! After breakfast you sneak up
the well-known avenue again, feeling very much as if
you had run away from school, and were coming back
in disgrace. This time, the verandah shrieks until the
natives run to the avenue gate to see what is the matter
with the man "papalangis," and then console you with
the prophecy that the schooner won't get away for another
week.

She does, though. In the middle of the afternoon
tea, the captain himself arrives, declines to have a cup,
and says it is really business this time, and he is
away. You go down that eternal avenue again,
followed by cheerful cries of "No goodbye! we'll keep
your place at dinner," and in half an hour the green and
purple hills of lovely Raratonga are separated from you
by a widening plain of wind-ruffled blue waves, and
the *Duchess* is fairly away to Savage Island.

"Miss G——, have you nearly done your book?"

"Pretty nearly—why?" I ask, looking up from the
pages of "John Herring."

We are a day or two out from Raratonga, but not
even one hundred of the six hundred miles that lie
between the Cook Group and lonely Niué is compassed

as yet. The winds have been lightest of the light, and from the wrong quarter too, until this morning, when we have "got a slant" at last. Now the *Duchess* is rolling along in her usual tipsy fashion at seven or eight knots an hour, and the china-blue sea is ruffled and frilled with snow. It is hot, but not oppressively so, and I have been enjoying myself most of the morning lounging on a pile of locker cushions against the deck-house, alternately reading, and humming to myself something from Kipling about :

> Sailing south on the old trail, our own trail, the out trail,
> Sliding south on the long trail, the trail that is always new.

The pirate captain has been at the wheel for the last two hours, but I have not taken much note of the fact. Our only mate left us in the Cook Group, for a reason not absolutely new in the history of the world (a pretty little reason she was, too); and our bo'sun, who has been giddily promoted to a rank that he describes as "chief officer," is not exactly a host in himself, though he is a white man. In consequence, the pirate and he have been keeping watch and watch since we sailed—four hours on and four hours off—and, as one or two of our best A.B.s declined to go down to Niué, and most of the others are bad helmsmen, the two whites have been at the wheel during the greater part of their watches.

I have grown quite accustomed to seeing one or other standing aft of the little companion that leads down to the cabin, lightly shifting the spokes in his hands hour after hour. It never occurred to me, however, that I was personally interested in the matter.

But we are in the South Pacific, and I have still a good many things to find out about the "way they do things at sea," here where the ocean is the ocean, and no playground for globe-trotting tourists.

"Are you nearly done?" asked the pirate again, shifting half a point, and throwing a glance at the clouds on the windward side. They are harmless little clouds, and only suggest a steady breeze.

"I have about half an hour's reading left," I answer.

"Then you'd better chuck the book into your cabin, for it's almost eight bells, and that begins your trick at the wheel," says the pirate calmly.

"My *what*?"

"Your trick. Your turn. Time you have to steer, see?"

"But good heavens! I never had a wheel in my hand in my life—I don't know how!"

"That's your misfortune, not your fault," says the pirate kindly. "You'll never have to say that again. There's eight bells now—come along. J—— and I have had too much of the wheel, and now we're well away from land is your time to learn."

And from thenceforth until we made the rocky coast of Niué, more than a week later, I spent a portion of every day with the polished spokes of the wheel in my hands, straining my eyes on the "lubber's point," or anxiously watching the swelling curves of the sails aloft in the windy blue, ready to put the wheel up the instant an ominous wrinkle began to flap and writhe upon the marble smoothness of the leaning canvas. At night, the smallest slatting of sail upon the mast would start me out of my sleep, with an uneasy fear that I was steering, and had let her get too close to the wind; and I deposed most of my prayers in favour of an evening litany that began: "North, north by east, nor'-nor'-east, nor'-east by north, nor'-east," and turned round upon itself to go backward in the end, like a spell said upside down to raise a storm.

Withal, the good ship left many a wake that would have broken the back of a snake, for the first day or two of my lessons, and the native A.B.s used to come and stand behind me when an occasional sea made the wheel kick, under the evident impression that they would be wanted before long. But I learned to steer—somehow—before we got to Niué, and I learned to lower away boats, and to manage a sixteen foot steer-oar, when we got becalmed, and spent the day rowing about among the mountainous swells, out of sheer boredom. And for exercise and sport, I learned to go up into the cross-trees and come down again by the ratlines or the back-stay, whichever seemed the handiest, wearing the flannel gymnasium dress I had brought for mountaineering excursions. It was very pleasant up there on a bright, salt-windy morning, when the *Duchess* swung steadily on her way with a light favouring breeze, her little white deck lying below me like a tea-tray covered with walking dolls, her masts at times leaning to leeward until my airy seat was swung far out across the water. Having a good head, I was never troubled with giddiness, and used to do a good deal of photographing from aloft, when the ship was steady enough to allow of it. That was seldom, however, for the *Duchess* had been built in New Zealand, where the good schooners do not come from, and had no more hold on the water than a floating egg. More than one sailing vessel turned out by the same builders had vanished off the face of the ocean, in ways not explained, by reason of the absence of survivors, but dimly guessed at, all the same; and I cannot allow that the pirate captain had any just cause of annoyance—even allowing for a master's pride in his ship—when I recommended him to have the schooner's name painted legibly on her keel before he should leave Auckland on his next northward journey, just " in case."

We were about a hundred and fifty miles off Niué, when the pirate came to me one windy morning, and asked me if I wanted to see something that had only once been seen before.

There was, of course, only one reply possible.

"Then keep a look-out, and you'll see it," said the pirate. "We're going to run right by Beveridge Reef, and it's been only once sighted. What's more, it's wrong charted, and I'm going to set it right. You've no idea what a lot of wrecks there have been on that d—— that dangerous place. Not a soul ever got away from one of them to tell what happened, either. They'd only know when things began drifting down to Niué, weeks after—timber and cargo, and so on—why, a lot of the houses in Niué are built out of wreckage—and then people would say that there'd been another wreck on Beveridge Reef. Some fool reported it as a coral island two miles across, once upon a time, but I'll bet he never saw it. If it had been, it wouldn't have been as destructive as it is."

Late in the day we sighted it. The pirate was aloft, swinging between heaven and earth, with a glass in his hand, calling out observations to the chief-officer-boatswain below. The crew were attending exclusively to the horizon, and letting the ship look after herself, according to the amiable way of Maories when there is anything interesting afoot. The weather was darkening down, and heavy squalls of rain swept the sea now and then. But there it was, clearly enough to be seen in the intervals of the squalls, a circle of white foam enclosing an inner patch of livid green, clearly marked off from the grey of the surrounding ocean. Here and there a small black tooth of rock projected from the deadly ring of surf, and—significant and cruel sight—two ships' anchors were plainly to be seen through the glass, as we neared the reef, lying fixed among the rock, so low in the water as only to be visible at intervals.

"A wicked place," said the captain, who had come down from his eyrie, and was giving orders for the preparation of a boat. "Couldn't see a bit of it at night—couldn't see it in broad daylight, if there was a big sea on. And wrong charted too. Think of the last minutes of those poor chaps the anchors belonged to!"

The sea and sky were really beginning to look nasty, and I did not want to think of it. But the pirate went on discoursing pleasantly of deaths and wrecks, while the men were putting various things into the whaleboat, and getting ready to lower away. He did not often have a passenger, but when he did, he evidently thought it his duty to keep her entertained.

We were very near to the reef now—so close that I was able to take a photograph of it, a little marred by the rainy weather. Meantime, the boat was being swung out, and the men were getting in. And now "a strange thing happened." Out of nowhere at all eight sharks appeared—large ones, too—and began to cruise hungrily about the *Duchess's* hull, their lithe yellowish bodies sharply outlined in the dark blue water, their evil eyes fixed on me, as I overhung the rail to look at them. "If only!" they said as plainly as possible, with those hideously intelligent green orbs. "If only——"

"What has brought those horrible brutes about us?" I asked.

"Those? oh, they're waiting to be fed, I suppose."

Pretty much all the ships that came this way before us have given them a good dinner. I bet they say grace before meat now every time they see a sail, which isn't often. Here, you Oki, put in that keg of beef."

"Where are you going?" I demanded with considerable interest, for the pirate captain never did things like any one else, and I scented an adventure.

"Going to find out what the inside of that lagoon is really like. No one ever put a boat into it yet. No, you can't be in it this time: very sorry, but——"

"What?"

"Well, you see, one isn't absolutely sure of getting back again, in a place like this. Didn't you see me put in grub and water and a compass? I don't think you'd like a boat voyage down to Niué, if we happened to miss the train. The mate has the course, and could take her on, if I came to grief. No, it isn't any use asking, I just can't. Lower away."

They lowered and——

Well, if the pirate had been a shade less determined about the number in the boat, there would have been a pretty little tragedy of the sea, that gusty afternoon. One more in the boat had certainly turned the scale. For the wind was continually getting up, and the wretched *Duchess* was rolling like a buoy, and the boat, as she touched the water, with the captain and three men in her, was caught by the top of a wave, and dashed against the side of the ship. In a flash she was overturned, with a badly damaged thwart, and was washing about helplessly among the waves, with the four men clinging to her keel. The sea took her past the schooner like a rag. I had only time to run to the stern, before she was swept out of hearing, but I heard the pirate call as he disappeared in the trough of a wave, "Get out your camera, here's the chance of your life!" Then the boat was gone, and for a moment the mate and I thought it was all over. "The sharks will have 'em if they don't sink!" declared that officer, straining over the rail, while the Maori crew ran aimlessly about the deck, shouting with excitement.

What happened during the next half-hour has never been very clear in my memory. The wind kept rising, and the afternoon grew late and dark. The overturned boat, with the four heads visible about her keel, drifted helplessly in the trough of the seas, at the mercy of waves and sharks. (I heard, afterwards, that the men had all kicked ceaselessly to keep them away, and that they expected to be seized any moment.) The wind screamed in the rigging, and drifts of foam flew up on deck, and the Maories ran about and shouted, and got in each other's way, and tried to heave ropes, and missed, and tried to launch a boat under the mate's direction, and somehow did not—I cannot tell why. And right in the middle of the play, when we seemed to be making some attempt to bear down upon the drifting wreck, a grey old man who had come on with us from the Cook Islands, but had kept to his berth through illness most of the time, burst out on deck with an astonishing explosion of sea language, and told us that we were nearly on to the reef. Which, it seems, every one had forgotten!

After that, things grew so lively on the poop that I got up on the top of the deck-house to keep out of the way, and reflect upon my sins. It seemed a suitable occasion for devotional exercises. The white teeth of the reef were unpleasantly near, the water was growing shoal. "Put a leadsman in the chains this minute!" yelled the grizzled passenger (who had been at sea in his time, and knew something of what was likely to happen

CLOSE SAILING 187

when you got a nasty reef on your lee side, with the wind working up). The auxiliary engine, meant for use on just such occasions, had been sick for some time. There was a very strong tide running, the wind had shifted while the ship's company were intent on the fate of the boat, and on the whole it looked very much as if the decorations already possessed by the notorious reef were likely to be increased by another pair of best quality British made anchors—*ours*.

A good many things happen on sailing ships—Pacific ships especially—that one does not describe in detail, unless one happens to be writing fiction. This is not fiction, so the occurrences of the next quarter of an hour must be passed over lightly. The ancient passenger took command of the ship. We got away from the reef by an unpleasantly close shave and bore down upon the boat, which the pirate captain had impossibly contrived to right by this time, paddling it along with one oar, while the men baled constantly. We got the captain and the men and the damaged boat on board, and a few "free opinions, freely expressed"—as a certain famous lady novelist would put it—were exchanged. Then the pirate, who was quite fresh, and very lively, demanded the second boat, and said he was bound to get into that place anyhow, and wouldn't leave till he did.

I rather think we mutinied at this juncture. I am sure I did, because I had been thinking over my sins for some time, and had come to the conclusion that there really were not many of them, and that I wanted a chance to accumulate a few more, preferably of an agreeable kind, before I faced the probability of decorating any Pacific coral reef with my unadorned and unburied skeleton. The grey-haired passenger and the mate mutinied too, upon my example, and the pirate, seeing that we were three to one, and moreover, that it was growing dark, made a virtue of necessity, and went off for a shift of clothes, giving orders to make all sail at once. And so we left the reef in the growing dusk, and no man has to this day disturbed the virgin surface of its stormy little lagoon with profanely invading oar.

Was there a fortune lying concealed beneath those pale green waves within the foaming jaws of the reef? I never heard. But there were some among our native crew who came from the far-off island of Penrhyn, where the pearl fisheries are, and they were strong in asserting their belief that the pirate might have been well paid for his exploration. It was just that sort of reef, said the pearl-island men, that most often contained good shell, and produced the biggest pearls, the first time of looking. An old, undisturbed atoll, where no one had ever thought of looking for shell, was the place where big pearls got a chance to grow. The first comer scooped in the prizes; afterwards, the shell itself and the smaller pearls were all that any one was likely to get.

However that might be, the talk, on the rest of the way down to Niué, ran much on pearls and pearl-shell, and I learned a good deal about these gold-mines of the Pacific—always making allowance for the inevitable Pacific exaggeration. Any man who can live a year among the islands, and restrain himself, in the latter part of his stay, from lying as naturally and freely as he breathes, deserves a D.S.O.

Stripped of flowers of fiction, the romance of the pearling trade was still interesting and fascinating enough. Pearls, in the Pacific, are obtained from a large bivalve that has a good deal of value in itself, being the material from which mother-o'-pearl is made. Prices, of course, fluctuate very much, as the shell is used in so many manufactures that depend on the vagaries of fashion; but the value may run to £200 a ton or over. When it gets down to £40 or less, it is hardly worth the expense of lifting and carrying. For the most part, however, it is worth a good deal more than this, and when it is at the highest, fortunes can be, and have been, made out of small beginnings, in a very short time. The pearls are an "extra," and not to be relied upon. There may be almost none in a big take of shell, there may be a few small ones, there may be a number of fine ones that will make the fortune of the lucky fisher. It is all a gamble, and perhaps none the less fascinating for that. Much of the best shell and the finest pearls in the Pacific, come from the Paumotus, which are French. Thursday Island, off the north of Queensland, was the great centre of the fishery until lately, but it has been almost fished out. The Solomons were reported to have a good deal of shell, and a rush took place to that part not long ago, but the yield was much exaggerated. There are a good many atolls about the Central Pacific in general, which contain more or less shell, and are generally owned and fished by Australian syndicates. Outlying reefs and islets, where no one goes, now and then turn out to be valuable. The news of a find travels apparently on the wings of the seagulls from group to group, for no such place ever remains secret for more than a very short time, and then, if the owner's title is not secure (a thing that may easily happen, in the case of an island that does not lie within the geographical limits of any of the annexed groups) there is sometimes trouble. Pearl-poaching is easy and profitable, if not very safe; and who is to tell ugly tales, a thousand miles from anywhere, out in the far Pacific?

(*The swift-winged schooner and the racing seas: decks foam-white beneath a burning sky: salt wind on the lips, and the fairy-voiced enchantress Adventure singing ever from beyond the prow!* "*O dreamers in the man-stifled town,*" *do you hear the wide world calling?*)

And so the pirate captain brought us up to Niué, and left me there, and sailed away with the ship to Auckland, where he gave over the command, and went (so it was said) to aid in the instruction of sea-going youth, somewhere further south. The Cook Islands shrieked with joyous amusement when they heard of the pirate's new rôle as the guide and mentor of tender boyhood—but I do not know, after all. The pirate was as full of mischief as an egg is full of meat, as full of fight as a sparrow-hawk, gifted with an uncanny faculty for plunging into every kind of risk that the wide seas of the earth could hold, and coming out unscathed and asking for more. He was assuredly not to be numbered among the company of the saints, but neither is the average "glorious human boy"—and on the principle of setting a thief to catch a thief, the pirate's new rôle may well have turned out a success.

We came up to Niué graced by a last touch of the piratical spirit. There was some blusterous weather as we neared the great island with its iron-bound, rocky coasts, towards which we had been making for so many days, but we swept up towards the land with every rag of canvas set, for that was the pirate captain's custom, and he would not break it. By-and-by, as I was standing on the main deck, holding on to the deckhouse, while I looked at the looming mass of blue ahead, the main squaresail gave way with a report like a gun, and began to thrash the foremast with streamers of tattered canvas. The pirate had it down in a twinkling, and got the men to bend on a new sail immediately. It went up to the sound of yelling Maori chants (for the crew liked this sort of excitement), and once more the ship fled on towards Niué with every sail straining against the gusty wind. Half-an-hour, and crack!—the new square-sail was gone too, and half of it away to leeward like a huge grey bird in a very great hurry. And the pirate, as we began to draw inshore, raged up and down the deck, like a lion baulked of its prey. To come up to Niué without every sail set was a disgrace that he had never yet encountered, and it evidently hit him hard that he had not another sail in the locker, and was forced to "carry on" as best he could without it.

Niué, or Savage Island, is no joke to approach. It is about forty miles round, and almost every yard of the whole forty is unapproachable, by reason of the precipitous cliffs, guarded by iron spears of coral rock, that surround it on every side. There are one or two places where an approach can be made, in suitable weather, with care, but it is quite a common thing for sailing vessels to beat on and off as much as a week, before they succeed in landing passengers or goods. We came up on a very gusty day, with the blow-holes in the cliffs spouting like whales as we went by, but the pirate captain ran us into the anchorage below Alofi as easily as if it had been perfect weather and an excellent harbour, and we put out a boat to land our goods, including myself. The pirate had not an ounce of caution in his body, but, as an old Irishman on one of the islands declared: "The divil takes care of his own, let him alone for that, and it's not the Pirate that he's goin' to let into any houle till he lets him into the biggest wan of all—mind that!"

CHAPTER X

How not to see the Islands—Lonely Niué—A Heathen Quarantine Board—The King and the Parliament—The Great Question of Gifts—Is it Chief-like ?—The New Woman in Niué—Devil-fish and Water-Snakes—An Island of Ghosts—How the Witch-Doctor died—The Life of a Trader.

LANDINGS on Pacific islands are not usually easy, but there are few approaches as bad as that of Niué, the solitary outlier of Polynesia. It is a difficult task to get within reasonable distance of the land in the first place, and when the ship has succeeded in manœuvring safely up to the neighbourhood of the cruel cliffs, the trouble is only beginning. There are no harbours worth the name on the island, although the cliffs show an occasional crack through which a boat may be brought down to the sea, and the circling reef is broken here and there. The best that a ship can do is to lie off at a safe distance, put out a boat, and trust to the skill of the crew to effect a landing on the wharf. In anything but really calm weather, communication is impossible. However, there are very many calm days in this part of the Pacific, so chances are fairly frequent.

It was not at all as calm as one could have wished when the *Duchess* put out her whaleboat to bring me ashore. But the pirate trusted to his luck, and was, as usual, justified. The boat passage proved to be a mere crack in the reef, through which the sea rushed with extreme violence, dancing us up and down like a cork. It was not difficult for our smart Maori crew to fend us off the knife-edged coral walls with their oars, as we manœuvred down towards the spider-legged little iron ladder standing up in the surf, and pretending to be a wharf. But when we got within an oar's length of the ladder, and the boat was leaping wildly on every swell, things got more exciting. The only way of landing on Niué is to watch your time at the foot of the ladder, while the men fend the boat off the coral, and jump on to the rungs at the right moment. A native standing on the platform at the top takes you by the arms as you rise, and snatches you into the air as the eagle snatched Endymion. Only, instead of going all the way to heaven, you land on the pier—or what passes for it—and find yourselves upon the soil of Niué.

Behind the pier rises a little pathway cut in the face of the rock, and leading up to the main street of the capital. Once up the path, we are fairly arrived in Savage Island.

It is not a place known to the globe-trotting tourist, as yet. Much of the Pacific has been "discovered" by the tripper element of recent years, but Niué is still almost inviolate. Once here, if one seeks the true spirit of the South Seas, one still may find it.

Travellers go in scores by every steamer to Samoa, to Fiji, to Honolulu, which are on the beaten track of "round-the-world." They drive up to Stevenson's villa, they make excursions to the Nuuanu Pali, they see a sugar plantation here, and a kava drinking there, and a native dance, specially composed to suit tourists' tastes, somewhere else. They stay a week in a fine modern hotel, drink green cocoanuts (and other things that are stronger), take photograghs of island girls wearing imported Parisian or Sydney costumes, and think they have seen the life of the islands. Never was there a greater mistake. The sweet South Seas do not so easily yield up their secret and their charm. The spell that for three hundred years has drawn the wandering hearts of the world across the ocean ploughed by the keels of Drake and Hawkins and Cook, of Dampier, Bougainville, and Bligh, will not unfold itself save to him who will pay the price. And the price to-day is the same in kind, though not in degree, as that paid by those old explorers and adventurers—hard travel, scanty food, loneliness, loss of money and time, forgetting the cities and civilisation. To know the heart of the South Seas, all these things must be encountered, and encountered willingly, with a love of the very hardship they may bring, strong as the seabird's love of the tossing waters and thunder-waking storm.

The typical British tourist—yes, even he—hears from far off, at times, the mysterious call of the island world, and tells himself that he will listen to it a little nearer, and enjoy the siren song sung to so many long before him. Hence his visits to the great Pacific ports that can be reached by liner; hence, in most cases, his gradually acquired conviction that the islands are, after all, very much like any other place in the tropics—beautiful, interesting, but—— Well, writer fellows always exaggerate: every one knows that.

Hotel dinners, big liners, shops, hired carriages, guides, and picture postcards—these things are death to the spirit of the South Seas. This is the first lesson that the island wanderer must learn. Where every one goes the bloom is off the peach. Leave the great ports and the steamers; disregard the advice of every one who knows anything (most people in island towns know everything, but you must not listen to them, for the jingling of the trade dollar has long since deafened their ears to the song of the mermaids on the coral beaches); take ship on a schooner, it does not much matter where; live in a little bungalow under the palms for weeks or months; ride and swim and feast with the brown people of the coral countries, as one of themselves; learn, if you do not already know, how to live on what you can get, and cook what you catch or pick or shoot, to sleep on a mat and wash in a stream, do without newspapers and posts, forget that there ever was a war anywhere, or an election, or that there will ever be a "season" anywhere again; and so perhaps, the charm of the island world will whisper itself in your waiting ear. What then? What happened to the men who ate the enchanted fruit of the lotus long ago? Well, no one ever said that the sweetness of the fruit was not worth all that it cost.

There are about five thousand native inhabitants on Niué, and and generally a score or so of whites—almost all traders. Alofi, the capital, possesses a few hundred of the former, and nearly all the latter. It is a winsome little spot, and I loved it the moment the wide grassy street first broke upon my view, as I climbed the narrow pathway from the shore.

The houses stand down one side, as is the invariable custom of South Sea towns. They are whitewashed concrete for the most part, built by the natives out of materials furnished by the coral reef. The roofs are plaited pandanus thatch, high and steep. The doors are mostly windows, or the windows doors—it would be hard to say which. They are simply long openings filled in with wooden slats, which can be sloped to suit the wind and weather. Mats and cooking pots and the inevitable Chinese camphor-wood box, for keeping clothes in, are all the furniture. Round the doorways grow palms and gay hibiscus, and cerise-flowered poinsettia, and here and there a native will have set up an odd decoration of glittering stalactites from the caves on the shore, to sparkle in the sun by his doorstep. The white men's houses have grass compounds in front for the most part, and many have iron roofs, glass windows, and other luxuries.

All these houses look the one way—across the wide, empty grassy street, between the stems of the leaning palms, to the sunset and the still blue sea. It is a lonely sea, this great empty plain lying below the little town. The *Duchess* calls twice a year, the mission steamer once, a trade steamer, ancient and worn out, limps across from Tonga, two hundred miles away, every ten or twelve months. That is all. The island itself owns nothing bigger than a whaleboat, and cannot as a rule communicate with any other place in case of emergency. Some few months before my visit, a trader had very urgent need to send a letter to Australia. After waiting in vain for something to call, he sighted an American timber brig on her way to Sydney, far out on the horizon. Hastily launching a native canoe, and filling it with fruit, he paddled three or four miles out to sea, in the hope of being seen by the ship. His signals were perceived, and the brig hove to, when the trader paddled up to her, offered his fruit as a gift, and begged the captain to take his letter. This the sailor willingly did, and still more willingly accepted the excellent Niué bananas and oranges that went with the missive. And so the post was caught—Niué fashion.

There is no doctor on the island as a rule, and if you want to die during the intervals between ships, you may do so unopposed. I am almost afraid to state how healthy the people of Niué are as a rule, in spite of—or can it be in consequence of?—this deprivation.

The "bush" overflows the town, after the charming way of bush, in this island world. Big lilies, bell-shaped, snowy petalled, and as long as your hand, spill over into the main street from the bordering scrub. The grass on the top of the cliff, the day I landed, was blazing with great drifts of fiery salvia, and starred with pink and yellow marigolds. About the houses were clumps of wild "foliage plants," claret and crimson leaved, looking like a nurseryman's bedding-out corner. The coco palm that I knew so well had a sister palm here, of a kind new to me—an exceedingly graceful tree twenty to thirty feet high, bearing small inedible berry-like fruits, and splendid fan-shaped leaves, of the shape and size once so familiar in the "artistic type of drawing-room at home. Pinnacles of fantastic grey rock, all spiked and spired, started up unexpectedly in the midst of the riotous green, and every pinnacle was garlanded cunningly with wreaths and fronds of flowering vines. There were mammee-apples and bananas beside most of the houses: yellow oranges hung as thickly in the scrub as ornaments on a Christmas tree, and one or two verandahs were decorated with the creeping trailers of the delicious granadilla. A land of peace and plenty, it looked in the golden rays of the declining sun, that windy blue afternoon. It proved alas, to be nothing of the kind: its soil is fertile, but so thinly scraped over the coral rock for foundation, that very little in the way of nutritious food will grow—it has no water save what can be gathered from deep clefts in the rocks, the bananas are scanty, the mammee-apples unsatisfying, and the "oranges" are for the most part citrons, drinkable, as lemons are, but little use for anything else. Indeed, Niué is a useless place altogether, and nobody makes fortunes there now-a-days, though one or two did well out of the "first skim" of its trading, a generation ago. Nor does any one grow fat there, upon a diet of tinned meats, biscuit, and fruit. Nor are there any marvellous "sights," like the volcanoes of Hawaii, or the tribe dancing and fire-walking of Fiji. Still, I loved Niué, and love it yet.

It was so very far away, to begin with. In other islands, with regular steamers, people concerned themselves to some degree about the doings of the outer world, and used to wonder how things were getting on, beyond the still blue bar of sea. Newspapers arrived, people came and went, things were done at set times, more or less. One was still in touch with the world, though out of sight.

But in Niué, the isolation was complete. There was no come and go. We were on the road to nowhere. Nobody knew when any communication with anywhere would be possible, so nobody troubled, and save for an occasional delirious day when a ship really did come in, and waked us all from our enchanted slumber for just so long as you might turn round and look about you before dropping off into dreams again, we were asleep to all that lay beyond the long horizon line below the seaward-leaning palms. Niué was the world. The rest was a cloudy dream.

I rented a little cottage in the heart of a palm-grove, when I settled down to wait for the problematical return of the *Duchess*, and see the life of Niué. It belonged to a native couple, Kuru and Vekia, who were well-to-do, and had saved money selling copra. The Niuéan, unlike every other Polynesian, is always willing and anxious to make a bargain or do a deal of any kind, and Kuru and his wife were as delighted to get the chance of a "let" as any seaside landlady. They moved their small goods out of the house most readily, and left me in full possession of the two rooms and the verandah and the innumerable doors and windows, with everything else to find for myself.

A general collection of furniture, taken up by a friendly white resident, resulted in the loan of a bed and a box and a table, three chairs, some cups and cutlery, and a jug and basin. These, with a saucepan lent by my landlady (who, as I have said, was rich, and possessed many superfluities of civilisation), made up the whole of my household goods. For two months I occupied the little house among the palms, and was happy. "Can a man be more than happy?" runs the Irish proverb, and answer there is none.

There were never, in all my island wanderings, such shadows or such sunsets, as I saw in lonely Niué. The little house was far away from others, and the palms stood up round it close to the very door. In the white, white moonlight, silver-clear and still as snow, I used to stay for half a night on my verandah, sitting cross-legged in the darkness of the eaves, and watching the wonderful great stars of shadow drawn out, as if in ink, round the foot of every palm-tree. The perfect circle of tenderly curving rays lay for the most part still as some wonderful drawing about the foot of the tree; but at rare intervals, when the hour was very late, and even the whisper of the surf upon the reef seemed to have grown tired and dim and far away, the night would turn and sigh in its sleep for just a moment, and all the palm-tree fronds would begin to sway and shiver up in the sparkling moon-rays, glancing like burnished silver in the light. Then the star at the foot would dance and sway as well, and weave itself into forms of indescribable beauty, as if the spirit of Giotto of the marvellous circles were hovering unseen in the warm air of this alien country that he never knew, and pencilling forms more lovely than his mortal fingers ever drew on earth. . . . Yes, it was worth losing one's sleep for, in those magic island nights.

In the daytime, I rode and walked a good deal about the islands, which is very fairly provided with roads, and tried to find out what I could about the people and their ways. There is not a more interesting island in the Pacific than Niué, from an ethnological point of view ; but my scientific knowledge was too contemptibly small to enable me to make use of my opportunities. This I regretted, for the place is full of strange survivals of ancient customs and characteristics, such as are seldom to be found among Christianised natives. The people are somewhat rude and rough in character ; indeed until about forty years ago, they were actually dangerous. Their island is one of the finest of natural fortresses, and they used it as such, declining to admit strangers on any pretext. Captain Cook attempted to land in 1777, but was beaten off before he had succeeded in putting his boat's crew ashore. Other travellers for the most part gave the place a wide berth.

When men of the island wandered away to other places (the Niuéan is a gispy by nature) they received no kindly welcome on attempting to come home. The Niuéan had an exceeding fear of imported diseases, and to protect himself against them, he thought out a system of sanitary precaution, all on his own account, which was surely the completest the world has ever seen. There was no weak link in the chain : no break through which measles, or cholera, or worse could creep, during the absence of an official, or owing to the carelessness of an inspector. Every person attempting to land on Niué, be he sick or well, stranger or native, was promptly killed! That was Niué's rule. You might go away from the island freely, but if you did, you had better not attempt to come back again, for the " sanitary officers " would knock your brains out on the shore. It was without doubt the simplest and best system of quarantine conceivable. Possibly as a result of this Draconian law, the people of Niué are remarkably strong and hardy to-day, though since the relaxation of the ancient rule, a certain amount of disease has crept in.

The people, though warlike and fierce, were never cannibals here at the worst. They did not not even eat their enemies when slain in battle. They enjoyed a fight very much, however, when they got the chance of one, and still remembered the Waterloo victory of their history, against the fierce Tongans, about two hundred years ago. The Tongans, until within the last half-century, seem to have been the Danes of the Pacific, always hunting and harrying some other maritime people, and always a name of terror to weak races. Tonga is the nearest land to Niué, being about three hundred miles away, so it was not to be expected that the Niuéans would escape invasion, and they were fully prepared for the Tongan attack when it did come. They did not attempt to meet force by force. There was one place they knew where the Tongans might succeed in landing, and near to this they laid a cunning plan for defence.

A trader took me down to see the spot one Sunday afternoon. It is one of the numerous caves of Niué, with a top open for the most part to the sky. The cave runs underneath the greenery and the creeping flowers of the bush—a long black gash just showing here and there among the leaves. The drop is forty or fifty feet, and an unwary foot might very easily stumble over its edge, even now.

On the day when the Tongan war canoes broke the level line of the sea horizon, the Niué men hastened to the shore, and prepared the cave in such a way as to set a fatal and most effective trap for their enemies. They cut down a mass of slight branches and leafy twigs, and covered the gulf completely, so that nothing was to be seen except the ordinary surface of the low-growing bush. When the enemies landed, the Niué men showed themselves on the farther side of the cave, as if fleeing into the woods. The Tongans, with yells of joy, rushed in pursuit, straight over the gulf—and in another moment were lying in crushed and dying heaps at the foot of the pit, while the men of Niué, dashing out of ambush on every side, ran down into the cave from its shallow end and butchered their enemies as they lay.

After this, it is said that the Tongans left Niué alone.

Because of the loneliness and inaccessibility of the place, the Savage Islanders have always been different from the rest of the Pacific. The typical "Kanaka" is straight-haired, light brown in colour, mild and gentle and generous in disposition, ready to welcome strangers and feast them hospitably. He is aristocratic to the backbone in his ideas, and almost always has a native class of nobles and princes, culminating in a hereditary king.

The Savage Islander is often frizzy-haired, and generally a darkish brown in colour. His manners are rather brusque, and he gives nothing without obtaining a heavy price for it. He has no chiefs, nobles, or princes, and

A LOCAL PARLIAMENT

does not want any. There is always a head of the State, who enjoys a certain amount of mild dignity, and may be called the King for want of a better name. The office is not hereditary, however, the monarch being elected by the natives who form the island Parliament. Meetings of this Parliament are held at irregular intervals; and the King, together with the British Resident Commissioner, takes an important part in the debates.

These are very formal affairs. The brown M.P.s who live, each in his own village, in the utmost simplicity of manners and attire, dress themselves up for the day in full suits of European clothing, very heavy and hot, instead of the light and comfortable cotton kilt they generally wear. They travel into Alofi and join the local members on the green before the public hall—generally used as a school-house. King Tongia joins them, the British Resident comes also, and for hour after hour, inside the great, cool hall, with its matted floor and many open window-embrasures, the talk goes on. This road is to be made, that banyan tree is to be removed, regulation pigsties are to be built in such a village, petitions are to be sent up to New Zealand about the tax on tobacco—and so on, and so on. The king is a tough old man; he has his say on most questions, and it is not considered generally good for health or business to oppose him too much; but of royal dignity he has, and asks for, none.

There is something quite American in the history of Tongia's elevation, some seven years ago. He had acted as Prime Minister to the late head of the State; and when the latter died he calmly assumed the reins without going through the formality of an election. This was not the usual custom, and some of the members remonstrated. Tongia told them, however, that he was in the right, and meant to stay on. When the captain of a ship died on a voyage, did not his chief mate take over command? The cases were exactly parallel, to his mind. This argument pleased the members, who had most of them been to sea, and Tongia was allowed to retain his seat, the objectors calming themselves with the thought of the sovereign's age—he was well over eighty at that time. "He is only the stump of a torch," they said; "he will soon burn out." But the stump is burning yet, and shows no symptoms of extinction. Tongia married a pretty young girl soon after his "election," settled down in the royal palace—a white-washed cottage with a palm-thatch roof—and seems likely to outlast many of his former opponents.

The powers of the king, limited as they are, have lessened since 1902, when New Zealand annexed Niué—a proceeding that had its humorous side, if one examines the map, for Niué is something like a thousand miles from Auckland. The Resident Commissioner who is responsible for the well-being of the island lives in a house much more like a palace than Tongia's modest hut, and is in truth the real ruler of the place. His work, however, is not overpowering. He is supposed to be judge and law-giver, among many other duties, but in Niué no one ever seems to do anything that requires punishment. There is nothing in the shape of a prison, if any one did. Innocent little crimes, such as chicken stealing with extenuating circumstances, or allowing pigs to trespass into somebody's garden, occasionally blot the fair pages of the island records, but a little weeding, or a day's work on the road is considered sufficient punishment for these. At the time of my stay, which lasted nearly two months, such a wave of goodness seemed to be passing over the island that the Resident complained he could not find enough crime in the place to keep his garden weeded, and declared that he really wished somebody would do something, and do it quick, or all his imported flowers would be spoiled!

Since the forties, missionaries have been busy in Savage Island, and there is no doubt that they have done their work effectively. The early traders, who arrived near the same time, also helped considerably in the civilisation of the natives. Drink has never been a trouble on Niué, and at the present date, no native ever tastes it, and strict regulations govern importation by the whites for their own use. The natives are healthy, although European diseases are by no means unknown. Skin diseases are so troublesome that many of the traders wash the money they get from the bush towns, before handling, and the new-comer's first days in the island are sure to be harassed by the difficulties of avoiding miscellaneous hand-shaking. Knowing what one knows about the prevalence of skin-troubles, one does not care to run risks; but the Niuéan, like all islanders, has unfortunately learned the habit of continual hand-shaking from his earliest teachers, and is never likely to unlearn it. So the visitor who does not want to encounter disappointed faces and puzzled inquiries, looks out old gloves to go a-walking with, and burns them, once he or she is settled in the place, and no longer a novelty.

There are manners in Niué—of a sort. "Fanagé fei!" is the greeting to any one met on the road, and it must not be left out, or the Savage Islanders will say you have no manners. It means, "Where are you going?" and it is not at all an empty inquiry, for you must mention the name of your destination in reply, and then repeat the inquiry on your own account, and listen for the answer. Riding across the island day by day, I used to pass in a perfect whirlwind of "Where-are-you-goings?"—calling out hastily, as the horse cantered over the grassy road, "Avatele," or "Mutelau," (names of villages) or "Misi Nicolasi" (Mrs. Nicholas, a trader's wife), and adding as I passed on: "Fanagé fei?" to the man or woman who had greeted me. There was generally a long story in reply, but I fear I was usually out of hearing before it was ended. My manners, out riding, must have struck Niué as decidedly vulgar.

It was during the first few days of my stay that I attained a distinction that I had never hoped to see, and that I am not at all likely to see again. I was made a headline in a copybook! If that is not fame, what is?

The native school-teacher—a brown, black-eyed and bearded man of middle age and dignified presence—had called at my house shortly after my arrival, to display his English and his importance, and welcome the stranger. He wanted, among a great many other things, to know what my name was, and how it was spelt. I wrote it down for him, and he carried it away, studying it the while. Next day, the copies set in the principal school for the youth of Niué consisted of my name in full, heading the following legend: "While this lady is in Niué, we must all be very good." Evidently a case of "Après moi le déluge!"

Sitting on a box in my cool little shady house of a morning, writing on my knee, with the whisper of the palms about the door, and the empty changeless blue sea lying below, I used to receive visitor after visitor, calling on different errands—some to sit on the verandah and look at me in silence; some to come in, squat on the floor, and discourse fluently for half an hour in a language I did not understand (they never seemed distressed by the absence of replies); some to sell curios; some to give dinners! You give dinners in Niué in a strictly literal sense. Instead of bringing the guest to the dinner, you take the dinner to the guest, and then wait to see it eaten. It generally consists of a baked fish wrapped in leaves, several lumps of yam, hot and moist, and as heavy as iron, a pudding made of mashed pumpkin and breadfruit, another made of bananas, sugarcane, and cocoanut, some arrowroot boiled to jelly, and the inevitable taro top and cocoanut cream—about which I must confess I was rather greedy. The rest of the dinner I used to accept politely, as it was set out on the floor, eat a morsel or two here and there, and afterwards hand over the remainder to Kuru and his wife, who were always ready to dispose of it. At the beginning, I used to offer gifts in return, which were always refused. Then, acting on the advice of old residents, I reserved the gift for a day or two, and presented it at the first suitable opportunity. It was always readily accepted, when offered after this fashion, and thus I learned one more lesson as to island etiquette.

"You'll see a lot of stuff in travel books," said an old resident to me, "about the wonderful generosity of the island people, all over the Pacific—how they press gifts of every kind on travellers, and won't take any return. Well, that's true, and it's not true. All the island people love strangers, and are new-fangled with every fresh face, and they do come along with presents, but as to not wanting a return, why, that isn't quite the case. They won't take payment, mostly, and there's very few places where they'll even take a present, right off. But they always expect something back, some time. I know that isn't what the books say, but books are mostly wrong about anything you've got to go below the top of things to see—and the traveller likes that pretty idea, of getting presents for nothing, too much to give it up easily. Still, you may take my word for it that the natives *will* take a return for anything and everything they give you, here and everywhere else, unless it's a drink of cocoanut, or a bit of fruit they offer you on the road, or maybe a bit of dinner, if you'd drop in on them at meals. Set presents you've got to pay for, and more than their value too, if you take them. I don't myself, I find native presents too expensive.

"What do you want to give? Oh, well, if a woman brings you in a dinner or two, give her a trade silk handkerchief, one of those shilling ones, some day. Or if they bring you baskets of fruit, give them a couple of sticks of tobacco. They'll take payment for fruit here, in that way, at any time. You'll need to give some things when you're going away, to the people you've seen most of—a few yards of cotton, or something of that kind. White people are expected to give presents, all over the islands—it needn't be dear things, but it ought to be something. If the lords and folk who have been round the Pacific in their yachts only heard what the natives say of them, because they didn't know that, they'd take care to bring a case or two of cheap stuff for presents next time. 'Not chief-like,' is what the natives say—and I ask you yourself, it isn't 'chief-like,' is it, to take all you can get, and give not a stick of niggerhead or an inch of ribbon in return? I'd think they'd be too proud—but then,

I'm not a tourist trotting round the globe, I'm only a man who works for his living.

"As for yourself, you take my advice, and say right out you don't want the dinners, when they bring them. Yes, it'll offend them, but you must either do that, or pay for stuff you don't want three days out of seven, or six days, more likely, if they think you're liberal-minded. You'll get no end of presents when you're going away, pretty things enough, and those will have to be paid for in presents, too. Better make it as cheap as you can, meantime.

"But those people who go travelling like princes, and load their cabins up with spears and clubs and tappa-cloths and shells the natives have given them everywhere they went—and not a farthing, or a farthing's worth, do they let it cost them from end to end—I tell you, they're a disgrace to England," concluded my informant hotly.

"I am quite sure it is simply because they do not know—how should they?" I asked, trying to defend the absent globe-trotters.

"Decent feeling ought to teach them!" declared the critic of manners, who was evidently not to be pacified.

I had my dinner to cook, so I went away, and left him still revolving the iniquities of travelling milords in his memory. But I did not forget the conversation, for it seemed to me that the facts about this matter of present-giving and taking ought to be known as widely as possible. In nearly two years of island travel that followed after those days, I had full opportunity of proving the truth of the statements made by my Niué acquaintance, and every experience only served to confirm them.

Travellers who visit the islands should note this fact, and lay in a stock of suitable goods in Sydney, which is the starting point for most Pacific travel. There are various firms who make a speciality of island trade, and these will usually sell any reasonable quantity at wholesale prices. The natives of the Pacific, in general, are not to be put off with worthless trifles as presents, nor do they care for beads, unless in the few groups still remaining uncivilised. They like best the sort of goods with which they are already familiar, and do not care for "imported" novelties. Silk handkerchiefs are liked everywhere, and they are easy to carry. Cotton or silk stuff is much valued. Imitation jewellery—brooches, pins, etc.—is valued quite as much as real, except in Niué, where the natives seem to have a natural craving and liking for precious metals. Tinned foods of all kinds, and sweets, are perhaps better appreciated than anything else. Tinned salmon in especial, is the safest kind of "tip" that can be given to any native, from a lordly Samoan chief, down to a wild "bushie" from the Solomons.

Withal, one must not take away the character of the island world for hospitality, because of its childlike fancy for presents. Many and many a destitute white man can tell of the true generosity and ungrudging kindness he has met with at the hands of the gentle brown men and women, when luck was hard and the whites would have none of him. They are not fair-weather friends, in the European sense of the word. True, when the weather is sunny with you, they will come round and bask in the warmth, and share your good luck. But when the rainy days come, they will share all they have with you, just as freely, and they will not look for presents, then.

THE NIUÉAN—A WORKER

The industries of the island filled up many a pleasant morning. Niué is supposed to be the most hard-working of all the Pacific islands, and certainly its people do not seem to eat the bread of idleness. Here, there is no lounging and dreaming and lotus-eating on the sounding coral shore—perhaps there isn't much shore anyway ; perhaps because the Savage Islander is not made that way. The food of the people consists largely of yams, and in a country which has hardly any depth of soil, these are hard to grow, and need care. The bananas are grown in the most wonderful way in the clefts of the coral rocks, so that they actually appear to be springing out of the stone. Copra is made in fair quantity, and many of the people spend the greater part of their time collecting a certain kind of fungus which is exported to Sydney, and used (or so report declares) for making an imitation of birds' nest soup in China.

The proportion of women on the island is very large, because there are always at least a thousand men, out of a total population of five thousand souls, away working elsewhere. The Niuéan is a bit of a miser, and will do anything for money. He engages, therefore, as a labourer in the plantations of Samoa, where the natives will not do any work they can avoid, or goes up to Malden Island to the guano pits, or takes a year or two at sea on an island schooner, or goes away as fireman on the missionary steamer—anything to make money. Meantime his womenkind stay at home and keep themselves. They work about the white people's houses, they act as stevedores to the ships, they fetch and carry all over the island. When I wanted two heavy trunks conveyed a distance of six miles one day, four sturdy Niué girls came to do the work ; slung the trunks on two poles, trotted away with them, and reached the end of the journey before my lazy horse had managed to carry me to my destination. They do an immense amount of plaiting work—mats, fans, baskets, and above all, hats, of which the annual export runs into thousands of dozens. These hats are made of fine strips of dried and split pandanus leaf; they much resemble the coarser kind of Panama, and give excellent shade and wear. They are worn over the whole Pacific, and a great part of New Zealand, and, I strongly suspect, are exported to England under the name, and at the price of second-grade Panamas. A clever worker will finish one in a day. Much of the plaiting is done in caves in the hot season, as the material must be kept fairly cool and moist.

When the Niué folks are not working, they idle a little at times, but not very much. They sing in chorus occasionally, but it is not an absorbing occupation with them, and they do not dance a great deal either, since the advent of missionary rule. Their chief amusement is an odd one—walking round the island. You can scarcely take a long ride without encountering a stray picnic party of natives, mostly women, striding along at a good round pace, and heavily laden with fruit, food, and mats. They always complete the journey—forty miles—in a day, picknicking on the roadside for meals, and seem to enjoy themselves thoroughly. The strenuous life, exemplified after this fashion, is certainly the last thing one would expect to find in the Pacific. But then, the great fascination of the island world lies in the fact that here, as nowhere else, "only the unexpected happens."

.   .   .   .   .

It is a day of molten gold, with a sea coloured like a sheet of sapphire glass in a cathedral window. I am busy washing up my breakfast things at the door (there is no false shame about the performance of domestic duties in the capital city of Niué) when a couple of native girls appear on the grass pathway, their wavy hair loose and flowing, their white muslin dresses kilted up high over strong brown limbs. Each carries a clean "pareo" in her hand. They are going for a swim, one of them informs me in broken English: will I come too?

Of course I will. I get out my own bathing dress, and follow the pair down the cliff, scrambling perilously from crag to crag, until we reach a point where it is possible to get down on to the narrow rocky ledge at the verge of the sea. Within the reef here there is a splendid stretch of protected water, peacock-blue in colour, immensely deep, and almost cold. There are no sharks about here, the girls tell me, and it is an excellent place for a swim.

Oh, for a Royal Academician to paint the picture made by the younger girl, as she stands on the edge of the rocks ready to leap in, dressed in a bright blue scarf that is wound round and round her graceful bronze body from shoulder to knee, and parting her full wavy hair aside with slender dark fingers! Beauty of form did not die out with the ancient Greeks: the Diana of the Louvre and the Medici Venus may be seen any day of any year, on the shores of the far-away islands, by those who know lovely line when they see it, and have not given over their senses, bound and blinded, to the traditions of the schools. If there is any man in the world to-day who can handle a hammer and chisel as Phidias did, let him come to the South Sea Islands and look there for the models that made the ancient Greek immortal. The sculptor who can mould a young island girl, Tahitian for the Venus type, Samoan for the Diana, or a young island chief, like Mercury, in bronze, will give the world something as exquisite and as immortal as any marvel from the hand of Phidias or Praxiteles.

My beautiful Niué girl was an exception, so far as her own island went. Niué women are strong and well made, but not lovely as a rule. Her companion was as sturdy as a cart-horse, but as plain as a pig. She smoked a huge pipe, chewed plug tobacco, and laughed like a hyena. They were truly a well-contrasted pair.

The reef was a good way off, so we all struck out for that, when we came up panting and blowing from our dive. The girls gave me a fine exhibition of under-water swimming now and then, slipping easily underneath the gleaming surface, and disappearing from view below, for so long a time that one became quite nervous. My pretty little friend persuaded me to accompany her once, and though I did not like it among the ugly-looking coral caves, I dived for a short time, and endeavoured to follow her flying heels.

Under water among the coral reefs! It sounds romantic, but it was not pleasant. Five feet beneath the surface, the light was as clear as day, and one could see all about one, far too much, for the things that were visible were disquieting. I knew extremely well that coral reefs are the haunt of every kind of unpleasant sea-beast, and I fancied Victor Hugo's "pieuvre" at the very least, within the gloomy arch of every cave. There were far too many fish also, and they were much too impertinent, and a fish in one's hair, even if harmless, is not nice. I had not gone down much over a fathom, when I turned, and began to beat upwards again looking eagerly at the light. And then I saw a thing that as nearly as possible made me open my mouth and drown myself.

It was merely a bunch of black waving trailers, coming

THE DELIGHTS OF DIVING

out of the dark of the rocks, and spreading between me and the pale-green light of day. I did not know what it was, and I do not know, to this day. And, like the runaway soldier in the poem, "I don't know where I went to, for I didn't stop to see." I was on the top of the water, twenty yards away, and swimming at racing speed, when I realised the fact that I was still alive, some moments later. And on the surface I stayed, for the rest of the swim. The native girls were exceedingly amused, for the islander fears nothing that is in the water or under it; but I did not mind their laughing.

One of them then, as she swam along, began laying her mouth to the surface of the water, and blowing bubbles, laughing all the time. She insisted that I should do it too, and I imitated her, at which she seemed delighted. "That what we doing, suppose some shark come," she explained, "shark he plenty frighten, no like that."

We practised this useful accomplishment for some time, and then went ashore again. I regret to say that I roused the amusement of my companions yet again, before we landed, by making hasty exclamations, and dodging rapidly away from the embraces of a black-and-white banded snake, about four feet long, that suddenly appeared from nowhere in particular, moving very swiftly, and seemed disposed to argue the right of way. The lagoon at Raratonga had not prepared me for the Zoological Garden in which one had to bathe at Niué.

"Snake he no harm," said my Venus Anadyomene, as she stood on the rock, with her bathing scarf in her hand, wringing it out in the calmest manner in the world. "Plenty-plenty snake stop there."

There were indeed plenty of snakes. One could see them any fine day from the top of the cliffs, gliding through the water below, or lying on the rocks in family parties of a score or two, conspicuous at a great distance, because of their handsome black-and-white banded skins. As to there being no harm—well, I never heard of any one in Niué being injured. But a boy in Fiji trod on one of these checkerboarded creatures, about that time, and died in half an hour from its bite. I am strongly inclined to think that the Niué snake is poisonous, like almost all sea-snakes, though it does not seem at all ready to attack.

What was it I saw under water? I never knew, but I guessed as much as I wanted, a day or two later, when I saw a native, fishing on the reef near my bathing-place, draw up a big devil-fish, with eight limp dangling arms over six feet long, and carry it away. A trader told me that he had once pulled up one himself, while out fishing in a light canoe, and that it seized hold of the little boat, and made such a fight that he barely escaped with his life. It is the pleasant habit of this fish, when attacked by a human being, to fling its hideous tentacles over his head and face, and force them up into eyes, nostrils, and mouth, so as to suffocate him, if he cannot master the creature.

"Do you think there were any sharks about the day I bathed?" I inquired.

"Well, if the girls were blowing, I should say there must have been. They wouldn't do it for fun altogether," he replied.

"Surely they wouldn't bathe, if they knew there were any about?"

"Oh, wouldn't they, though! *They* don't mind them. No native is afraid of anything in the sea."

I believed this with reservations, until a day came in another island, when I nearly furnished a dinner

AN UNLOOKED-FOR DANGER

for a shark myself, and thenceforth gave up bathing in unprotected tropical waters, for good. It was in Rakahanga, many hundreds of miles nearer the Line, and I had left the schooner to enjoy a walk and a bathe. A native Rakahangan girl, who had never seen a white woman before, and was wildly excited at the thought of going bathing with this unknown wonder, found a boat for me, and allowed me to pick my own place in the inner lagoon of the island. I chose a spot where the lagoon narrowed into a bottle-neck communicating with the sea, and we started our swim. The girl, however, much to my surprise, would not go more than a few yards from the boat, and declined to follow me when I struck out for the open water. I had been assured by her, so far as my scanty knowledge of Maori allowed me to understand, that there were no sharks, so her conduct seemed incomprehensible, until a stealthy black fin, shaped like the mainsail of a schooner, rose out of the water a few score yards away, and began making for me!

The native girl was first into the boat, but I was assuredly not long after her. The black fin did not follow, once I was out of the water. But the heat of that burning day, far up towards the Line, was hardly enough to warm me, for half an hour afterwards.

I found, on asking the questions that I should have asked first of all, that the bottle-neck entrance of the lagoon was a perfect death-trap of sharks, and that more than one native had been eaten there.

"Why on earth did the girl tell me there were none and why did she venture into such a place herself?" I asked.

"Well," said the only white man on the island, "I should think she knew that any shark will take a white person, and leave a native, if there's a choice. And if you had that red bathing-dress on that you're carrying, why, you were simply making bait of yourself!"

"But why should she want to see me killed?"

"Oh, she didn't. She only wanted to have the fun of a bathe with a white woman, and just took the chances!"

So much about bathing, in the "sunny isles of Eden." One is sorry to be obliged to say that it is one of the disappointments of the Pacific. Warm, brilliant water, snowy coral sands, and glancing fish of rainbow hues, are charming accompaniments to a bath, no doubt, but they are too dearly paid for when snakes, sharks, sting-rays, and devil-fish have to be counted into the party.

. . . . . .

Nothing in curious Niué is quite so curious as the native fancies about ghosts and devils. In spite of their Christianity, they still hold fast to all their ancient superstitions about the powers of evil.

Every Savage Islander believes, quite as a matter of course, that ghosts walk the roads and patrol the lonely bush, all night long. Some are harmless spirits, many are malignant devils. After dark has fallen, about six o'clock, no one dares to leave his house except for some very important errand; and if it is necessary to go out so late as nine or ten o'clock, a large party will go together—this even in the town itself. Every native has a dog or two, of a good barking watchdog breed, not to protect property, for theft is unknown, but to drive away ghosts at night! Devil possession is believed in firmly. When a man takes sick, his neighbours try, in a friendly manner, to "drive the devil out of him." Perhaps they hang him up by his thumbs; possibly they put his feet in boiling water, causing fearful scalds; or they may drive sharks' teeth into him here and there. But the most popular method is plain and simple squeezing, to squeeze the devil out! This often results in broken ribs, and occasionally in death. It is a curious fact, in connection with this " squeezing," that the natives are remarkably expert " masseurs," and can " drive the devil" out of a sprain, or a headache, or an attack of neuralgia, by what seems to be a clever combination of the "pétrissage" and " screw" movement of massage. This, they say, annoys the devil so much that he goes away. Applied to the trunk, however, and carried out with the utmost strength of two or three powerful men, Savage Islander massage is (as above stated) often fatal—and small wonder!

When a man has died, from natural or unnatural causes, a great feast is held of baked pig and fowl, yams, taro, fish, and cocoanuts. Presents are given to the dead man's relatives, as at a wedding, and other presents are returned by them to the men who dig the grave. The corpse is placed in a shallow hole, wrapped in costly mats; and then begins the ghostly life of the once-loved husband or father, who now becomes a haunting terror to those of his own household. Over his grave they erect a massive tomb of concrete and lime, meant to discourage him, so far as possible, from coming out to revisit the upper world. They gather together roots of the splendid scarlet poinsettia, gorgeous hibiscus, and graceful wine-coloured foliage plants, and place them about his tomb, to make it attractive to him. They collect his most cherished possessions—his " papalangi " (white man's) bowler hat, which he used to wear on Sundays at the five long services in the native church; his best trousers; his orange-coloured singlet with pink bindings; his tin mug and plate—and place them on the grave. Savage Island folk are very avaricious and greedy; yet not a soul will dare to touch these valuable goods; they lie on the grave, in sun and storm, until rotted or broken. If it is a woman's grave, you may even see her little hand sewing-machine (almost every island in the Pacific possesses scores of these) placed on the tomb, to amuse the ghost in its leisure hours. There will be a bottle of cocoanut hair-oil, too, scented with "tieré" flowers, and perhaps a little looking-glass or comb—so that we can picture the spirit of the dark-eyed island girls, like mermaids, coming forth at night to sit in the moonlight and dress their glossy hair—if ghosts indeed have hair like mortal girls!

Mosquito-curtains, somewhat tattered by the wind, can be seen on many graves, carefully stretched over the tomb on the regulation uprights and cross-pieces, as over a bed. This is, no doubt, intended to help the ghost to lie quiet, lest the mosquitoes should annoy it so much that it be driven to get up and walk about. Certainly, if a Savage Island ghost does walk, it is not because every care is not taken to make it (as the Americans would say) "stay put."

There are no graveyards on the island. Every man is buried on his own land, very often alongside the road, or close to his house. The thrifty islanders plant onions and pumpkins on the earth close about the tomb, and enjoy the excellent flavour imparted to these vegetables by the essence of dead ancestor which they suck up through the soil. In odd contradiction to this economical plan, a "tapu" is placed upon all the cocoanut trees owned by the deceased; and for a year or more valuable nuts are allowed to lie where they fall, sprouting into young plants, and losing many tons of copra annually to the island. Groups of palms unhealthily crowded

AN ILL-REPUTED ROAD 221

together, bear witness everywhere to the antiquity of this strange practice.

The main, and indeed the only good road, across the island, owns a spot of fearsome reputation. On a solitary tableland, swept by salt sea-winds, stand certain groups of clustered cocoa-palms, sprung from tapu's nuts on dead men's lands. Here the natives say, the ghosts and devils have great power, and it is dangerous to walk there at night alone, even for white men, who take little account of native spirits. Many of the white traders of the island are shy of the spot; and some say that when riding in parties across the island at night, their horses shy and bolt passing the place, and exhibit unaccountable fear. Only a year or two ago, a terrible thing happened in this desolate spot, as if to prove the truth of local traditions. There was one native of the island, a "witch-doctor," learned in charms and spells, who professed not to be afraid of the devils. He could manage them, he said; and to prove it, he used sometimes to walk alone across the island at night. One morning, he did not return from an excursion of this nature. The villagers set out in a body to look for him in the broad light of the tropical sun. They found him, at the haunted spot, lying on the ground dead. His face was black, and his body horribly contorted. The devils had fought him, and conquered him—so the natives said. And now no gold would induce a Savage Islander to pass the fatal spot after dark.

I asked the white missionary doctor resident at the time of my visit on the island, if he could account for the death. He said that he had not held a post-mortem, and therefore could not say what the cause might be; but the appearance of the corpse was undoubtedly as described by the natives.

Being anxious to investigate the truth of these stories, I determined to spend a night on the spot, and see what happened. The natives were horrified beyond measure at the idea; and when an accident on a coral reef laid me up from walking exercise until just before the schooner called again at the island to take me away—thus preventing me from carrying out the plan—they were one and all convinced that the fall was the work of devils, anxious to prevent me from meddling with their doings!

The problem, then, remained unsolved, and rests open to any other traveller to investigate. But as Savage Island lies far off the track of the wandering tourist, its ghosts are likely to remain undisturbed in their happy hunting-grounds for the present.

Mrs. Joe Gargery would certainly have liked Niué, for it is a place where there is none of the "pompeying" so obnoxious to her Spartan soul. And yet, if you stay there long, you will find out that Savage Island practises certain of the early Christian virtues, if it has dropped a few of its luxuries manufactured by civilisation. If you want a horse to ride across the island—a gentle, native creature that goes off at both ends, like a fire-cracker, when you try to mount, biting and kicking simultaneously, and, when mounted, converts your ride into a sandwich of jibbing and bolting, you will call in at the nearest trader's, and tell him you want his horse and his neighbour's saddle and whip. All these will appear at your door, with a couple of kindly messages, in half an hour. You will time your arrival at the different villages so as to hit off some one's meal-hours, walk in, ask for a help of the inevitable curried tin, and carry off a loaf of bread or a lump of cake, if your host happens to have baked that morning and you have not. When a ship comes in—perhaps the bi-yearly steamer from Samoa, with real mutton and beef in her ice-chest—and the capital gorges for two days, you, the stranger within their gates, will meet hot chops walking up to your verandah between two hot plates, and find confectioners' paper bags full of priceless New Zealand potatoes, sitting on your doorstep. You will learn to shed tears of genuine emotion at the sight of a rasher of bacon, and to accept with modest reluctance the almost too valuable gift of one real onion. Hospitality among the white folk of Savage Island is hospitality, and no mistake, and its real generosity can only be appreciated by those who know the supreme importance assumed by "daily bread," when the latter is dependent upon the rare and irregular calls of passing ships.

For, like a good many Pacific Islands, this coral land is more beautiful than fertile. Its wild fantastic rocks, which make up the whole surface of the island, produce in their clefts and hollows enough yam, taro, banana, and papaw to feed the natives; but the white man wants more. Tins are his only resource—tins and biscuits, for flour does not keep long, and bread is often unattainable. Fowls or eggs can seldom be bought, for the reason that some one imported a number of cats many years ago; these were allowed to run wild in the bush, and have now become wild in earnest, devouring fowls, and even attacking dogs and young pigs at times. Why, then, if the island is valueless to Europeans, and the life hard, do white men live in Savage Island and many similar places? For the reason that fortunes have been piled up, in past years, by trading in such isolated spots, and that there is still money to be made, though not so much as of old. Trading in the Pacific is a double-barrelled sort of business. You settle down on an island where there is a good supply of copra (dried cocoa-nut kernel, manufactured by the natives). You buy the copra from the islanders at about £8 a ton, store it away in your copra-house until the schooner or the steamer calls, and then ship it off to Sydney, where it sells at £13 to £14 a ton. Freight and labour in storing and getting on board, eat into the profits. But, in addition to buying, the trader sells. He has a store, where cheap prints, violent perfumes, gaudy jewellery, tapes and buttons and pins and needles, tins of beef, shoes, etc., are sold to the natives at a price which leaves a very good profit on their cost down in Auckland.

The laws of all the Pacific Colonies forbid the white trader to buy from the natives except with cash; but, as the cash comes back to him before long over the counter of the store, it comes to much the same in the end as the old barter system of the early days, out of which money used to be quickly and easily made. Sometimes the trader, if in a small way of business, sells his copra to captains of calling ships at a smaller price than the Auckland value. But nowadays so many stores are owned by big Auckland and Sydney firms that most of the stuff is shipped off for sale in New Zealand or Australia. "Panama" hats, already mentioned, are a very important article of commerce here. Every island has some speciality of its own besides the inevitable copra; and the trader deals in all he can get. The trader's life is, as a rule, a pleasant one enough. Savage Island is one of the worst places where he could find himself; and yet the days pass happily enough in that solitary outlier of civilisation. There is not much work to do; the climate is never inconveniently hot; the scenery, especially among the up-country primæval forests, is very lovely. There is a good deal of riding and bathing, a little shooting, and a myriad of wild and fantastic caves to explore when the spirit moves one. The native canoes are easy to manage and excellent to fish from.

It is traditional in Savage Island for the few white people—almost all rival traders—to hang together, and live in as friendly a manner as a great family party. If the great world is shut out, its cares are shut away, and life sits lightly on all. No one can be extravagant ; no one can "keep up appearances" at the cost of comfort ; no one is over-anxious, or worried, or excited over anything—except when the rare, the long-expected ship comes in, and the natives rend the air with yells of joy, and the girls cocoanut-oil their hair, and the white men rush for clean duck suits and fresh hats, and the mails come in, and the news is distributed, and cargoes go out, and every one feasts from dawn till dusk, and all the island is in a state of frantic ebullition for at least three days. Then, indeed, Niué is alive.

We were all getting hungry when the *Duchess* came in again, after nearly two months' absence, for provisions were short, and most of us had come down to eating little green parrots out of the bush, and enjoying them, for want of anything better. It was certainly tantalising to see the ship off the island beating about for three days and more, before she was able to approach, but that is an usual incident in Niué. She came up at last, and I got my traps on board, and paid my bills, and carried away the model canoes and shell necklaces, and plaited hats and baskets, that were brought me as parting presents, and gave a number of yards of cotton cloth, and a good many silk handkerchiefs, in return. And so the big sails were hoisted once more with a merry rattling and flapping, and away we went, northward a thousand miles, to desolate, burning Penrhyn and Malden Island.

CHAPTER XI

A Life on the Ocean Wave—Where They kept the Dynamite—How far from an Iced Drink?—The Peacefulness of a Pacific Calm—A Golden Dust Heap—Among the Rookeries—Sailing on the Land—All about Guano.

THE pirate captain was gone when the schooner reappeared off Niué, and a certain ancient mariner had taken his place. Things were not quite so exciting on the *Duchess* under the new régime, but the order which reigned on board was something awful; for the ancient mariner had been a whaling captain in his day, and on whaling ships it is more than on any others a case of "Growl you may, but go you must," for all the crew. The ancient mariner was as salty a salt as ever sailed the ocean. He had never been on anything with steam in it, he was as tough as ship-yard teak, and as strong as a bear, though he was a grandfather of some years' standing, and he was full of strange wild stories about the whaling grounds, and odd happenings in out-of-the-way corners of the Pacific —most of which he seemed to consider the merest commonplaces of a prosaic existence.

We suffered many things from the cook, in the course of that long burning voyage towards the Line. The *Duchess's* stores were none of the best, and the cook dealt with them after a fashion that made me understand once for all the sailor saying: "God sends meat, and the devil sends cooks." Pea-soup, salt pork and beef, plum duff, ship's biscuit, sea-pie —this was the sort of food that, in the days before I set foot on the *Duchess*, I had supposed to form the usual table of sailing vessels. I fear it was a case of sea-story-books, over again. What we did get was "tinned rag" of a peculiarly damp and viscous quality, tea that usually tasted of cockroaches, biscuit that was so full of copra bugs we had to hammer it on the table before eating it, an occasional tin of tasteless fruit (it ran out very soon), and bread that was a nightmare, for the flour went musty before we were out a week, and the unspeakable cook tried to disguise its taste with sugar. Board-of-trade limejuice, which is a nauseous dose at best, we were obliged by law to carry, and I think we must have run rather near scurvy in the course of that long trip, for the amount of the oily, drug-flavoured liquid that the mates and myself used to drink at times, seemed to argue a special craving of nature. But *à la guerre comme à la guerre*—and one does not take ship on a Pacific wind-jammer expecting the luxuries of a P. and O.

We were not going direct to Malden, having to call first at Samoa and Mangaia. Three days of rough rolling weather saw us in Apia, about which I have nothing to say at present, since I paid a longer visit to Stevenson's country later on. We had about forty native passengers to take on here for the Cook Islands and Malden. There was nowhere to put them, but in the South Seas such small inconveniences trouble nobody.

I am very strongly tempted here to tell about the big gale that caught us the first night out, carried away our lifeboat, topsail, topgallant, and main gaff, swamped the unlucky passengers' cabin, and caused the Cingalese steward to compose and chant all night long a litany containing three mournful versicles: "O my God, this is too much terrible! O my God, why I ever go to sea! O my God, I never go to sea again!" But in the Pacific one soon learns that sea etiquette makes light of such matters. So the wonderful and terrible sights which I saw once or twice that night, clinging precariously to anything solid near the door of my cabin, and hoping that the captain would not catch me out on deck, must remain undescribed. Nearly seven weeks were occupied by this northern trip—time for a mail steamer to go out from London to New Zealand, and get well started on the way home again. We were, of course, entirely isolated from news and letters; indeed, the mails and papers that we carried conveyed the very latest intelligence to islands that had not had a word from the outer world for many months. Our native passengers, who were mostly going up to Malden Island guano works as paid labourers, evidently considered the trip one wild scene of excitement and luxury. The South Sea Islander loves nothing more than change, and every new island we touched at was a Paris or an Ostend to these (mostly) untravelled natives. Their accommodation on the ship was not unlike that complained of by the waiter in "David Copperfield." They "lived on broken wittles, and they slept on the coals." The *Duchess* carried benzine tins for the feeding of the futile little motor that worked her in and out of port, and the native sleeping place was merely the hold, on top of the tins.

"Do you mind the dynamite remaining under your bunk?" asked the ancient mariner, shortly after we left Samoa.

"*Under my bunk?*"

"Yes—didn't you know it was there? The explosives safe is let into the deck just beneath the deck cabin. I'll move it if you're nervous about it—I thought I'd tell you, anyways. But it's the best place for it to be, you see, right amidships." And the ancient mariner, leaning his six foot two across the rail, turned his quid, and spat into the deep.

"What do we want with dynamite, anyhow?" asked the bewildered passenger, confronted with this new and startling streak of local colour.

"*We* don't want none. The Cook Islands wants it for reefs."

"Oh, leave it where it is—I suppose it's all the same in the end where it starts from, if it did blow up," says the passenger resignedly. "What about the benzoline in the hold, though?"

"Every one's got to take chances at sea," says the captain, easily. "The mates have orders to keep the natives from smokin' in the hold at night."

And at midnight, when I slip out of my bunk to look on and see what the weather is like (it has been threatening all day), a faint but unmistakable odour of island tobacco greets my nose, from the opening of the main hatch! Benzoline, dynamite, natives smoking in the hold, one big boat smashed, one small one left, forty native passengers, five whites, and three hundred miles to the nearest land!

Well, *à la guerre comme à la guerre*, and one must not tell tales at sea. So I don't tell any, though tempted. But I am very glad, a week later, to see the Cook Islands rising up out of the empty blue again. We have had head winds, we have been allowanced as to water, we are all pleased to have a chance of taking in some fruit before we start on the thousand miles run to Malden—and above all, we leave that dynamite here, which is a good thing; for really we have been putting rather too much strain on the good nature of the "Sweet little cherub that sits up aloft, to keep guard o'er the life of poor Jack," this last week or two.

If proof were wanted that the cherub's patience is about at an end, our arrival at Mangaia furnishes it—for we do take fire after all, just a couple of hundred yards from shore!

It does not matter now, since half the natives of the island are about the ship, and the case of explosives has just been rowed off in our only boat, and the blaze is put out without much trouble. But, two days ago!

Well, the sweet little cherub certainly deserved a rest.

. . . . .

Now the *Duchess's* bowsprit was pointed northwards, and we set out on a thousand miles' unbroken run up to Malden Island, only four degrees south of the Line. For nine days we ploughed across the same monotonous plain of lonely sea, growing a little duller every day, as our stores of reading matter dwindled away, and our fruit and vegetables ran out, and the memory of our last fresh mess became only a haunting, far-off regret. Squatting or lying about the white-hot poop in the merciless sun—which burnt through our duck and cotton clothing, and scorched the skin underneath, but was at least a degree better than the choking Hades of a cabin below—we used to torture each other with reminiscences and speculations, such as " They have real salt beef and sea-pie and lobscouse and pea-soup, and things like that, every day on Robinson's schooner; no tinned rag and musty flour "; or " How many thousand miles are we now from an iced drink ? " This last problem occupied the mates and myself for half a morning, and made us all a great deal hotter than we were before. Auckland was about 2,300 miles away, San Francisco about 3,000 as far as we could guess. We decided for Auckland, and discussed the best place to buy the drink, being somewhat limited in choice by the passenger's selfish insistence on a place where she could get really good iced coffee. By the time this was settled, the captain joined in, and informed us that we could get all we wanted, and fresh limes into the bargain, only a thousand miles away, at Tahiti, which every one had somehow overlooked. Only a thousand ! It seemed nothing, and we all felt (illogically) cheered up at the thought.

Late in the afternoon we came near attaining our wish for a temperature of thirty-two degrees in rather an unexpected way. The bottom of the Pacific generally hovers about this figure, some miles below the burning surface, which often reaches the temperature of an ordinary warm bath ; and the *Duchess* had a fairly narrow escape of going down to look for a cool spot without a return ticket. A giant waterspout suddenly formed out of the low-hanging, angry sky that had replaced the clear heat of the morning. First of all, a black trunk like an elephant's began to feel blindly about in mid-air, hanging from a cloud. It came nearer and nearer with uncanny speed, drawing up to itself as it came a colossal cone of turbulent sea, until the two joined together in one enormous black pillar, some quarter of a mile broad at the base, and probably a good thousand feet high, uniting as it did the clouds and the sea below. Across the darkening sea, against the threatening, copper-crimson sunset, came this gigantic horror, waltzing over leagues of torn-up water in a veritable dance of death, like something blind, but mad and cruel, trying to find and shatter our fragile little ship. Happily, the dark was only coming, not yet come; happily, too, the wind favoured us, and we were able to tack about and keep out of the way, dodging the strangely human rushes and advances of the water-giant with smartness and skill. At one time it came so close that the elephant trunk —now separately visible again—seemed feeling about over our heads, although the captain afterwards said it had been more than three hundred yards away—and the immense maelstrom underneath showed us the great wall of whirling spindrift that edged its deadly circle, as plain as the foam about our own bows. Every one was quiet, cool, and ready; but no one was sorry when the threatening monster finally spun away to leeward and melted into air once more. A waterspout of this enormous size, striking a small vessel, would snap off her masts like sticks of candy, kill any one who happened to be on deck, and most probably sink the ship with the very impact of the terrible shock.

"One doesn't hear much about ships being sunk by waterspouts," objected the sceptical passenger to this last statement.

"Ships that's sunk by waterspouts doesn't come back to tell the newspapers about it," said the captain darkly.

Life on a South Sea schooner is not all romance. For the officers of the ship it is a very hard life indeed. Native crews are the rule in the South Seas, and native crews make work for every one, including themselves. Absolutely fearless is the Kanaka, active as a monkey aloft, good-natured and jolly to the last degree, but perfectly unreliable in any matter requiring an ounce of thought or a pennyworth of discretion, and, moreover,

THE ART OF SEAMANSHIP   233

given to shirk work in a variety of ingenious ways that pass the wit of the white man to circumvent. Constant and keen supervision while at sea, unremitting hurry and drive in port, are the duties of a South Sea mate, coupled with plenty of actual hard work on his own account. I have known a case where a small schooner was leaking badly, many days from port, and almost constant pumping was required. The pump broke while in use; and the watch, delighted to be released, turned in at eight bells without having done their spell, and without reporting the accident. The water gained steadily, but that did not trouble them; and when the mate discovered the accident, and set them to mend the pump at once, they were both surprised and grieved!

"Watch and watch" is the rule on small sailing-vessels; four hours on and four hours off, day and night, except for the "dog watches," four to six and six to eight in the evening, which create a daily shift in order that each man may be on watch at a different time on successive days. Always provided, of course, that the ship has any watches at all! I *have* sailed in a Pacific schooner where the crew spent most of their time playing the accordion and the Jew's harp, and slept peacefully all night. In the daytime there was generally some one at the wheel; but at night it was usually lashed, and the ship was let run, with all sails set, taking her chances of what might come, every soul on board being asleep. One night the cook came out of his bunk to get a drink from the tank, and found the vessel taken aback. The whole spirit of South Sea life breathes from the sequel. He told nobody! The galley was his department, not the sails; so he simply went back to his bunk. In the morning we fetched up off the northern side of an island we had intended to approach from the south; having, strange to say, somehow escaped piling our bones on the encircling reef, and also avoided the misfortune of losing our masts and getting sunk.

If there is a good deal of hard work on most schooners, and something of risk on all, there is also plenty of adventure and romance, for those who care about it. One seldom meets an island skipper whose life would not furnish materials for a dozen exciting books. Being cut off and attacked by cannibals down in the dangerous western groups; swimming for dear life away from a boat just bitten in two by an infuriated whale; driving one native king off his throne, putting another on, and acting as prime minister to the nation; hunting up a rumour of a splendid pearl among the pearling islands, and tracking down the gem, until found and coaxed away from its careless owner at one-tenth Sydney market prices —these are incidents that the typical schooner captain regards as merely the ordinary kind of break to be expected in his rather monotonous life. He does not think them very interesting, as a rule, and dismisses them somewhat briefly, in a yarn. What does excite him, cause him to raise his voice and gesticulate freely, and induce him to "yarn" relentlessly for half a watch, is the recital of some thrilling incident connected with the price of cargo or the claims made for damaged stuff by some abandoned villain of a trader. There is something worth relating in a tale like that, to his mind!

The passenger on an island schooner learns very early to cultivate a humble frame of mind. On a great steam liner he is all in all. It is for him almost entirely that the ships are built and run; his favour is life or death to the company. He is handled like eggs, and petted like a canary bird. Every one runs to do his bidding; he is one of a small but precious aristocracy waited on hand and foot by he humblest of serfs. On a schooner, however, he is ou. ted from his pride of place most completely by the car,·o, which takes precedence of him at every point; so th. t he rapidly learns he is not of nearly so much value as a fat sack of copra, and he becomes lowlier in mind than he ever was before. There is no special accommodation for him, as a rule ; he must go where he can, and take what he gets. If he can make himself useful about the ship, so much the better ; every one will think more of him, and he will get some useful exercise by working his passage in addition to paying for it.

Here is a typical day on the *Duchess*.

At eight bells (8 a.m.) breakfast is served in the cabin. The passenger's own cabin is a small deck-house placed amidships on the main deck. The deck is filled up with masses of cargo, interposing a perfect Himalayan chain of mountains between the main deck and the poop. It is pouring with tropical rain, but the big main hatch yawns half open on one side, because of the native passengers in the hold. On the other side foams a squally sea, unguarded by either rail or bulwark, since the cargo is almost overflowing out of the ship. The *Duchess* is rolling like a porpoise, and the passenger's hands are full of mackintosh and hat-brim. It seems impossible to reach the poop alive ; but the verb " have to " is in constant use on a sailing-ship, and it does not fail of its magical effect on this occasion. Clawing like a parrot, the passenger reaches the cabin, and finds the bare-armed, bare-footed mates and the captain engaged on the inevitable " tin " and biscuits. There is no tea this morning, because the cockroaches have managed to get into and flavour the brew; and the cabin will none of it. The captain has sent word by the native steward that he will " learn " the cook—a strange threat that usually brings about at least a temporary reform—and is now engaged in knocking the copra-bugs out of a piece of biscuit and brushing a colony of ants off his plate. Our cargo is copra, and in consequence the ship resembles an entomological museum more than anything else. No centipedes have been found this trip so far; but the mate stabbed a big scorpion with a sail-needle yesterday, as it was walking across the deck; and the cockroaches—as large as mice, and much bolder—have fairly "taken charge." The captain says he does not know whether he is sleeping in the cockroaches' bunk, or they in his, but he rather thinks the former, since the brutes made a determined effort to throw him out on the deck last night, and nearly succeeded!

It grows very warm after breakfast, for we are far within the tropics, and the *Duchess* has no awnings to protect her deck. The rail is almost hot enough to blister an unwary hand, and the great sails cast little shade, as the sun climbs higher to the zenith. The pitch does not, however, bubble in the seams of the deck, after the well-known fashion of stories, because the *Duchess*, like most other tropical ships, has her decks caulked with putty. A calm has fallen—a Pacific calm, which is not as highly distinguished for calmness as the stay-at-home reader might suppose. There is no wind, and the island we are trying to reach remains tantalisingly perched on the extreme edge of the horizon, like a little blue flower on the rim of a crystal dish. But there is plenty of sea —long glittering hills of water, rising and falling, smooth and foamless, under the ship, which they fling from side to side with cruel violence. The great booms swing and slam, the blocks clatter, the masts creak. Everything loose in the cabins toboggans wildly up and down the floor. At dinner, the soup which the cook has struggled to produce, lest he should be "learned," has to be drunk out of tin mugs for safety. Every one is sad and silent, for the sailor hates a calm even more than a gale.

Bonitos come round the ship in a glittering shoal by-and-by, and there is a rush for hooks and lines. One of our native A.B.s produces a huge pearl hook, unbaited, and begins to skim it lightly along the water at the end of its line, mimicking the exact motions of a flying-fish with a cleverness that no white man can approach. Hurrah! a catch! A mass of sparkling silver, blue, and green, nearly twenty pounds weight, is swung through the air, and tumbled on deck. Another and another follows; we have over a hundred pounds weight of fish in half an hour. The crew shout and sing for delight. There are only seven of them and five of us, but there will not be a scrap of that fish left by to-morrow, for all the forecastle hands will turn to and cook and eat without ceasing until it is gone; after which they will probably dance for an hour or two.

To every one's delight, the weather begins to cloud over again after this, and we are soon spinning before a ten-knot breeze towards the island, within sight of which we have been aimlessly beating about for some days, unable to get up. Our crew begin to make preparations. Tapitua, who is a great dandy, puts two gold earrings in one ear, and fastens a wreath of cock's feathers about his hat. Koddi (christened George) gets into a thick blue woollen jersey (very suitable for Antarctic weather), a scarlet and yellow *pareo* or kilt, and a pair of English shoes, which make him limp terribly; but they are splendid squeakers, so Koddi is happy. (The Pacific islander always picks out squeaking shoes if he can get them, and some manufacturers even put special squeakers into goods meant for the island trade.) Ta puts on three different singlets—a pink, a blue, and a yellow—turning up the edges carefully, so as to present a fine display of layered colours, like a Neapolitian ice; and gums the gaudy label off a jam tin about his bare brown arm, thus christening himself with the imposing title of "Our Real Raspberry." Neo is wearing two hats and three neck-handkerchiefs; Oki has a cap with a "P. & O." ribbon, and Union Steamship Company's jersey, besides a threepenny-piece in the hollow of each ear. Truly we are a gay party, by the time every one is ready to land.

And now after our thousand mile run, we have arrived at Malden.

Malden Island lies on the border of the Southern Pacific, only four degrees south of the equator. It is beyond the verge of the great Polynesian archipelago, and stands out by itself in a lonely stretch of still blue sea, very seldom visited by ships of any kind. Approaching it one is struck from far away by the glaring barrenness of the big island, which is thirty-three miles in circumference, and does not possess a single height or solitary tree, save one small clump of recently planted cocoanuts. Nothing more unlike the typical South Sea island could be imagined. Instead of the violet mountain peaks, wreathed with flying vapour, the lowlands rich with pineapple, banana, orange, and mango, the picturesque beach bordered by groves of feathery cocoanuts and quaint heavy-fruited pandanus trees, that one finds in such groups as the Society, Navigator's, Hawaiian, and Cook Islands, Malden consists simply of an immense white beach, a little settlement fronted by a big wooden pier, and a desolate plain of low greyish-green herbage, relieved here and there by small bushes bearing insignificant yellow flowers. Water is provided by great condensers. Food is all imported, save for pig and goat flesh. Shade,

WHERE MONEY HAS BEEN MADE 239

coolness, refreshing fruit, pleasant sights and sounds, there are none. For those who live on the island, it is the scene of an exile which has to be endured somehow or other, but which drags away with incredible slowness and soul-deadening monotony.

Why does any one live in such a spot? More especially, why should it be tenanted by five or six whites and a couple of hundred Kanakas, when many beautiful and fertile islands cannot show nearly so many of either race; quite a large number, indeed, being altogether uninhabited? One need never look far for an answer, in such a case. If there is no comfort on Malden Island, there is something that men value more than comfort—money. For fifty-six years it has been one of the most valuable properties in the Pacific. Out of Malden Island have come horses and carriages, fine houses and gorgeous jewellery, rich eating, delicate wines, handsome entertainments, university education and expensive finishing governesses, trips to the Continent, swift white schooners, high places in Society, and all the other desirables of wealth, for two generations of fortunate owners and their families. Half-a-million hard cash has been made out of it in the last thirty years, and it is good for another thirty. All this from a barren rock in mid-ocean! The solution of the problem will at once suggest itself to any reader who has ever sailed the Southern Seas—guano!

This is indeed the secret of Malden Island's riches. Better by far than the discovery of a pirate's treasure-cave, that favourite dream of romantic youth, is the discovery of a guano island. There are few genuine treasure romances in the Pacific, but many exciting tales that deal with the finding and disposing of these unromantic mines of wealth. Malden Island itself has had an interesting history enough. In 1848, Captain Chapman, an American whaling captain who still lives in Honolulu, happened to discover Malden during the course of a long cruise. He landed on the island, found nothing for himself and his crew in the way of fruit or vegetables, but discovered the guano beds, and made up his mind to sell the valuable knowledge as soon as his cruise was over. Then he put to sea again, and did not reach San Francisco for the best part of a year. Meantime, another American, Captain English, had found the island and its treasure. Wiser than Captain Chapman, he abandoned his cruise, and hurried at once to Sydney, where he sold the island for a big price to the trading firm who have owned it ever since.

This is the history of Malden Island's discovery. Time, in the island, has slipped along since the days of the Crimea with never a change. There is a row of little tin-roofed, one-storeyed houses above the beach, tenanted by the half-dozen white men who act as managers; there are big, barn-like shelters for the native labourers. Every three years the managers end their term of service, and joyfully return to the Company's great offices in Sydney, where there is life and companionship, pleasant things to see, good things to eat, newspapers every day, and no prison bar of blue relentless ocean cutting off all the outer world. Once or twice in the year one of the pretty, white island schooners sails up to Malden, greeted with shrieks and war-dances of joy; discharges her freight of forty or fifty newly indentured labourers, and takes away as many others whose time of one year on the island has expired. On Malden itself nothing changes. Close up to the equator, and devoid of mountains or even heights which

ON MALDEN ISLAND

could attract rain, its climate is unaltered by the passing season. No fruits or flowers mark the year by their ripening and blossoming, no rainy season changes the face of the land. News from the outer world comes rarely; and when it does come, it is so old as to have lost its savour. Life on Malden Island for managers and labourers alike, is work, work, all day long; in the evening, the bare verandah and the copper-crimson sunset, and the empty prisoning sea. That is all.

The guano beds cover practically the whole of the island. The surface on which one walks is hard, white, and rocky. This must be broken through before the guano, which lies a foot or two underneath, is reached. The labourers break away the stony crust with picks, and shovel out the fine, dry, earth-coloured guano that lies beneath, in a stratum varying from one to three feet in thickness. This is piled in great heaps, and sifted through large wire screens. The sifted guano—exactly resembling common sand—is now spread out in small heaps, and left to dry thoroughly in the fierce sun. There must not be any trace of moisture left that can possibly be dispersed; for the price of the guano depends on its absolute purity and extreme concentration, and purchasers generally make careful chemical tests of the stuff they buy.

When dried, the guano is stored away in an immense shed near the settlement. If it has been obtained from the pits at the other side of the island, eight miles away, it will be brought down to the storehouse by means of one of the oddest little railways in the world. The Malden Island railway is worked, not by steam, electricity, or petrol, but by sail! The S.E. trade-wind blows practically all the year round on this island; so the Company keep a little fleet of land-vessels, cross-rigged, with fine large sails, to convey the guano down to the settlement. The empty carriages are pushed up to the pits by the workmen, and loaded there. At evening, the labourers climb on the top of the load, set the great sails, and fly down to the settlement as fast as an average train could go. These "land-ships" of Malden are a bit unmanageable at times, and have been known to jump the rails when travelling at high speed, thus causing unpleasant accidents. But the Kanaka labourers do not mind a trifle of that kind, and not even in a S.E. gale would they condescend to take a reef in the sails.

As it is necessary to push these railway ships on the outward trip, the managers generally travel on a small railway tricycle of the pattern familiar at home. This can be driven at a fair speed, by means of arm levers. Across the desolate inland plain one clatters, the centre of a disk of shadowless grey-green, drenched clear of drawing and colour by the merciless flood of white fire from above. The sky is of the very thinnest pale blue; the dark, deep sea is out of sight. The world is all dead stillness and smiting sun, with only the thin rattle of our labouring car, and the vibration of distant dark specks above the rookeries, for relief.

The dark specks grow nearer and more numerous, filling the whole sky at last with the sweep of rushing wings and the screams of angry bird voices. We leave the tricycle on the rails and walk across the thin, coarse grass, tangled with barilla plants, and low-growing yellow-flowered shrubs, towards the spot where the wings flutter thickest, covering many acres of the unlovely, barren land with a perfect canopy of feathered life. This is the bird by which the fortunes of Malden have been made—the smaller man-o'-war bird. It is about the size of a duck, though much lighter in build. The back is black, the breast white, the bill long and hooked. The bird has an extraordinarily rapid and powerful flight. It might more appropriately be called the "pirate" than the "man-o'-war" or "frigate" bird, since it uses its superior speed to deprive other seabirds of the fish they catch, very seldom indeed exerting itself to make an honest capture on its own account. Strange to say, however, this daring buccaneer is the meekest and most long-suffering of birds where human beings are concerned. It will allow you to walk all through its rookeries, and even to handle the young birds and eggs, without making any remonstrance other than a petulant squeal. The parents fly about the visitors' heads in a perfect cloud, sweeping their wings within an inch of our faces, screaming harshly, and looking exceedingly fierce, with their ugly hooked bills and sparkling black eyes. But that is their ordinary way of occupying themselves; they wheel and scream above the rookery all day long, visited or let alone. Even if you capture one, by a happy snatch (not at all an impossible feat) you will not alarm the others, and your prisoner will not show much fight.

The eggs lie all over the ground in a mass of broken shells, feathers, and clawed-up earth. Those birds never build nests, and only sit upon one egg, which is dirty white, with brown spots. The native labourers consider frigate-bird eggs good to eat, and devour large numbers, but the white men find them too strong. The birds are also eaten by the labourers, but only on the sly, as this practice is strictly forbidden, for the reason that illness generally follows. The frigate-bird, it seems, is not very wholesome eating.

It is not in the insignificant deposits of these modern

rookeries that the wealth of the island lies, but in the prehistoric strata underlying the stony surface crust already mentioned. There are three strata composing the island—first the coral rock, secondly the guano, lastly, the surface crust. At one time, the island must have been the home of innumerable myriads of frigate-birds, nesting all over its circumference of thirty-three miles. The birds now nest only in certain places, and, though exceedingly thick to an unaccustomed eye, cannot compare with their ancestors in number.

The schooner called on a Sunday, and so I could not see the men at work. One of the managers, however, showed me over the labourers' quarters, and told me all about their life. There is certainly none of the "blackbirding" business about Malden. Kidnapping natives for plantation work, under conditions which amount to slavery, is unfortunately still common enough in some parts of the Pacific. But in the Cook Group, and Savage Island, where most of the labourers come from, there is no difficulty in obtaining as many genuine volunteers for Malden as its owners want. The men sign for a year's work, at ten shillings a week, and board and lodging. Their food consists of rice, biscuits, yams, tinned beef, and tea, with a few cocoanuts for those who may fall sick. This is "the hoigth of good 'atin" for a Polynesian, who lives when at home on yams, taro root, and bananas, with an occasional mouthful of fish, and fowl or pig only on high festival days.

The labourers' quarters are large, bare, shady buildings fitted with wide shelves, on which the men spread their mats and pillows to sleep. A Polynesian is never to be divorced from his bedding; he always carries it with him when travelling, and the Malden labourers each come to the island provided with beautifully plaited

A PENALTY OF LABOUR 245

pandanus mats, and cushions stuffed with the down of the silk-cotton tree. The cushions have covers of "trade" cottons, rudely embroidered by the owner's sweetheart or wife with decorative designs, and affectionate mottoes.

From 5 a.m. to 5 p.m. are the hours of work, with an hour and three-quarters off for meals. There is nothing unpleasant about the work, as Malden Island guano is absolutely without odour, and apparently so dry and fine when taken from the pits, that one wonders at the necessity for further sifting and drying. Occasionally, however, one of the workers develops a peculiar intestinal trouble which is said to be caused by the fine dust of the pits. It is nearly always fatal, by slow degrees. Our schooner carried away one of these unfortunates—a Savage Island man who had come up to Malden in full health and strength only a few months before. He was the merest shadow or sketch of a human being—a bundle of bones clad in loose brown skin, with a skull-like face, all teeth and eye-sockets—he could not stand or walk, only creep along the deck; and he was very obviously dying. Poor fellow! he longed for his own home above everything—the cool green island, sixteen hundred miles away, where there were fruit and flowers in the shady valleys, and women's and children's voices sounding pleasantly about the grassy village streets, and his own little pandanus-thatched cottage, with his "fafiné" and the babies at the door, among the palms and oranges above the sea. But the schooner had a two months' voyage to make yet among the Cook and other groups, before Savage Island could be reached; and Death was already lifting his spear to strike. We left the poor fellow as a last chance on Penrhyn Island, a couple of hundred miles away, hoping that the unlimited cocoanuts he could obtain there might do him some good, and that by some fortunate chance he might recover sufficiently to take another ship, and reach Niué at last.

The guano of Malden Island is supposed to be the best in the world. It is extremely rich in super-phosphates, and needs no "doctoring" whatever, being ready to apply to the land just as taken from the island. As the company are obliged to guarantee the purity of what they sell, and give an exact analysis of the constitutents of every lot, they keep a skilled chemist on the island, and place a fine laboratory at his disposal. These analyses are tedious to make, and require great accuracy, as a mistake might cause a refusal of payment on the part of the purchaser. The post of official chemist, therefore, is no sinecure, especially as it includes the duties of dispenser as well, and not a little rough-and-ready doctoring at times.

The temperature of the island is not so high as might be expected from the latitude. It seldom goes above 90° in the shade, and is generally rendered quite endurable, in spite of the merciless glare and total absence of shade, by the persistent trade-wind. Mosquitoes are unknown, and flies not troublesome. There are no centipedes, scorpions, or other venomous creatures, although the neighbouring islands ("neighbouring," in the Pacific, means anything within three or four hundred miles) have plenty of these unpleasant inhabitants. The white men live on tinned food of various kinds, also bread, rice, fowls, pork, goat, and goat's milk. Vegetables or fruit are a rare and precious luxury, for the nearest island producing either lies a thousand miles away. Big yams, weighing a stone or two apiece and whitewashed to prevent decay, are sent up from the Cook Islands now and then; but the want of really fresh vegetable food is one of the trials of the island. It is not astonishing to hear that the salaries of the Malden officials are very high. A year or two on the island is a good way of accumulating some capital, since it is impossible to spend a penny.

The native labourers generally leave the island with the greatest joy, glad beyond expression to return to their sweet do-nothing lives at home. Why they undertake the work at all is one of the many puzzles presented by the Polynesian character. They have enough to eat and enough to wear, without doing any work to speak of, while they are at home. Usually the motive for going to Malden is the desire of making twenty-five pounds or so in a lump, to buy a bicycle (all South Sea Islanders have bicycles, and ride them splendidly) or to build a stone house. But in most cases the money is "spreed" away in the first two or three days at home, giving presents to everybody, and buying fine clothes at the trader's store.

So the product of the year's exile and hard work is simply a tour among the island—in itself a strong attraction—a horribly hot suit of shoddy serge, with a stiff white shirt, red socks, and red tie, bought up in Malden from the company out of the labourer's wages, and proudly worn on the day the schooner brings the wanderer home to his lightly clad relatives—a bicycle, perhaps, which soon becomes a scrap-heap; or, possibly a stone house which is never lived in. The company has the labour that it wants, and the money that the labour produces. Every one is satisfied with the bargain, doubtless; and the far-away British farmer and market-gardener are the people who are ultimately benefited.

CHAPTER XII

Pearl-fishing at Penrhyn—The Beautiful Golden-Edge—Perils of the Pearl Diver—A Fight for Life—Visit to a Leper Island—A God-forsaken Place—How they kept the Corpses—The Woman who sinned—A Nameless Grave—On to Merry Manahiki—The Island of Dance and Song—Story of the Leper and his Bird—Good-bye to the *Duchess*.

A DAY or two after leaving Malden we sighted Penrhyn, lying five degrees further south, but for some unexplained reason a very much hotter place than Malden. Penrhyn is an island that is famous all over the South Sea world, and not unknown even in Europe. Its pearl-shell and pearls, its strange, wild, semi-amphibious natives, and its melancholy leper station, make it a marked spot upon the Pacific map ; and a certain rather fictitious value attaching to its stamps has made the name of the island familiar to all stamp collectors at home. The general impression conveyed to the voyager from kinder and fairer islands is that Penrhyn is a place "at the back of God-speed," a lonely, sultry, windy, eerie spot, desolate and remote beyond description.

It is an atoll island, consisting merely of a strip of land some couple of hundred yards in width, enclosing a splendid lagoon nine miles long. The land is white coral gravel ; nothing grows on it but cocoanut and pandanus and a few insignificant creepers. Fruit, vegetables, flowers, there are none. The natives live entirely on cocoanut and fish. They are nominally Christianised, but the veneer of Christianity is wearing uncommonly thin in places. They are reckless and daring to a degree, notable even among Pacific Islanders. Any Penrhyn man will attack a shark single-handed in its own element, and kill it with the big knife he usually carries. They are, beyond comparison, the finest swimmers in the world; it is almost impossible to drown a Penrhyn Islander. He will swim all day as easily as he will walk. You may often meet him out fishing, miles from shore, without a boat, pushing in front of him a small plank that carries his bait, lines, and catch. Some of the fish he most fancies seldom come to the surface. To catch these he baits his line, dives, and swims about underneath the water for a minute or two at a time, trailing the bait after him, and rising to the surface as often as a fish takes it.

Of his pearl-diving exploits I shall speak later. The deadly surf that breaks upon the outer reef has no terrors for him. Among the small boys of the island there is a favourite feat known as "crossing a hundred waves," which consists in diving through ninety-nine great rollers, just as they are about to break, and rushing triumphantly to shore on the back of the hundredth. The old warlike, quarrelsome character of the islanders—no doubt originally due to scarcity of food —still lurks concealed under an outward show of civility. Penrhyn was the only South Pacific island I have visited where I did not care to walk alone in the bush without my little American revolver. The four or five white traders all keep firearms ready to hand in their stores. There has been no actual trouble of recent years, but there are narrow escapes from a free fight every now and then, and every man must hold himself ready for emergencies. It is only eight years since there was such an outbreak of hostilities in Penrhyn that a man-of-war had to be sent up to protect the traders.

I was kindly offered the use of a house during the week the *Duchess* spent in Penrhyn lagoon repairing sails and rigging, and generally refitting after the stormy weather that we had experienced on several occasions. But Penrhyn is rotten with undeclared leprosy, the water is not above suspicion, and flies abound in myriads. So I slept on the ship, and by day wandered about the desolate, thin, sun-smitten woods of the island, or flew over the green lagoon in one of the marvellously speedy pearling sloops of the traders. These boats are about a couple of tons each, with a boom as big, in proportion, as a grasshopper's leg. They are as manageable as a motor car, and faster than most yachts. It is a wonderful sight to see them taking cargo out to the schooners, speeding like gulls over the water, and turning round in their tracks to fly back again as easily as any gull might do. Pearling was almost "off" at the time of the *Duchess's* visit, since a good part of the lagoon was tabooed to allow the beds to recover.

The pearls are rather a minor consideration at Penrhyn. The shell is of beautiful quality, large and thick, with the much-valued golden edge; but pearls are not plentiful in it, and they are generally of moderate size. Some very fine ones have been found, however; and gems of ordinary value can always be picked up fairly cheaply from the divers. The Penrhyn lagoon is the property of the natives themselves, who sell the shell and the pearls to white traders. Christmas Island and some other Pacific pearling grounds are privately owned, and in these places there is a great deal of poaching done by the divers.

The great buyers of pearls are the schooner captains.

There are three or four schooners that call at Penrhyn now and then for cargo; and every captain has a nose for pearls like that of a trained hound for truffles. In the Paumotus, about Penrhyn, Christmas Island, and the Scillies (the Pacific Scillies, not those that are so familiarly known to English readers), they flit from island to island, following up the vagrant rumours of a fine pearl with infinite tact and patience, until they run it to ground at last, and (perhaps) clear a year's income in a day by a lucky deal. San Francisco and Sydney are always ready to buy, and the typical Pacific captain, if he is just a bit of a buccaneer, is also a very keen man of business in the most modern sense of the word, and not at all likely to be cheated. Three native divers, famous for their deep-water feats, came out in a pearling sloop with us one afternoon, and gave a fine exhibition.

The bed over which we halted was about ninety feet under the surface. Our three divers stripped to a " pareo " apiece, and then, squatting down on the gunwale of the boat with their hands hanging over their knees, appeared to meditate. They were " taking their wind," the white steersman informed me. After about five minutes of perfect stillness they suddenly got up and dived off the thwart. The rest of us fidgeted up and down the tiny deck, talked, speculated, and passed away the time for what seemed an extraordinarly long period. No one, unfortunately, had brought a watch; but the traders and schooner captains all agree in saying that the Penrhyn diver can stay under water for full three minutes; and it was quite evident that our men were showing off for the benefit of that almost unknown bird, the "wahiné papa." At last, one after another, the dark heads popped up again, and the divers, each carrying a shell or two, swam back to the boat, got on board, and presented their catch to me with the easy grace and high-bred courtesy that are the birthright of all Pacific Islanders—not at all embarrassed by the fact that all the clothes they wore would hardly have sufficed to make a Sunday suit for an equal number of pigeons.

As a general rule, the divers carry baskets, and fill them before coming up. Each man opens his own catch at once, and hunts through the shell for pearls. Usually he does not find any; now and then he gets a small grey pearl, or a decent white one, or a big irregular "baroque" pearl of the "new art" variety, and once in a month of Sundays he is rewarded by a large gleaming gem worth several hundred pounds, for which he will probably get only twenty or thirty.

Diving dresses are sometimes used in Penrhyn; but in such an irregular and risky manner that they are really more dangerous than the ordinary method. The suit is nothing but a helmet and jumper. No boots are worn, no clothing whatever on the legs, and there are no weights to preserve the diver's balance. It sometimes happens—though wonderfully seldom—that the diver trips, falls, and turns upside down, the heavy helmet keeping him head-downwards until the air all rushes out under the jumper, and he is miserably suffocated. The air pump above is often carelessly worked in any case, and there is no recognised system of signals, except the jerk that means "Pull up."

"They're the most reckless devils on the face of the earth," said a local trader. "Once let a man strike a good bed of shell, and he won't leave go of it, not for Father Peter. He'll stick down there all day, grabbin' away in twenty fathom or more till he feels paralysis comin' on——"

"Paralysis?"

"Yes—they gets it, lots of 'em. If you was to go down in twenty fathom—they can do five and twenty, but anything over is touch and go—and stay 'alf the day, you'd come up 'owling like anything, and not able to move. That's the way it catches them; and then they must get some one to come and rub them with sea water all night long, and maybe they dies, and maybe they're all right by morning. So then down they goes again, just the same as ever. Sometimes a man'll be pulled up dead at the end of a day. How does that happen? Well, I allow it's because he's been workin' at a big depth all day, and feels all right; and then, do you see, he'll find somethin' a bit extra below of him, in a holler like, and down he'll go after it; and the extra fathom or two does the trick.

"Sharks? Well, I've seen you poppin' at them from the deck of the *Duchess*, so you know as well as I do how many there are. Didn't 'it them, even when the fin was up? That's because you 'aven't greased your bullet, I suppose. You want to, if the water isn't to turn it aside. But about the divers? Oh! they don't mind sharks, none of them, when they've got the dress on. Sharks is easy scared. You've only got to pull up your jumper a bit, and the air bubbles out and frightens them to fits. If you meet a big sting-ray, it'll run its spine into you, and send the dress all to—I mean, spoil the dress, so's the water comes in, and maybe it'll stick the diver too. And the big devilfish is nasty; he'll 'old you down to a rock; but you can use your knife on him. The kara mauaa is the worst; the divers don't like him. He's not as big as a shark, but he's downright wicked, and he's a mouth on him as big as 'alf his body. If one comes along, he'll bite an arm or leg off of the man anyways, and eat 'im outright if e's big enough to do it. Swordfish? Well, they don't often come into the lagoon; it's the fishing canoes outside they'll go for. Yes, they'll run a canoe and a man through at a blow easy enough: but they don't often do it. If you wants a canoe, I'll get you one; and you needn't mind about the swordfish. As like as not they'll never come near you.

"About the divin'?—well, I think the naked divin' is very near as safe as the machine, takin' all things. Worst of it is, if a kara mauaa comes along, the diver can't wait his time till it goes. No, he doesn't stab it—not inside the lagoon, because there's too many of them there, and the blood would bring a whole pack about. He gets under a ledge of rock, and 'opes it'll go away before his wind gives out. If he doesn't, he gets eat."

Did Schiller, or Edgar Allen Poe ever conjure up a picture more ghastly than that of a Penrhyn diver, caught like a rat in a trap by some huge, man-eating shark, or fierce kara mauaa—crouching in a cleft of the overhanging coral, under the dark green gloom of a hundred feet of water, with bursting lungs and cracking eyeballs, while the threatening bulk of his terrible enemy looms dark and steady, full in the road to life and air? A minute or more has been spent in the downward journey; another minute has passed in the agonised wait under the rock. Has he been seen? Will the creature move away now, while there is still time to return? The diver knows to a second how much time has passed; the third minute is on its way; but one goes up quicker than one comes down, and there is still hope. Two minutes and a half; it is barely possible now, but—— The sentinel of death glides forward; his cruel eyes, phosphorescent in the gloom, look right

A LIVING DEATH

into the cleft where the wretched creature is crouching, with almost twenty seconds of life still left, but now not a shred of hope. A few more beats of the labouring pulse, a gasp from the tortured lungs, a sudden rush of silvery air bubbles, and the brown limbs collapse down out of the cleft like wreaths of seaweed. The shark has his own.

There is a "Molokai," or Leper Island, some two miles out in the lagoon, where natives afflicted with leprosy are confined. The Resident Agent—one of the traders—broke the rigid quarantine of the Molokai one day so far as to let me land upon the island, although he did not allow me to approach nearer than ten or twelve yards to the lepers, or to leave the beach and go inland to the houses that were visible in the distance. Our boatmen ran the sloop close inshore, and carried the captain and myself through the shallow water, carefully setting us down on dry stones, but remaining in the sea themselves. A little dog that had come with the party sprang overboard, and began swimming to the shore. It was hurriedly seized by the scruff of its neck, and flung back into the boat. If it had set paw on the beach it could never have returned, but would have had to stay on the island for good.

Very lovely is the Molokai of Penrhyn; sadly beautiful this spot where so many wretched creatures have passed away from death in life to life in death. As we landed, the low golden rays of the afternoon sun were slanting through the pillared palm stems and quaintly beautiful pandanus fronds, across the snowy beach, and its trailing gold-flowered vines. The water of the lagoon, coloured like the gems in the gates of the Heavenly City, lapped softly on the shore; the perpetual trade wind poured through the swaying trees, shaking silvery gleams from the lacquered crests of the palms. In the distance, shadowed by a heavy pandanus grove, stood a few low brown huts. From the direction of these there came, hurrying down to the beach as we landed, four figures—three men and a woman. They had put on their best clothes when they saw the sloop making for the island. The woman wore a gaudy scarlet cotton frock; two of the men had white shirts and sailor's trousers of blue dungaree—relics of a happier day, these, telling their own melancholy tale of bygone years of freedom on the wide Pacific. The third man wore a shirt and scarlet "pareo," or kilt. Every face was lit up with delight at the sight of strangers from the schooner; above all, at the marvellous view of the wonderful "wahiné papa." Why, even the men who lived free and happy on Penrhyn mainland did not get the chance of seeing such a show once in a lifetime! There she was, with two arms, and two legs, and a head, and a funny gown fastened in about the middle, and the most remarkable yellow shoes, and a ring, and a watch, which showed her to be extraordinarily wealthy, and a pale smooth face, not at all like a man's, and hair that was brown, not black—how odd! It was evidently as good as a theatre, to the lonely prisoners!

Bright as all the faces of the lepers were at that exciting moment, one could not mistake the traces left by a more habitual expression of heavy sadness. The terrible disease, too, had set its well-known marks upon every countenance. None of those who came out to see us had lost any feature; but all the faces had the gross, thickened, unhuman look that leprosy stamps upon its victims. The woman kept her arm up over her head, to hide some sad disfigurement about her neck. One of the men walked slowly and painfully, through an affection of the hip and leg. There were nine lepers in all upon the island; but the other five either could not, or did not, wish to leave their huts, and the agent refused to break the quarantine any further than he had already done. What care the wretched creatures are able to give one another, therefore, what their homes are like, and how their lives are passed, I cannot tell. Three of the lepers were accompanied by their faithful dogs. They are all fond of pets, and must have either a dog or a cat. Of course the animals never leave the island. We exchanged a few remarks at the top of our voices, left a case of oranges (brought up from the Cook Islands, a thousand miles away), and returned to our boat. The case of oranges was eagerly seized upon, and conveyed into the bush.

"They will eat them up at once," I said.

"Not they," said one of our white men. "They'll make them into orange beer to-night, and get jolly well drunk for once in their miserable lives. Glad to see the poor devils get the chance, say I." And so—most immorally, no doubt—said the "wahiné papa" as well.

The lepers are fed from stores furnished by a small Government fund; and the trader who fulfils the very light duties of Resident Government Agent generally sends them over a share of any little luxury, in the way of oranges, limes, or yams, that may reach the island. None the less, their condition is most miserable, and one cannot but regard it as a crying scandal upon the great missionary organisations of the Pacific that nothing whatever is done for the lepers of these northern groups. The noble example of the late Father Damien, of

Hawaii, and of the Franciscan Sisters who still live upon the Hawaiian Molokai, courting a martyr's death to serve the victims of this terrible disease, seems to find no imitators in the islands evangelised by British missionaries. Godless, hopeless, and friendless, the lepers live and die alone. That their lives are immoral in the last degree, their religion, in spite of early teaching, almost a dead letter, is only to be expected. Penrhyn is not alone in this terrible scourge. Rakahanga, Manahiki, and Palmerston—all in the same part of the Pacific—are seriously affected by the disease. Palmerston I did not see; but I heard that there is one whole family of lepers there, and some stray cases as well.

The island belongs to the half-caste descendants (about 150 in number) of Masters, a "beachcomber" of the early days, who died a few years ago. These people are much alarmed at the appearance of leprosy, and have segregated the lepers on an island in the lagoon. They are anxious to have them removed to the Molokai at Penrhyn, since the family came originally from that island; but no schooner will undertake to carry them. In Rakahanga, the lepers are not quarantined in any way, but wander about among the people. There are only a few cases as yet; but the number will certainly increase. This may also be said of Manahiki, for although very serious cases are isolated there, the lepers are allowed, in the earlier stages, to mix freely with every one else, and even to prepare the food of a whole family. The New Zealand Government, it is believed, will shortly pass a law compelling the removal of all these cases to the Molokai at Penrhyn. No Government, however, can alleviate the wretched condition of these unfortunate prisoners, once sent to the island. That remains for private charity and devotion.

AN ISLAND OF GLOOM

A God-forsaken, God-forgotten-looking place is Penrhyn, all in all. When sunset falls upon the great desolate lagoon, and the tall cocoanuts of the island stand up jet black against the stormy yellow sky in one unbroken rampart of tossing spears, and the endless sweep of shadowy beach is empty of all human life, and clear of every sound save the long, monotonous, never-ceasing cry of the trade wind in the trees, it needs but little imagination to fancy strange creatures creeping through the gloom of the forest—strange, ghastly stories of murder and despair whispering in the gathering night. Death in every form is always near to Penrhyn; death in the dark waters of the lagoon, death from the white terror of leprosy, and death at the hands of men but quarter civilised, whose fingers are always itching for the ready knife. And at the lonely sunset hour, when old memories of the life and light of great cities, of welcoming windows shining red and warm through grey, cold northern gloamings come back to the wanderer's mind in vivid contrast, the very wings of the " Shadow cloaked from head to foot " seem to shake in full sight above these desolate shores. Yet, perhaps, the intolerable blaze of full noon upon the windward beaches strikes a note of even deeper loneliness and distance. The windward side of Penrhyn is uninhabited; the sea that breaks in blinding white foam upon the untrodden strand, wreathed with trailing vines of vivid green, is never broken by a sail. The sun beats down through the palm and pandanus leaves so fiercely that the whole of the seaward bush is but a shadeless blaze of green fire. Nothing stirs, nothing cries; the earth is silent, the sea empty; and a barrier of thousands of long sea miles, steadily built up, day by day, through many weeks, and only to be passed again by the slow demolishing, brick by brick, of the same great wall, lies between us and the world where people live. Here there is no life, only an endless dream ; not as in the happy southern islands, a gentle sunrise dream of such surpassing sweetness that the sleeper asks nothing more than to dream on thus for ever ; but a dark-hour dream of loneliness, desolation, and utter remoteness, from which the dreamer cannot awaken, even if he would. Why do men—white men, with some ability and some education—live in these far-away infertile islands ? There is no answer to the problem, even from the men themselves. They came, they stayed, they do not go away—why, they do not know. That is all.

The land extent of Penrhyn is only three square miles, though the enclosed lagoon is a hundred. The population is little over four hundred souls; there are three or four white traders, as a rule. There is no resident white missionary. The island is one of those that have been annexed by New Zealand, and is therefore British property. It is governed by the Resident Commissioner of the Cook Group, who visits it about once a year.

Until two or three years ago, the Penrhyn Islanders used to keep their dead in the houses, hanging up the corpse, wrapped in matting, until it was completely decayed. This hideous practice was put an end to by the Representatives of British Government, much to the grief of the natives, who found it hard to part with the bodies of their friends, and leave them away in the graveyard they were bidden to choose. As the best substitute for the old practice, they now build little houses, some four feet high, over the tombs of their friends, and live in these houses for many months after a death, sitting and sleeping and even eating on the tomb that is covered by the thatch or iron roof of the grave-house. The graveyard is in consequence a strange and picturesque sight, almost like a village of some pigmy folk. A few plain concrete graves stand above the remains of white men who have died in the island, and one headstone is carved with the initials—not the name—of a woman. There is a story about that lonely grave; it was told to me as I lingered in the little "God's Acre" at sunset, with the light falling low between the palms and the lonely evening wind beginning to wail from the sea.

The woman was the wife of a schooner captain, a man of good family and connections, who liked the wild roving life of the Pacific, yet managed to retain a number of acquaintances of his own class in Auckland and Tahiti. His wife was young and handsome, and had many friends of her own. On one of the schooner's visits to Penrhyn, the man was taken suddenly ill, and died in a very short time, leaving his wife alone. It seems that at first she was bewildered by her loss, and stayed on in the island, not knowing what to do, but before many months she had solved the problem after a fashion that horrified all the whites—she married a Penrhyn native! good-looking and attractive, but three-quarters savage, and left the island with him.

Several children were born to the pair, but they were given to the husband's people. At last he took a native partner, and deserted his English wife. She left the islands, and went down to Auckland; but her story had travelled before her, and Auckland society closed its doors. To Tahiti, where morals are easy, and no one frowns upon the union, temporary or permanent, of the white man and the brown woman, she went, hoping to be received as in former days. But even Papeëte, "the sink of the

Pacific," would have none of the white woman who had married a brown man. Northwards once more, to lonely Penrhyn, the broken-hearted woman went, wishing only to die, far from the eyes of her own world that had driven her out. A schooner captain, who called there now and then, cast eyes upon her—for she was still young, and retained much of her beauty—and asked her, at last, if she would become his wife, and so redeem in some degree her position ; but she had neither heart nor wish to live longer, so she sent the kindly sailor away, and soon afterwards closed her eyes for ever on the blue Pacific and the burning sands, the brown lover who had betrayed her, and the white lover who came too late. The traders buried her, and kindly left her grave without a name ; only the initials of that which she had borne in her first marriage, and the date of her death. So, quiet and forgotten at last, lies in lonely Penrhyn the woman who sinned against her race and found no forgiveness.

It was a relief to leave Penrhyn, with all its gloomy associations, and see the schooner's head set for the open sea and merry Manahiki. But we seemed to have brought ill-luck away with us, for there was what the captain called " mean weather " before we came within hail of land again, and the *Duchess* got some more knocking about.

It was on account of this that Neo, our native bo'sun, hit an innocent A.B. over the head with a belaying-pin one afternoon, and offered to perform the same service for any of the rest of the crew who might require it. The men had been singing mission hymns as they ran about the deck pulling and hauling—not exactly out of sheer piety, but because some of the hymns, with good rousing choruses, made excellent chanties. They were hauling to the tune of " Pull for the shore, brothers ! "

when a squall hit the ship, and out of the fifteen agitated minutes that followed, the *Duchess* emerged minus her jib-boom. When things had quieted down, Neo started to work with the belaying-pin, until he was stopped, when he offered, as a sufficient explanation, the following:

"Those men, they sing something made bad luck, I think, jib-boom he break. Suppose they sing, 'Pull for 'em shore' some other time, I break their head, that I telling them!"

The next time a chanty was wanted, "Hold the Fort!" took the place of the obnoxious tune, and Neo's lessons were not called for.

And so, in a day or two we came to Rakahanga and Manahiki (Reirson and Humphrey Islands), and stopped there for another day or two, before we spread our wings like the swallows, to fleet southward again.

It was certainly globe-trotting, not proper travelling. To flit from group to group, taking in cargo, and then hurrying off again, is the way not to understand the places one sees, and I was more than half inclined to leave the *Duchess* here, and stop over for a month or two on the chance of another schooner turning up. But the dinner that the solitary trader ate when he came on board made me change my mind. He looked like a man half-famished, and he certainly acted like one. There was hardly a thing on the island to eat at present, he said; the natives had only enough fish for themselves, and the turtle weren't coming and his stores were almost out, and he had been living on biscuit and cocoanuts for weeks. There was leprosy in both islands, and one did not dare to touch native pork or fowl. On the whole, I thought I would be contented to "globe-trot," on this occasion, and see what I could in a day or two,

The islands are about twenty-five miles apart, and very much like one another. They each own an area of about two square miles, and a population of some four hundred natives. And there is nothing in the whole Pacific prettier.

Coming up to Manahiki, one sees first of all a snowy shore and a belt of green tossing palms, just like any other island. As the ship coasts along, however, making for the village, the palm-trees break and open out here and there, and through the breaks one sees—paradise! There is a great sheet of turquoise-green water inside, and on the water an archipelago of the most exquisite little plumy, palmy islets, each ringed round with its own pearly girdle of coral sand. Every gap in the trees frames in a picture more lovely than the last—and, as we approach the village, the dainty little brown island canoes that all the Pacific wanderers know so well, begin to dot the jewel-bright surface of the inner lake, and gleams of white and rose and scarlet dresses, worn by the rowers of the tiny craft, sparkle on the water like gems. At last the vessel comes to anchor before a wide white, sloping beach, with brown-roofed huts clustering behind, and we reached merry Manahiki.

The island has long enjoyed a reputation for peculiar innocence and simplicity, coupled with piety of a marked description. Well, one does not care to destroy any one's illusions, so the less said about Manahiki's innocence and simplicity the better. The islanders are, at all events, a kindly and a cheerful people, and their home is the neatest and best kept island in the Pacific. A palm-bordered road of finest white sand, beautifully kept, and four miles long, runs without a bend or break from one end of the island to the other—this portion of the atoll forming a separate island, and containing most of the scanty population.

THE ADVANTAGE OF A JAIL

The village stands about midway—a collection of quaint little houses deeply thatched with plaited pandanus leaf, and walled with small, straight saplings set side by side and admitting a good deal of light and air. The houses are unwindowed as a rule. Rakahanga, the sister island, is extremely like Manahiki in formation and architecture. It, however, enjoys the additional advantage of a jail, which is built of crossed saplings, looks much like a huge bird-cage, and certainly could not confine any one who made the smallest attempt to get out. But, as criminals are unknown in these islands, and petty offences are visited by fine instead of imprisonment, the jail is not expected to do real service, being merely a bit of "swagger," like the white-washed stone houses possessed by one or two wealthy natives, who, Pacific fashion, never think of living in them.

Within, the ordinary houses are extremely simple. The floor of white coral gravel reflects and intensifies the soft diffused light that enters through the walls. There may be a native bedstead, laced across with "sinnet"—plaited cocoanut fibre—and provided with a gay patchwork quilt, and a few large soft mats of pandanus leaf, ingeniously split, dried, and plaited. There will certainly be a pile of camphor-wood trunks, containing the clothes of the household; a dozen or so cocoanut shells, for drinking and eating purposes; a few sheath-knives, and a small quantity of much-cherished crockery. In a corner, you may find a heap of flying-fish ready cleaned for baking in the oven-pit outside, and a number of green, unhusked cocoanuts, for drinking. You may possibly see some ship's biscuits, too, bought from the one white resident of the island, a trader; and there will also be some lumps of white, soft pith, shaped like large buns—the "sponge" or kernel of the old cocoanut, which grows and fills up the shell after the water has dried away, and the nut commenced to sprout. But there will be no bananas, no oranges, no mangoes, granadillas, pineapples, yam, taro or ti root, bread-fruit or maupei chestnuts, as in the fertile volcanic islands. Manahiki is a coral island pure and simple, and has no soil at all, nothing but sand and white gravel, out of which the cocoa-palm and a few small timber trees spring, in a manner that seems almost miraculous to those accustomed to the rich, fertile soil of Raratonga or Tahiti. Cocoanut and fish are the food of the Manahikian, varied by an occasional gorge of turtle-meat, and a feast of pig and fowl on very great occasions. There is, therefore, not much work to do in the island, and there are few distractions from the outside world, since trading schooners only call two or three times a year at best. Some copra-drying is done and a few toy canoes, baskets, and other curiosities are made, to find a precarious sale when a schooner comes in and the captain is inclined to speculate.

But time never hangs heavy on the Manahikian's hands. He is the most accomplished dancer and singer in the whole South Pacific, and the island is inordinately vain of this distinction. All South Sea islanders sing constantly, but in Manahiki, the tunes are much sweeter and more definite than in most other islands; and the impromptu variations of the " seconds " are really wonderful. The voices, too, are exceptionally good. The women's are rather hard and piercing, but those of the men are often magnificent. The time is as perfect as if beaten out by a metronome, and false notes are almost unknown.

Men and women alike seem incapable of fatigue when singing. The mere white man will feel tired and husky after going through the choruses of *The Messiah* or *The Creation*. A Manahikian, if he were acquainted with oratorio music, would run through both, *fff*, and then "take on" *Tannhäuser*, following up with another Wagnerian opera, and perhaps a cantata thrown in. By this time, it would be dusk, and the chorus would probably stop to eat a cartload of cocoanuts before beginning on the whole *Nibelungen Ring* cycle for the night. About midnight the Resident Agent, a clever half-caste, who has European ideas about the value of sleep, would probably send out the village policeman with a stick to induce the singers to go to bed; and, quite unfatigued, they would rise up from their cross-legged squatting posture on the ground, and go, remonstrant, but compelled.

Happily for the Resident Agent and the trader, however, European music is not known in Manahiki, and when a singing fit seizes the people, they can generally be stopped after about a day, unless somebody has composed something very new and very screaming. If the two ends of the village have begun one of their musical competitions, there may also be difficulty in bringing it to a period; for the rival choruses will sing against each other with cracking throats and swelling veins, hour after hour, till both sides are completely exhausted.

Dancing, however, is the Manahikian's chief reason for existing. The Manahikian dances are infinitely superior to those of most other islands, which consist almost altogether of a wriggle belonging to the *danse du ventre* family, and a little waving of the arms. The Manahiki dance has the wriggle for its groundwork, but there are many steps and variations. Some of the steps are so rapid that the eye can hardly follow them, and a camera shutter which works up to $\frac{1}{100}$ of a second does not give a sharp result. The men are ranged in a long row, with the women opposite; there is a good deal of wheeling and turning about in brisk military style, advancing, retreating, and spinning round. The men dance very much on the extreme tips of their toes (they are, of course, barefooted) and keep up this painful posture for an extraordinary length of time. Every muscle in the whole body seems to be worked in the "fancy" steps; and there is a remarkable effect of general dislocation, due to turning the knees and elbows violently out and in.

The women, like Miss Mercy Pecksniff, seem chiefly to favour the "shape and skip" style of locomotion. There is a good deal of both these, a great deal of wriggle, and plenty of arm action, about their dancing. They manœuvre their long, loose robes about, not at all ungracefully, and do some neat step-dancing, rather inferior, however, to that of the men.

Both men and women dress specially for the dance, so the festival that was organised to greet our arrivals took some time to get up, as all the beaux and belles of the village had to hurry home and dress. The women put on fresh cotton loose gowns, of brilliant pink, purple, yellow, white and green, oiled their hair with cocoanut oil scented with the fragrant white tieré flower, and hung long chains of red and yellow berries about their necks. About their waists they tied the dancing girdle, never worn except on these occasions, and made of twisted green ferns. The men took off their cool, easy everyday costume, of a short cotton kilt and gay coloured singlet, and attired themselves in shirts and heavy stuff trousers (bought from the trader at enormous expense, and considered the acme of smartness). Both sexes crowned

THE FASCINATION OF THE DRUM

themselves with the curious dancing headdress, which looks exactly like the long-rayed halo of a saint, and is made by splitting a palm frond down the middle, and fastening it in a half-circle about the back of the head.

The music then struck up and the dancers began to assemble. The band consisted of two youths, one of whom clicked a couple of sticks together, while the other beat a drum. This does not sound attractive; but as a matter of fact, the Manahiki castanet and drum music is curiously weird and thrilling, and arouses a desire for dancing even in the prosaic European. On board our schooner, lying half a mile from shore, the sound of the measured click and throb used to set every foot beating time on deck, while the native crew frankly dropped whatever they were at, and began to caper wildly. Close at hand, the music is even more impressive; no swinging waltz thundered out by a whole Hungarian band gets "into the feet" more effectively than the Manahiki drum.

A much-cherished possession is this drum. It is carved and ornamented with sinnet, and topped with a piece of bladder; it seems to have been hollowed out of a big log, with considerable labour. The skill of the drummers is really remarkable. No drumsticks are used, only fingers, yet the sound carries for miles. While drumming, the hands rise and fall so fast as to lose all outline to the eye; the drummer nods and beats with his foot in an ecstasy of delight at his own performance; the air is full of the throbbing, rhythmical, intensely savage notes. The dancers at first hesitate, begin and stop, and begin again, laugh and retreat and come forward undecidedly. By-and-by the dancing fervour seizes one or two; they commence to twirl and to stamp wildly, winnowing the air with their arms. Others join in, the two rows are completed, and Manahiki is fairly started for the day. Hour after hour they dance, streaming with perspiration in the burning sun, laughing and singing and skipping. The green fern girdles wither into shreds of crackling brown, the palm haloes droop, the berry necklaces break and scatter, but on they go. The children join in the dance now and then, but their small frames weary soon; the parents are indefatigable.

Perhaps both ends of the settlement are dancing; if that is so, the competitive element is sure to come in sooner or later, for the feeling between the two is very like that between the collegers and oppidans at Eton, each despising the other heartily, and ready on all occasions to find a cause for a fight. They will dance against each other now, striving with every muscle to twinkle the feet quicker, stand higher on the tips of the toes, wriggle more snakily, than their rivals. Evening comes, and they are still dancing. With the night, the dance degenerates into something very like an orgy, and before dawn, to avoid scandal, a powerful hint from the native pastor and the agent causes the ball to break up.

Do the dancers go to bed now, lie down on their piled up sleeping mats, and compose themselves to slumber? By no means. Most of them get torches, and go out on the reef in the dark to spear fish. Cooking fires are lighted, and there is a hurried gorge in the houses; everywhere, in the breaking dawn, one hears the chuck-chuck of the husking-stick preparing cocoanuts, and smells the savoury odour of cooking fish. The dancers have not eaten for at least twenty-four hours, perhaps more. But this feast does not

THE NATIVE DANCE

last long, for just as the sun begins to shoot long scarlet rays up through the palm trees, some one begins to beat the drum again. Immediately the whole village pours out into the open, and the dance is all on again, as energetic as ever. The trading schooner is three weeks over-due, and the copra on which the island income depends is not half dried; there is not a fancy basket or a pandanus hat ready for the trader; the washing of every house is hopelessly behindhand, and nobody has had a decent meal since the day before yesterday. No matter! the Manahikians are dancing, and it would take an earthquake to stop them.

Late in the second day, they will probably give out and take a night's rest. But it is about even chances that they begin again the next morning. In any case, no day passes in Manahiki or Rakahanga without a dance in the evening. Regularly at sunset the drum begins to beat, the fern girdles are tied on (relics, these, of heathen days when girdles of grass or fern were all that the dancers wore), the palm haloes are twisted about the glossy black hair, and the island gives itself up to enjoyment for the evening.

There is a dancing-master in Manahiki, a most important potentate, who does nothing whatever but invent new dances, and teach the youth of the village both the old dances and the new. He is to be seen in one of my photographs, standing beside the drummer, and regarding the dance with a severely critical eye.

We stopped overnight at the island, so I had time for a good walk along the beautiful coral avenue, which is indeed one of the loveliest things in the island world. It was Sunday, and all the natives were worshipping in the exceedingly ugly and stuffy concrete church, under the guidance of the native pastor, so I had the place almost to myself. Far away from everywhere, sitting in a ruinous little hut under the trees by the inner lagoon, I found a lonely old man, crippled and unable to walk. He was waiting until the others came back from church, staring solemnly into the lagoon the while, and playing with a heap of cocoanut shells. By-and-by he would probably rouse up, drag himself into the hut, and busy himself getting ready the dinner for the family against their return home, for he was an industrious old man, and liked to make himself useful so far as he could, and his relatives were very glad of what small services he could render in washing and cooking.

What was the matter with the poor old man? He was a leper!

That is the way of the islands, and no white rule can altogether put a stop to it. The half-caste who acts as agent for the Government of New Zealand had hunted out a very bad case of leprosy a year or two before, and insisted on quarantining it in a lonely part of the bush. This was all very well, but the leper had a pet cock, which he wanted to take with him, and the agent's heart was not hard enough to refuse. Now the leper, being fed without working, and having nothing to do, found the time hanging heavy on his hands, so he taught the cock to dance—report says, to dance the real Manahiki dances—and the fame of the wondrous bird spread all over the island, and as far as Rakahanga, so that the natives made continual parties to see the creature perform, and quarantine became a dead letter. Still the agent had not the heart to take the cock away, but when he saw the leper's end was near, he watched, and as soon as he heard the man was dead, he hurried to the quarantined hut, set it on fire, and immediately slaughtered the cock. An hour later, half the island was out at the hut, looking for the bird—but they came too late.

. . . . . .

We have been two days at merry Manahiki, and the cargo is in, and the Captain has ordered the *Duchess* —looking shockingly cock-nosed without her great jib-boom—to be put under sail again. As the booms begin to rattle, and the sails to rise against the splendid rose and daffodil of the Pacific sunset, Shalli, our Cingalese steward, leans sadly over the rail, listening to the thrilling beat of the drum that is just beginning to throb across the still waters of the lagoon, now that evening and its merry-making are coming on once more.

"He plenty good place, that," says Shalli mournfully. "All the time dancing, singing, eating, no working—he all same place as heaven. O my God, I plenty wish I stopping there, I no wanting any heaven then!"

With this pious aspiration in our ears, we spread our white wings once more—for the last time. Raratonga lies before us now, and from Raratonga the steamers go, and the mails and tourists come, and the doors of the great world open for us again. So, good-bye to the life of the schooner.

CHAPTER XIII

The Last of the Island Kingdoms—Fashions in Nukualofa—The King Who was shy—His Majesty's Love Story—Who got the Wedding-Cake?—The Chancellor goes to Jail—Bungalow Housekeeping—The Wood of the Sacred Bats—By the Tombs of the Tui-Tongas—A "Chief" Kava-party—The Waits!—Mariner's Cave—The Cave of the Swallows—To Samoa.

SOME weeks afterwards, after a round of three thousand miles, I found myself in Tonga, better known as the Friendly Islands. The distance from the Cook Group was only one thousand or less, as the crow flies, but the steamers flew down to Auckland, and then back again, which naturally added to the journey. Pacific travel is a series of compromises. The British Resident of Niué, which is only three hundred miles from Tonga, wanted to get to the latter place about that time, and when I met him at Nukualofa, the Tongan capital, he had had to travel two thousand four hundred miles to reach it! But no one is ever in a hurry, under the shade of the cocoanut tree.

Who has heard of Tongatabu? who knows where the "Friendly Islands" are? You will not find them very readily in the map, but they are to be found nevertheless, about one thousand miles to the north-east of New Zealand. And if you take the steamer that runs every month from Auckland to Sydney, touching at the "Friendly" or Tongan Group, on the way, you will

THE ONE ISLAND KINGDOM 275

find yourself, in four days, set down on the wharf of Nukualofa, the capital of the island of Tongatabu, and the seat of the oddest, most comic-opera-like monarchy that the world ever knew.

Thirty years ago—even twenty—the Great South Seas were scattered over with independent island states, ruled by monarchs who displayed every degree of civilisation, from the bloodthirsty monster, Thakomban of Fiji and Jibberik, the half-crazy tyrant of Majuro, up to such Elizabeths of the Pacific as Liluokalani of Hawaii, and Queen Pomaré of Tahiti. Now there is but one island kingdom left; but one native sovereign, who still sits on his throne unembarrassed by the presence of a British Resident, who is ruler in all but name. Hawaii has fallen to America; France has taken the Marquesas and Tahiti; England has annexed the Cook Islands and dethroned the famous Queen Makea; Germany and America have partitioned Samoa between them; the rich archipelago of Fiji has been added to the British Colonies. This accounts for almost all of the larger and richer island groups, distinguished by a certain amount of original civilisation, and leaves only one unseized—Tonga, or the Friendly Islands, over which England has maintained a protectorate since 1900.

The Tongan Archipelago was discovered by Captain Cook in 1777, and by him named the "Friendly Islands," on account of the apparently friendly disposition of the natives. He sailed away from the group unaware that beneath their seemingly genial reception, the Tongans had been maturing a plot to murder him and seize his ship. Treachery, it is true, has never been an essential part of the Tongan character; but they are, and always have been, the most warlike of all Pacific races, and it is probable that they thought the character of the deed excused by the necessities of a military race who feared injury from a superior power.

After Cook's visit the world heard very little of Tonga until 1816, when Mariner's "Tonga Islands," the history of a young sailor's captivity among the natives of the group, fairly took the reading world by storm. It is still a classic among works of travel and adventure. Since the islands were converted to Christianity their history has been uneventful. One king—George Tubou I.—reigned for seventy years, and only died at last, aged ninety-seven, of a chill contracted from his invariable custom of bathing in the sea at dawn! His great-grandson, George Tubou II. succeeded, inheriting through his mother's side, as the Tongan succession follows the matriarchal plan. It is this king—aged thirty-four, six feet four in height, and about twenty-seven stone weight—who now sits upon the last throne of the Island Kings, and rules over the only independent state left in the Pacific.

When Britain assumed a Protectorate over Tonga in 1900, it was done simply to prevent any other nation annexing the rich and fertile group, with its splendid harbour of Vavau which lay so dangerously near Fiji. The Germans, who had maintained a kind of half-and-half Protectorate for some time, ceded their rights in exchange for those possessed by England in Samoa, and Tonga then became safe from the incursions of any foreign nation whose interests, trading and territorial, might be hostile to those of Britain.

Perhaps as a consequence of all those negotiations, the Tongas have a high opinion of their own importance. When the war between China and Japan broke out, Tonga politely sent word to Great Britain that she intended to remain neutral, and not take any part in the affair. Great Britain's reply, I regret to say, is not recorded.

The Tongans are a Christianised and partially civilised, if a coloured, race, numbering about 20,000. They are of a warm brown in hue, with dense black, wiry hair (usually dyed golden red with lime juice), tall, well-made frames, and immense muscular development. As a nation, they are handsome, with intelligent faces, and a dignity of pose and movement that is sometimes unkindly called the "Tongan swagger." In education, many of them would compare favourably with the average white man, so far as mere attainments go; although a course of instruction at the local schools and colleges, amounting to very nearly the standard of an English "matriculations," does not prevent its recipient from believing firmly in the holiness of the sacred Tongan bats, feeding himself with his fingers, and walking about his native village naked as Adam, save for a cotton kilt.

There is not only a King in Tonga, but a real palace, guards of honour, a Parliament, a Prime Minister, a Chancellor of the Exchequer, and a large number of public officials. All these are Tongan natives. The king's guards are apt to make an especially vivid impression upon the newcomer, as he walks up the wharf, and sees the scarlet-coated sentry pacing up and down opposite the guard-room, with his fellows, also smartly uniformed, lounging inside. If the stranger, however, could have witnessed the scene on the wharf as soon as the steamer was signalled—the sudden running up of a dozen or two of guards who had been amusing themselves about the town in undress uniform (navy-blue kilt, red sash, buff singlet), the scrambling and dressing *coram publico* on the grass, getting into trousers, boots, shirt, tunic, forage cap, and the hurried scuffle to get ready in time, and make a fine appearance to the steamer folk—he might think rather less of Tonga's military discipline.

Beyond the wharf lies the town, straggling over a good mile of space, and consisting of a few main streets and one or two side alleys, bordered by pretty verandahed, flowery houses. The pavement is the same throughout —green grass, kept short by the constant passing of bare feet. There are a good many trading stores, filled with wares suited to native tastes—gaudy prints, strong perfumes, cutlery, crockery, Brummagen jewellery. The streets are busy to-day—busy for Nukualofa, that is. Every now and then a native passes, flying by on a galloping, barebacked horse, or striding along the grass with the inimitable Tongan strut; for it is steamer day, and the monthly Union steamer boat is the theatre, the newspaper, the society entertainment, the luxury-provider of all the archipelago. On the other twenty-nine or thirty days of the month, you may stand in the middle of a main street for half an hour at a time, and not see a single passer-by, but steamer day galvanises the whole island into life.

The sand of the beach beside the wharf is as white as snow; it is pulverised coral from the reef, nothing else. Great fluted clam-shells, a foot long and more, lie about the strand, among the trailing pink-flowered convolvulus vines that wreathe the shore of every South Sea island. Unkempt pandanus trees, mounted on quaint high wooden stilts, overhang the green water; among the taller and more graceful cocoa-palms, Norfolk Island pines, odd, formal, and suggestive of hairbrushes, stand among feathery ironwoods and spreading avavas about the palace of the king. Quite close to the wharf this latter is placed—a handsome two-storeyed building, with wide verandahs and a tower. Scarlet-coated sentries march up and down all day at its gates; it is surrounded by a wall, and carefully guarded from intruders. George Tubou II. is among the shyest of monarchs and hates nothing so much as being stared at; so on steamer days there is little sign of life to be seen about the palace.

I happened to arrive in Tonga at an interesting historical crisis, and was promised an audience with the retiring monarch.

After a week or two, however, the promise was suddenly recalled, and the visitor informed that the king declined to see her, then or at any other time. A little investigation revealed the cause. The High Commissioner of the Western Pacific had recently come over from Fiji, to remonstrate with the Tongan monarchy concerning certain unconstitutional behaviour, and a British man-of-war had accompanied him. I, being the only other person on the island from "Home," had naturally been seeing a good deal of the formidable stranger. This was enough for the king. There was a plot to deprive him of his throne, he was certain; and it was obvious that I was in it, whatever I might choose to say to the contrary. There was no knowing what crime I might not be capable of, once admitted to the Royal Palace. George Tubou II. is six feet four, and twenty-seven stone weight, but he is distinctly of a nervous temperament; and his fears of Guy Fawkes-ism kept possession of his mind during the whole of my stay; so that the carefully averted face of a fat, copper-coloured sort of Joe Sedley, driving very fast in a buggy, was all I saw of Tonga's king.

There is no one, surely, in the world who quite

comes up to George of Tonga for a "guid conceit o' himsel'." When he wished to provide himself with a queen, some six or seven years ago, he first applied to the Emperor of Germany, to know if there was a German Princess of marriageable age whom he could have! The Kaiser politely replied in the negative. King George then sent proposals to a princess of Hawaii who was as well educated as any white lady, and used to diplomatic society in Washington. This also failing, he turned his attentions to his own country; and then began the most extraordinary love-story ever told under the Southern Cross—a story that could have happened nowhere on the globe, except in the comic-opera country of Tonga.

There were two eligible princesses of the royal line of Tonga—Princess Ofa and Princess Lavinia. The king appears to have proposed to them both, and then found himself unable to decide between the two. They were both of high rank, both good-looking after the portly Tongan fashion, and both very willing to be queen, reign over the fine palace, order lots of silk dresses from Auckland, wear the queen's crown of Tonga (supposed to be gold, but rather inclined to suspicious outbreaks of verdigris), and see the natives get off their horses and kneel on the ground, when the royal state carriage drove by.

But the king kept both princesses in the agonies of suspense ever present, and hope constantly deferred for months—until the wedding-day was fixed, the wedding-cake (ordered three years before from a New Zealand confectioner, for the German Princess who was not to be had) patched up and fresh coloured, the wedding-dress provided, at the expense of the Government of Tonga, (according to custom) and actually made! Not till the

THE ROYAL WEDDING

very night before the wedding did his dilatory Majesty at last declare his intentions, and fix upon the princess he had last proposed to, whom nobody expected him to take—Lavinia. It is a sober fact that the wedding invitation cards, sent out at the last minute, were printed with a blank for the bride's name, which was added with a pen!

Lavinia, overjoyed at her good luck, got into the Governmentally provided wedding dress next day, and (as the fairy tales say) "the wedding was celebrated with great pomp!" There is no sense of humour in Tonga. If there had been, the king could hardly have selected the means of consolation for Ofa's disappointment that he actually did choose, in sending her the bottom half of his wedding cake, as soon as the ceremony was over. Princess Ofa was not proud; she had been beating her head on the floor-mats all morning and pulling out handfuls of her long black hair, but when the consolatory cake arrived, she accepted it promptly and ate it.

There are generally illuminations on the night of a royal wedding. Tonga was not behind-hand in this matter, but the illuminations were of rather an unusual kind, being nothing less than numbers of burning native houses, set on fire by the indignant friends of the jilted Princess Ofa. The friends of the new queen retaliated in kind; and for nearly a week, arson became the recognised sport of the island. This excess of party feeling soon died down, however, and the newly married couple were left to honeymoon in peace.

An infant princess was born in due time, and not very long after, Queen Lavinia died. Here was Princess Ofa's chance, if Fate had permitted; but Ofa herself was dead, leaving no eligible princess to console the widowed king.

For more than five years the monarch (who is still only thirty-four, has lived alone, a mark for every husband-hunting princess in the Pacific. A princess related to an ancient island monarchy, invited herself to stay in the palace one recent Christmas. King George received her pleasantly, entertained her for some weeks, and then sent her home with a big packet of fine tobacco and a barrel of spirits, to console her for the non-success of her visit—which may be accounted for by the fact that she is rather older than the king himself, and by no means so lovely as she was. A favoured candidate is a certain princess of the royal family of Tahiti. She has been described to the king as handsome, and at least sixteen stone weight, both of which claims are quite correct. King George really wants a European princess, but as soon as he has been convinced for the second time that this is impossible, it is hoped that he will decide on the Tahitian princess, and elevate her to the Tongan throne, since he admires fat women exceedingly.

One of the most remarkable things in this remarkable country is the Parliament. It would take too long to record the history of this assembly's birth and development; but the chapter has been a notable one in Tongan history. The Parliament usually consists of the King and Prime Minister, the Chancellor of the Exchequer, the Chief Justice, and a score or two of important chiefs, some of whom inherit by birth, while others are returned by their native villages. At the time of my visit, there were a couple of vacancies in this remarkable assembly, since the High Commissioner of the Western Pacific (Governor of Fiji) had just deported the Prime Minister and the Chancellor of the Exchequer to Fiji, on account of certain proceedings which resulted in emptying Tonga's public treasury and leaving nothing to show for it.

A TAX ON THE CAPITAL

Their absence did not greatly matter, however, as it is a rule of the Tongan Constitution, that Parliament shall not meet oftener than once in three years. An excellent and practical reason lies at the root of this seemingly peculiar law. Tongatabu is a small island, only twenty miles long; and when the Members of Parliament,—dressed in new cotton kilts, with smart large floor-mats tied round their waists with sinnet (cocoanut fibre plait), and violet, sea-green, or lemon silk shirts on their brown backs—arrive from the outer villages and islands in Nukualofa with all their relatives, for the beginning of the session, something very like a famine sets in. The whole Parliament, also its sisters, aunts, and grandpapas, has to be fed at public expense, while it stays in the capital arranging the affairs of the nation; and as the length of its sitting is always regulated by the amount of provisions available, and never ends until the last yam, the last skinny chicken, the last sack of pineapples, is eaten up, it is easy to understand why the capital does not care to undergo such a strain any oftener than it can help.

A new Prime Minister and Chancellor of the Exchequer were appointed before long, and it was made a condition of the latter office, that the Chancellor should understand a reasonable amount of arithmetic. There was also a rigid rule made about the keeping of the key of the Government safe in some suitable place. A good deal of trouble was caused by the last Chancellor's losing it, one day when he was out fishing on the coral reef! There was a duplicate, but the Chancellor had carefully locked it up in the safe, to make sure it should not be lost! The poor old gentleman nearly got sunstroke hunting about the coral reef for the key until he found it. If it had been carried away by the tides, the safe must have remained closed until an expert from Auckland could be brought up to open it. As the Chancellor of the Exchequer did not know how much he had in it, or how much he had spent in the last quarter, it can readily be understood that the public accounts acquired an entirely superfluous extra tangle or two during the absence of the lost key.

Tonga enjoys one of the finest climates in the Pacific. The heat is never excessive, and the air is generally bright and invigorating. Fevers are unheard of, and the few white residents of the islands enjoy splendid health. As for the Tongans themselves, they dispute with the Fijians the palm of being physically the finest and strongest people in the whole Pacific; and no one has ever thought of challenging their claim to be the most intellectual of all the brown island races. Their carriage is superb, though only its extreme *aplomb* and ease save it from degenerating into an actual swagger. Their dress displays the most perfect taste in the South Seas. It consists, among the men, of a short tunic ("vala") of fine cashmere or silk, occasionally of cotton, on working days—draped with all the grace of an antique statue, and worn with a wide sash, and a thin, close-fitting singlet or shirt. The Tongan woman generally wears a garment that is suggestive of the Greek *chiton*— a loose sleeveless dress reaching to a point midway between waist and knee. Underneath is seen a tunic similar to that of the men, but a little longer. The colours chosen by both sexes are exquisite. No artist could design more beautiful combinations than those I have often seen flitting about the grassy streets of Nukualofa, Tonga's capital. A finely made giant strides by, in a navy-blue vala, cream-coloured silk shirt, and vivid sea-green sash. Another wears a pale blue vala and shirt, and a sash of royal blue. A third is in white and lemon colour girdled with orange ; another wears a white vala, a pale green shirt, and a sash of violet silk. A tall, self-possessed young woman, her hair dyed golden red with lime, and worn coiffed high above the forehead, with a fall of natural curls down her back, has a scarlet and yellow vala under her short brown silk gown, while her companion—smaller and merrier faced, with the melting black eyes of " The Islands "—wears and looks charming in, a pale-blue gown over a vala of daffodil yellow. These are the fashions of Tonga ; and they offer a feast for artistic souls and pencils, that cannot be matched under the Southern Cross.

Tonga is very seldom visited by travellers, except for an hour or two during the steamer's stay in port, and it is hardly ever seen by British tourists. I could not discover that any English lady had ever made a stay there, except myself, and the wife of a local Church dignitary. There are, of course, a few Colonial residents. But the English traveller leaves Tonga out altogether, which is really a pity—for his sake. As for the islands, they can do very well without tourists, and would not be the better for them.

There was no hotel save a plain and simple public-house, at the time of my stay, though I understand this defect has been remedied. I had therefore to set up housekeeping on my own account. The tiny bungalow I took for my stay of four weeks in the island, was a real South Sea home. It stood almost on the white coral sand of the beach, and close to the cool green waters of the lagoon ; it was shaded by palms and scarlet-blossomed " flamboyant " trees, and it was nearly all door and window and verandah. Its carpets were plaited pandanus-leaf mats ; the ornaments in the sitting-room were foot-long fluted clam-shells off the beach, filled with wild red and yellow hibiscus flowers, poignantly perfumed frangipani stars, and the sweet pink blossoms of the South Sea oleander. The back kitchen had generally a bunch of bananas hanging from the roof, a pile of green cocoanuts for drinking, under the window, a mound of yellow papaws, or tree-melons, in a corner, some custard-apples and mangoes, and a big basket of pineapples, bought at the door for fourteen a shilling, or picked by myself during a drive through the bush.

There was not much else, besides bread and tea. I almost lived on fruit, and could not help wondering what the inhabitants of temperate latitudes, who fear ill consequences from a dozen plums or a double handful of strawberries, would have thought of my uncounted mangoes and bananas, and five or six pineapples a day. Only children, at home in England, really know how much fruit can safely be undertaken by the human digestive organs. Wise children! and foolish elders, who have forgotten so soon.

The transparent waters of the lagoon outside, lapping idly under the leaves of overhanging palm and pandanus, were not so cool as they looked, under the hot midday sun; and if one did not want a tepid sea-bath, it was best to wait till night. Then, what a luxury it was, after the heat of the day (for Tonga, though cool for the tropics, is nevertheless tropical), to float about in the dim lagoon, under a glow of stars that lit up the sky almost as brightly as an English moon, the dark shining water bearing one to and fro with the swell from the reef, the land growing farther and farther away, the palms on the thin pale shore-line standing out small and black, like Indian ink sketches, against the lucid purple of the midnight sky! Willingly indeed one would have passed the whole night out there, swimming, and floating in a warm dark sea of stars—stars above and stars below—if nature had not given out after an hour or two, and demanded a return to the solid earth. Sharks? Well, they had "hardly ever" been seen inside the reef. Stingarees, with their immense ugly bodies buried in the sand at the bottom, and their cruel barbed tails ready to strike? Yes, they had been seen, but not often; and in tropic waters you learn to take the chances like every one else, and enjoy yourself without thinking of the "might-be's."

It was the hot season, but not too hot for riding or driving, and I spent many mornings exploring about the island. To the Wood of the Bats, about eleven miles from Nukualofa, one drives in a springy little colonial buggy, driving over mile after mile of rather uneven grass road, along avenues of blossoming orange trees, through groves of bananas and breadfruit and tall mango trees, past straggling native villages with neat little fancy-work houses made of woven reeds and thatch, until, in the distance, one begins to hear a loud screaming, squeaking, and chattering noise. This is the Wood of the Bats that we are coming to, and that is some of their usual conversation. Under the trees—there are over twenty of them, avavas, like great cedars, ironwoods, mangoes; all big forest trees, and all covered with bats as thick as a currant bush with currants—the squeaking and squealing grows almost deafening. Thousands of great flying-foxes, with dark furry bodies as big as cats, big spreading wings (now folded tightly up) and sharp, keen fox-like heads, hang upside down on every tree, waiting for the night to come, and whiling away the time by quarrelling and swearing. They are all bad, these bats; they are ugly, dirty, vicious, destructive and greedy—yet they are strictly tabooed by the natives, and no one dares to kill a single one. It is believed that the prosperity of Tonga is inextricably associated with the bats, and that, if they ever deserted the wood, the country would fall. They are sacred, and must not be touched.

Every evening, punctually at five o'clock, the bats take wing, and rise from the trees like a screaming cloud of evil spirits. The sky is blackened with their bodies as they go, and scattered all over with the long streaming flights of separate bats that divide away from the main body. They are off to feed—to feed all night upon the bananas and pineapples and mangoes of the unhappy islanders, who lose thousands of pounds' worth of fruit and trade every year, but dare not revenge themselves. Just at dawn, they will return, screaming and shoving rudely as they settle down in the trees once more, squabbling for upper berths, and trying to push into a nice comfortable place amidships of a particular bough, by biting the occupant's toes until he lets go. They may have flown forty or fifty miles in the night, visited islands more than twenty miles away, and devastated the plantations of Tonga from end to end. They have worked hard for their suppers, and now they will doze and squabble all day, once more, until evening.

A few miles from the Wood of Bats, in the midst of exquisite scenery, stands a famous avava known as Captain Cook's Tree. It was under this tree that the great explorer called together all the natives, on his discovery of the islands in 1777, and addressed them by means of an interpreter. The account of this will be found in "Cook's Voyages." The tree is still in splendid condition, in spite of its age, which must amount to many hundred years. Pigs were brought to Tonga by

Cook in this same year, and a few of the original breed are still to be seen in the island—tall, gaunt, hump-backed creatures with immense heads and long noses, contrasting oddly with the smaller and fatter kinds introduced by later voyagers.

The burial-place of the Tui Tongans made an object for another drive. Before the introduction of Christianity, in early Victorian days, the Tongans had two kings, an ordinary earthly king, who did all the hard work of governing, and a heavenly king, the Tui Tonga, who was supposed to be of divine descent, and was worshipped as a god. For many centuries, the Tui Tongas were buried in great oblong raised enclosures, three-terraced, and built of rough-hewn, closely fitted slabs from the coral reef. Two of these great tombs still remain, hidden in tangled thickets of low bush, and considerably worn by age. I had no means of measurement, but judged the larger one to be about fifty yards by thirty, the smaller somewhat less. The state of the coral slabs, and the great trees that have grown up rooted among them, suggest that the tombs are extremely old. Tradition among the natives takes them back beyond the recollection of any of their ancestors; they cannot say when or why they were built. The construction—a double terrace, each step about five feet high—and the carefully arranged oblong shape, seem to point to some special significance long since forgotten. There is also a "trilithon" erection of three large blocks of stone, some miles away, concerning which island traditions are silent. It could not have been constructed by hand labour alone; some mechanical device must have been employed to raise the centre stone to its present position. The ancient Tongans, however, knew nothing of mechanics, and an interesting problem is therefore set for antiquarians to solve. The height of the side supports is about twenty feet, and the centre cross-piece, which rests in a socket on each side, is a little less in length.

The beautiful and interesting sea-caves—some swarming with birds, others celebrated for their lovely colouring and formation—which are found in the windward side of the island, I was unable to see, owing to the bad weather of the rainy season, during which my visit was made.

A "Chief" kava-party, however, got up for my benefit, consoled me for the loss of the caves. Kava is the great national drink of Tonga, as of many other South Sea Islands. It is made from the hard woody root of the Piper methysticum and is exhilarating and cooling, but not actually intoxicating. In taste, it is extremely unpleasant till one gets used to it, being peppery, soapy, and dishwatery as to flavour. I had drunk kava before, however, and learned to recognise its pleasanter properties; also, the old custom of chewing the kava-root, before infusing it, which still obtains in some parts of Samoa, has been quite given up in Tonga, and the pounding is done with stones.

The scene was weird and strange in the last degree. I was the only white person present. We all squatted on the mats in the chief's house, the natives in their valas and loose short gowns, with white scented flowers in their hair; I in a smart demi-toilette evening dress, because I was the special guest, and the chief's family would expect me to honour them by "dressing the part." The only light was a ship's hurricane lantern, placed on the floor, where it threw the most Rembrandtesque of shadows upon the silent circle of brown, glittering-eyed faces, and upon the rapt ecstatic countenances of the kava-makers, as they went through all the

A KAVA PARTY

details of what was evidently an ancient religious ceremony, very savage, very native, and not at all "missionary," despite the church membership of all the performers. There were loud sonorous chants and responses, elaborate gymnastics, with the great twist of hibiscus fibre that was used to strain the kava after it was pounded, and water poured on; something very like incantations, and finally, a wild religious ecstasy on the part of the kava-maker, who worked himself almost into a fit, and at last sank back utterly exhausted, with the bowl of prepared kava before him. This bowl was a standing vessel as big as a round sponge bath, carved, legs and all, from one block of a huge forest tree-trunk, and exquisitely polished and enamelled by many years of kava-holding. Its value was beyond price.

The calling of names now began—first the chief's, then mine, then the other guests. There is great ceremony observed at kava-drinkings, and an order of precedence as strict as that of a German Court. As my name was called, I clapped my hands once, took the cocoanut bowl from the girl who was serving it, and swallowed the contents at a draught. The next name was then called, and the next drinker drank as I did. It is very bad manners to act otherwise. The girl who served the kava walked round our squatting circle in a doubled-up posture that must surely have made her back ache; but custom forbade her to stand erect while serving.

After the long ceremony was ended, the dignified white-haired chief held a conversation with me, by means of an interpreter; and told me that there were four ways of kava-drinking, each with its appropriate etiquette. That which I had seen was the most important and elaborate of the four, very seldom used, and only permitted to chiefs. We exchanged a good many stately compliments through the interpreter, and I then took my departure.

It is near the end of my visit, and in a few more days the steamer takes me on to Haapai and Vavau and beautiful, steamy-hot Samoa. But this is Christmas morning, and one can think of nothing else.

Nothing? Well, those who know what it is to spend that day of days under a burning tropic sky, with palms and poinsettia for Christmas garlandry, instead of holly and mistletoe, know just what thoughts fly homewards across twelve thousand miles of sea, and how far they are concerned with the sunny, lonely Christmas of the present —how far with the dark and stormy Christmases of the past, when snow and winter reigned outside, but summer, more brilliant than all the splendours of southern world, was within, and in the heart. But it is of the Tongan Christmas day that I have to tell.

I was awakened very early by—the waits! Whatever one expects under the Southern Cross, one certainly does not expect that, and yet there they were, a score of boys and youths playing merry tunes under my window, and pausing now and then to see if I was not awake to come out and give them their Christmas " tip."

I dressed hastily, and came on to the verandah. The music of the band, which had puzzled me a good deal, now turned out to be produced solely by mouth-organs, blown by a number of youths dressed exactly alike in black valas, white linen jackets, and white uniform caps. The soul of the Tongan loves a uniform above everything, and all the bands in the islands—of whom there are an astonishing number—wear specially made costumes of a rather military type.

It was frightfully hot, for Christmas is midsummer here, and the day was exceptionally warm in any case.

CHRISTMAS CELEBRATIONS

But the "waits," standing out in the burning sun, did not seem to feel the heat at all. They blew lustily away at their mouth-organs, playing English dance music, Tongan songs, missionary hymns, in wonderful time and harmony, and with the inimitable Tongan verve and swing, poor though the instruments were. The performance was quite worth the gift they expected, I listened as long as they cared to play. Then they collected their dues, and went off to serenade a white trader, who, I strongly suspected, had been celebrating Christmas Eve after a fashion that would not tend to make him grateful for an early call.

For me, Christmas had begun on the previous evening, when I went to the midnight Mass at the church upon the shore, among the palms and the feathery ironwood trees. In the crystal-clear moonlight, what a brilliant scene it was! Even outside the church, the decorations could be seen for miles, since they consisted of thousands and thousands of half-cocoanut-shells, filled with cocoanut oil, and provided with a wick of twisted fibre, which when lit, burnt with a clear ray like a star, illuminating the walls of the churchyard, the outlines of the doors and the ridges of the roof—even the winding walks about the building, too, and the low-growing trees—with a perfect Milky Way of dancing light.

Within, all the colours of a coral reef (which includes every hue of a rainbow, and many more) were in full blaze about the tremendous, unbroken floor, where the natives stood or sat cross-legged, dressed in all their gayest finery. There was a heavy scent of perfumed cocoanut oil, orange-blossom, and frangipani flowers and a rich glow of lights; and the waves of gorgeous melody that burst forth now and again with the progress of the service were like the billows of Time breaking upon the shores of Eternity. Of all the choral singing that I heard in the Pacific, that of Tonga was incomparably the fullest, the most splendid, and most majestic. The singers of Manahiki are sweeter and stranger, those of the Cook Islands more varied and soft, but the Tongan music is, for sheer magnificence and volume, unsurpassable.

The women, in their graceful tunics, with their elaborately dressed hair, and their fine, dignified presence, were all unlike the soft sensuous languorous syrens of Tahiti and Raratonga. They do not encourage familiarity, even from white women, and their moral character is much higher than that of their sisters in the far Eastern Pacific. Women are treated with more respect in Tonga than in any part of the Pacific. They have little to do in the way of household work, and almost no field work. The men save them most of the hard labour, on the undeniable ground that hard work makes a woman ugly, and they do not care for ugly wives!

Nearly every one wore a mat tied round the waist, partly concealing the gay dress—in spite of the extreme heat of the night. Some of the mats were new and clean, but most were old, ragged, and dirty. This curious custom is a relic of ancient heathen days in Tonga, when a handsome dress of any kind, worn by a commoner, was apt to arouse the dangerous envy of a chief, and in consequence, a native who was wearing his " best " generally tied the dirtiest old mat that he could get over all, so that he might not look too rich! The reason has long since vanished, but the custom remains in a modified form. A mat, tied round the waist with strong sinnet cord, is considered a correct finish to the gayest of festival costume in Tonga of to-day, and, as far as I was able to ascertain, its absence, on occasions of ceremony, is considered rather vulgar.

The service was enlivened by the presence of a very large and extremely loud brass band. Brass is a passion with the Tongan musician, and he certainly makes the most of it. The effects produced are a little monotonous to a European ear, but, none the less, impressive and fine.

After the midnight mass, I went home in the bright moonlight, the gentle stir of the trade-wind, the soft rustle of the ironwood trees, falling with a pleasantly soothing effect upon ears a little strained and tired by the strenuous character of the Tongan music. Next morning came the waits, and in the afternoon there were games and sports of a rather too familiar Sunday-school pattern, at the various mission stations. I did not trouble to attend any of them, as the Pacific native is certainly least interesting when most intent on copying the ways and fashions of the white man. The cricket matches which came off at various intervals during the few weeks of my stay, were well worth seeing, however, for the Tongan is a magnificent cricketer, and has often inflicted bitter defeat on the best teams that visiting men-of-war could put in the field against him.

The politically disturbed state of the island was interesting in one way, but a serious disadvantage in another, since it prevented my obtaining much information about many interesting native customs that I should have been glad to investigate. I am afraid that I deserved the worst that scientifically minded travellers could say of me, in Tonga, for I merely spent the time enjoying myself after the pleasant island fashion, and not in research or geographical note-taking, even so far as was possible. Yet, after all, what are the islands, if not a Garden of Indolence, a lotus-land, a place where one dreams, and wanders, and listens to the murmuring reef-song, and

sleeps under the shade of a palm, and wakes but to
dream again? Does one degenerate, in such a life?
Why, yes, of course—constantly, surely, and most
delightfully.

"*Be good, and you will be happy, but you won't have a
good time,*" says "Pudd'nhead Wilson," one of the wisest of
modern philosophers. In the islands, one is not good, in
the ordinary Dr. Wattian sense of the term, and perhaps
one is not happy—though if so, one never finds it out. But
the good time one does have, and it is very good indeed.
And if you do not believe me, dear sensible reader, never
be tempted to go and try, for it is very likely that the
good time and your own goodness would mutually cancel
one another, and you would be unvirtuous and bored all
in one. The islands are not for all, and the gateway to
the "Tir-na'n-Oge" is now, as ever, hard to find.

The big Union steamer, with her ice, and her
"cuisine" (cooking is never cooking, on board a passenger
vessel), and her dainty little blue and white cabins, and
her large cool saloon glittering with crystal and gilding,
came in in due time, and I went away with her to Samoa.
The three days' run was broken by two calls in the
Tongan group—one at Haapai, and one at Vavau.

Of Haapai, a long, low, wooded island, with a few
hundred native inhabitants, and one or two whites, we
saw nothing but the king's palace—a great, square, two-
storeyed, verandahed building, which is never lived in—
and the Wesleyan chapel, which has some of the finest
sinnet work in the Pacific to show. This sinnet work is
quite distinctive of the islands, and is very beautiful and
artistic. It is not one of the "curios" known to the
markets and collections of civilisation, because it is always
done *in situ*, and cannot be removed. At first sight, it
looks like remarkably good chip carving, done on the

capitals of pillars, and about the centres of supports and beams, in various shades of red, black, brown, and yellow. Looking closer, one sees that it is much more remarkable than carving, being a solid mass of interwoven sinnet plait, as fine as very thin twine, wound and twisted into raised patterns by the clever fingers of the natives. In the church at Haapai, the sinnet plaiting is very fine and elaborate, and certainly well worth seeing. The captain of the steamer, who acted as our guide, made sure we had all seen it, and then took us a wild, hot, hurried walk across the island, to the coral beach at the other side, and past the palace, and along an endless cocoanut avenue, which was very pretty, but——

We wanted our afternoon tea, and we mutinied at that point, and insisted on going back to the ship. This grieved our commander, who conceived that his duties to the Company required he should ensure every passenger saw everything that was to be seen on the whole voyage, and shirked nothing—but we threatened to overpower and maroon him, if he did not take us back, so he returned, lecturing learnedly about the cutting off of the " Port-au-Prince," in Haapai, by the natives, in seventeen hundred and I-forget-when. We ought to have been listening—but we wanted our tea, and we weren't.

We reached Vavau just before dark, barely in time to admire the wonderful windings and fiords, the long blue arms and bright green islets, of this Helen among island harbours. Vavau is celebrated for its beauty through all the South Sea world, and its loveliness has not been one whit exaggerated.

In the early morning—at half-past five, to be precise—the energetic captain routed all the passengers out of their bunks, and compelled them, by sheer force of character, to follow him, groaning and puffing, up a hill five hundred feet high, and exceedingly precipitous—a mere crag, in fact—that overlooked the harbour. We did not want to go, but none of us were sorry we had been compelled, when we did get to the top and saw that matchless harbour lying extended at our feet, mile after mile of land-locked fiord and palmy headland and exquisite green island, all set in a stainless mirror of flaming blue, and jewelled, where the shallows lightened to the shore, with flashes of marvellous colour shot up from the coral reef lying underneath. Rose and amethyst and violet, and malachite green and tawny yellow—they were all there, painting the splendid sweep of the harbour waters with hues that no mortal brush could reproduce, or pen describe. We stayed there long, and even the thought of breakfast, generally a moving call, did not hurry us away.

In the afternoon, the captain had business to attend to, so he turned out one of the officers to act as guide, and sent us all off to see the Cave of the Swallows, and Mariner's Cave, on the other side of the harbour.

If the Cave of the Swallows were situated on any European coast, it would be as tourist-ridden a spot as the Blue Grotto of Capri, or any other of the thousand famous caves through which holiday-making travellers are dragged each summer season—and would consequently be despoiled of half its loveliness. But it is very far away, in the South Sea Islands, and though a passenger steamer does visit Vavau once a month there are usually no tourists—only a missionary and a trader or two. So the lovely place lies undisturbed almost all the time, and you shall not find, when you row across the harbour to see it, that you have to wait your turn in a crowd of other boats, full of romping and larking trippers, with the guide of every party keeping a sharp look-out to see that no one takes longer than he ought going over the " sight "—so long as his charges remain outside.

Instead of this, we glide silently under a noble archway some fifty feet high, and enter a great, still, ocean sanctuary, that looks as if no wandering oar had ever profaned its peace, since first the white man came to these far-off isles. Outside, the water is Prussian blue in colour, and over a thousand feet deep, but within the arch of the cave the bottom shoots up till it is within a hundred feet of the glass-clear surface on which we float, hanging above the silver-coloured coral reefs of the deep sea-bed, like birds hanging in air. The roof and walls of the cave are brilliant verdigris green, the water-floor, that curves so closely in and out of the numerous arches and recesses, where mysterious shadows creep, is sapphire shot with fire. At one side of the cave there is a dark winding corridor leading to depths unknown. We glide down this a little way, and there before us opens out—surely, a temple and a shrine! The water-floor spreads and broadens here into the carpet of a high, still, secret inner cave, in the centre of which springs up a splintered pedestal—shattered, one fancies, by the blow that broke the image that must surely once have stood in this strange sea-shrine. From an unseen rift in the roof, far above, a white ray of sun strikes down into the cave, and falls like a blast from an offended heaven upon the broken pedestal.

There is a geological explanation, no doubt, but we shall not look for it, for this is a wonder that would have delighted Victor Hugo himself, who drew the scenery of the "Toilers of the Sea." And Victor Hugo's pen would be needed by any one who would adequately describe the spot.

There is a rock in the outer cave, that sounds like a church bell when struck with an oar, and this delights the boatmen greatly, though they have heard it every time the steamer came up to Vavau. It is, indeed, a solemn and beautiful sound, and well suited to the place.

Going back to the ship, we are shown the spot where the famous Mariner's Cave opens out, under water. There is nothing whatever to be seen, since the entrance is six feet under water at low tide. The story was first told to the world in Mariner's " Tonga," published 1802, and was utilised by Byron in his poem of " The Island." A young chief, it was said, was chasing a turtle one day, and saw the creature dive. He followed it, and was surprised to find that, on rising after his dive, he had reached an under-water cave of considerable size, to which there was no outlet save the one by which he had come in. Giving up the turtle, he dived again, returned to the surface, and did not trouble himself about the cave until, some months later, it occurred to him as an excellent place for an elopement—the parents of the girl he loved having refused to give her to him. So it came about that the young chief's sweetheart disappeared, and no one knew what had become of her until one day a boating party, to their intense amazement, saw what appeared to be the ghost of the girl rising from the heart of the waves. The apparition stared round, saw the intruders, and immediately disappeared. She was seen no more, but the story caused so much talk, that in the end the true secret came out, and it was discovered that the chief had hidden his lady-love in the cave, diving down with food to her day by day, and even bringing torches, safely wrapped in leaves. The stern parents, touched by so much devotion, relented, and the chief triumphantly brought home his bride at last in full day.

Mariner, who was interested in the ancient tale, succeeded in reaching the cave himself, and found it as represented. He surmised that there was an air supply, passing through invisible cracks in the rock above, for the air seemed to keep fresh. There was something like a rough couch of stone at one end, where the imprisoned girl had made her bed. No light whatever penetrated the cavern.

Since Mariner's time, very few Europeans have succeeded in entering the cave, which is extremely difficult to get into, owing to the length of the passage under water, and the currents of the tides. About thirty years ago, Captain Luce, of H.M.S. *Esk*, succeeded in entering the cave, but rose too soon on going out, and lacerated his back so badly against the coral spears under water, that he died in a few days. Since then, I heard that one white man had gone safely in and returned, but no one seemed to know who, or when. None of our party, at all events, felt tempted to make the trial.

The steamer was ready to start when we got back, so we hurried on board, and started away for Samoa. There was much more to see in Vavau, but the only way of seeing it was to stop over for a month and remain in the village. For this no one had time. I was giving a month to each group of islands, which is little enough in the Pacific—but I knew very well that, unless I had had a vessel of my own, or a year or two extra to spend, it was impossible to see all that could be seen.

Tofoa, for instance, one of the Tongan Group, which is an active volcano, and, naturally, not inhabited—what could be more interesting than a call there? But uninhabited volcanoes do not furnish cargo for steamship companies, so all we could see was a smear of smoke in the far distance, as we steamed on our way to Apia, the capital of the "Navigators" Group, better known, since the days of Stevenson, as Samoa.

CHAPTER XIV

Stevenson's Samoa—What happened when It rained—Life in a Native Village—The Albino Chief—A Samoan " Bee "—The Tyranny of Time—Fishing at Midnight—Throwing the Presents—My Friend Fangati—The Taupo Dances—Down the sliding Rock—" Good-bye, my Flennie !"

WHEN I woke up in the morning, the ship was still, and the familiar chatter of island tongues, and splashing of island paddles, audible outside the ports, told that we had reached Apia.

Dressing is always a rush, under such circumstances. I hurried out on the deck in even quicker time than usual, and hastened to enjoy a good look at the little island that has been made famous the wide world over, by the genius of the great writer who passed his latest years in exile among those palmy hills.

Upolu, Stevenson's island, is the second largest in the Samoan Group, being forty miles by eight. Savaii is a little wider. Tutuila is smaller. The six other islands are of little importance.

Apia and Stevenson's home have been written about and described, by almost every tourist who ever passed through on the way to Sydney. There is little therefore to say that has not been said before. Every one knows that Apia is a fair-sized, highly civilised place, with hotels and shops and band promenades, and that Vailima, Stevenson's villa, is a mile or two outside. Every one has heard of the beautiful harbour of Apia itself, with the blue over-hanging hills, and the dark wooded peak rising above all, on the summit of which the famous Scotsman's tomb gleams out like a tiny pearl —"under the wide and starry sky." Since the disturbances of 1899, most people have been aware that England has absolutely relinquished any rights she had in Samoa, and that the islands are now divided between Germany and America—Upolu being among the possessions of the former.

Perhaps some people have forgotten that Samoa is a fairly recent discovery, having been first sighted by Bougainville in 1768. It is supposed that the natives originally came from Sumatra. During the last six hundred years, they were frequently at war with the Tongans and Fijians, and from the latter learned the horrible practice of cannibalism—which, however, they abandoned of their own accord a good while before the coming of the first missionaries in 1833.

They are a singularly beautiful race, and most amiable in character. They are all Christianised, and a great number can read and write. Tourists have done their best to spoil them, but outside the towns there is much of the ancient simplicity and patriarchal character still to be found.

About two dozen Samoan gentlemen—I call them gentlemen, because in manners and demeanour they really deserved the name, and many were actual chiefs—had come on board the steamer, and were walking about the deck when I came out. The air was like hot water, and there was not a breath of wind. All the same, the Samoan gentleman were quite cool, for they wore nothing at all but a British bath-towel with red edges, tied round the waist in the universal kilt style of the Pacific. In the Cook Group, the garment is called a pareo, and is made of figured cotton. In Tonga, it is a vala, and is usually cashmere. In Samoa the name is changed to lava-lava, and the thing may be either a piece of plain coloured cotton, or the bath-towel above mentioned, which is considered a good deal smarter—but the costume itself is the same all through.

Most of the men had their short-cut hair plastered snow-white with lime, because it was Saturday. Almost every Samoan limes his hair on Saturdays, partly to keep up the yellow colour produced by previous applications, partly for hygienic reasons that had better be left to the imagination.

All the visitors displayed an incomparable self-possession and dignity of bearing, not at all like the "Tongan swagger," but much more akin to the manner of what is known in society as "really good people." Coupled to the almost complete absence of clothes, and the copper skins, it was enough to make one perfectly giddy at first. But afterwards, one grew used to it, and even came to compare the average white man's manner disadvantageously with the unsurpassable self-possession and calm of the unclothed native.

Then came boats and landing and hotels, and the usual one-sided South Sea town, with little green parrakeets tweedling cheerfully among the scarlet flowers of the flamboyant trees, and looking very much as if they had escaped from somewhere. And behold, as we were making our way to the hotel, a heavy waterspout of hot-season rain came on, whereupon the street immediately became a transformation scene of the most startling character.

The roadway had been full of natives in their best clothes, come down to see the passengers—some in bath-towels, like the visitors to the steamer, but many in the cleanest of shirts and cotton tunics, and scores of pretty Samoan girls in civilised gowns of starched and laced muslin, trimmed hats, and gay silk ribbons. The rain began to spout, as only tropical rain can, and immediately things commenced to happen that made me wonder if I were really awake. Under the eaves of houses, beneath umbrellas, out in the street without any shelter at all, the Samoans rapidly began undressing. Smart white shirts, frilled petticoats, lacy dresses, all came off in a twinkling, and were rolled up into tight bundles, and stowed away under their owners' arms, to protect the precious garments from the rain. Then down the street, with bare brown legs twinkling as they ran, and bodies covered merely by the " lava-lava," scurried the bronze ladies and gentlemen who had looked so smart and dressy a few brief seconds before. Some of the girls, who could not get an inch of shelter under which to undress, merely pulled their fine frocks up under their arms, and ran down the street looking like very gay but draggled tulips set on two long brown stalks. It was the oddest transformation scene that I had ever been privileged to look on at, and it sent the passengers of the ship into such screaming fits of laughter that they forgot all about keeping themselves dry, and landed in the hotel in the condition of wet seaweed tossed up by the waves. So we arrived in Samoa.

There is no use in relating at length how I drove out to see Stevenson's much described villa at Vailima—now in the possession of a wealthy German merchant, and much altered and spoiled—and how I did *not* climb the two thousand feet up to his tomb above the harbour, and was sorry ever after. Rather let me tell how, tired of the civilised section of the island, I took ship one day in an ugly little oil-*launch*, and sailed away to see the life of a native village, down at Falepunu. There is not much real native life now to be seen in the capital; for, although the "faa Samoa" (ancient Samoan custom) is very strong all over the islands, in Apia it is at a minimum, and the influence of the white man has much increased since Stevenson's day. Besides, how can one study native customs, dining at a *table d'hôte* and living in a great gilt and glass hotel, situated in the midst of a busy street?

So it was very gladly that I saw the wide blue harbour of Apia open out before me, and melt into the great Pacific, the "league long rollers" tossing our little cockle shell about remorselessly as we headed out beyond the reef, and began to slant along the coast, Upolu's rich blue and green mountains unfolding in a splendid panorama of tropic glory, as we crept along against the wind towards Falefa, our destined port, nearly twenty miles away. Here and there, white threads of falling water gleamed out against the dark mountain steeps; and the nearer hills, smooth and rich and palmy, and green as a basket of moss, parted now and then in unexpected gateways, to show brief glimpses of the wildly tumbled lilac peaks of far-away, rugged inner ranges. A day of gold and glitter, of steady, smiting heat, of beauty that was almost too beautiful, as hour after hour went by, and found the glorious panorama still unrolling before eyes that were well-nigh wearied, and bodies that wanted shelter and food.

But even a little oil-launch cannot take all day to cover twenty miles; so it was still early in the afternoon when we glided into the harbour of Falefa, and came to a stop in the very heart of Paradise.

How to picture Falefa, to the dwellers in the far grey north! how to paint the jewel-green of the water, the snow-white of the sand, the overhanging palms that lean all day to look at their own loveliness in the unruffled mirror below ; the emerald peaks above, the hyacinth peaks beyond, the strangely fashioned outrigged canoes, with their merry brown rowers, skimming like long-limbed water-flies about the bay ; the far-away sweetness and stillness and unlikeness of it all ! And the waterfall, dropping down seventy feet of black precipitous rock right into the sea's blue bosom—and the winding, shady fiords, where the water is glass-green with reflections of shimmering leaves—and the little secluded brown houses, domed and pillared after the Samoan fashion, that ramble about among the long avenues of palm—surely, even in all the lovely South Sea Islands, there never was a lovelier spot than this harbour of Falefa !

We three—a half-caste Samoan lady, a New Zealand girl, and myself—landed on the beach and gave over our things to a native boy, to carry up to the great guest-house at Falepunu, a mile further on. Every Samoan village has its guest-house, for the free accommodation of passing travellers, but few have anything that can compare with the house where we were to stay—my companions for the night only, myself for a week.

A Samoan house, owing to the heat of the climate, is a roof and nothing more, the walls being omitted, save for the posts necessary to support the great dome of the roof. It is well worth looking at and admiring all the same. Fine ribs made of strong flexible branches run diagonally from eaves to crown, only an inch or two apart, and curved with exquisite skill to form the arching dome. Over these, at an acute angle, are laid similar ribs in a second layer, forming a strong, flexible

THE GUEST-HOUSE

lattice. At just the right intervals, narrow, curved beams cross behind these, and hold them firm. The centre of the house displays three splendid pillars, made from the trunks of three tall trees; these support the roof-tree, and are connected with the sides of the dome by several tiers of slender beams, beautifully graded in size and length. The guest-house of Falepunu belongs to a high chief, and is in consequence exceptionally handsome. Its roof-tree is fifty feet from the floor, and the width of the house, on the floor-level, is the same. Forty wooden pillars, each seven feet high, support this handsome dome, every inch of which is laced and latticed and tied together with the finest of plaited cocoanut fibre, stained black, red, and yellow, and woven into pattern like elaborate chip carving.

There is not a nail used in the construction of the house. One wet afternoon I attempted to count the number of thousand yards of sinnet (plaited cocoanut fibre) that must have been used in this colossal work, and gave it up in despair. The number of the mats used in forming the blinds was more calculable. Each opening between the pillars was surmounted by seven plaited cocoanut-leaf mats, fastened up under the eaves into a neat little packet. These could be dropped like a venetian blind, whenever rain or wind proved troublesome. The total number of mats was two hundred and seventy-three.

The floor of a Samoan house consists of a circular terrace, raised some two feet above the level of the ground. It is surrounded by a shallow ditch, and it is made of large and small stones, closely fitted together, and covered with a final layer of small white coral pebbles from the beach. This forms the carpet of the house, and is known as "Samoan feathers," from the fact that it also forms everybody's bed at night, covered with a mat or two.

The chief, Pula-Ulu, and his wife, Iva, who were in charge of the guest-house, in the absence of its owner, received us joyfully, and proceeded to make a feast for us at once. Fowls were killed, baked bread-fruit and taro brought from the ovens outside (which were simply pits dug in the ground, and filled with hot stones), and oranges and pineapples plucked from the nearest grove. We sat crosslegged on the mats, and ate till we could eat no more; then, "faa Samoa," we lay down where we were to rest and doze away the hot hours of the afternoon.

In the evening, Iva lit a big ship's hurricane lamp, and set it on the floor; and half Falepunu came in to call. In rows and rows they sat on the floor-mats, their brown, handsome faces lit up with interest and excitement, fanning themselves ceaselessly as they sat, and asking endless questions of the half-caste lady, who interpreted for the others. I, as coming from London, was the heroine of the hour, for the Samoans are all greatly interested in "Beritania" (Britain) and, in spite of the German annexation, still prefer the English to any other nation.

The inevitable question: "Where was my husband?" followed by: "Why had I not got one?"—in a tone of reproachful astonishment—was put by almost every new-comer. The half-caste visitor explained volubly; but the villagers still looked a little puzzled. The Samoans have in almost every village a "taupo" or "Maid of the Village," whose office it is to receive guests, and take a prominent part in all public ceremonies and festivals. But she only holds office for a very few years, until she marries, and she is always surrounded, when travelling, by a train of elderly attendants. An unmarried woman who had money of her own, who wandered about alone, who held office in no village, here or at home, this was decidedly a puzzle to the Falepunu folk, whose own women all marry at about fourteen. They had seen white women travelling with their husbands, but never one who had ventured from Beritania all alone!

There was evidently some difficulty, at first, in "placing" me according to Samoan etiquette, which is both complex and peculiar. A white woman with her husband presents no difficulty, since the "faa Samoa" always gives the superior honour to the man, and therefore the woman must only receive second-class ceremony. In my case, the question was solved later on, by classing me as a male chief! I was addressed as "Tamaite" (lady), but officially considered as a man; therefore I was always offered kava (the national drink of Samoa, never given to their own women, and not usually to white women), and the young chiefs of the district came almost every evening to call upon me in due form, sitting in formal rows, and conversing, through an interpreter, in a well-bred, gracious manner, that was oddly reminiscent of a London drawing-room. The women did not visit me officially, although I had many a pleasant bathing and fishing excursion in their company.

On the first evening the callers stayed a long time—so long, that we all grew very weary, and yearned for sleep. But they kept on coming, one after another; and by-and-by half-a-dozen young men appeared, dressed in kilts of coloured bark-strips; adorned with necklaces of scarlet berries and red hibiscus flowers, and liberally cocoanut-oiled. In the centre of the groups was the most extraordinary figure I had ever seen—a white man, his skin burned to an unwholesome pink by exposure, his hair pure gold, extremely fine and silky, and so thick as to make a huge halo round his face when shaken out. His eyes were weak, and half shut, and I was not surprised to hear that he was not really of white descent, being simply a Samoan albino, born of brown parents. This man, being the son of a chief, took the principal figure in the dance that was now got up for our amusement. The seven men danced on the floor-mats, close together, the albino in the centre, all performing figures of extraordinary agility, and not a little grace. The music was furnished by the other spectators, who rolled up a mat or two, and beat time on these improvised drums, others clapping their hands, and chanting a loud, sonorous, measured song.

At the end of the dance, the performers, streaming with perspiration (for the night was very hot) and all out of breath, paused for our applause. We gave it liberally, and added a tin or two of salmon, which was joyfully received, and eaten at once. All Samoans love tinned salmon, which, by an odd perversion, they call "peasoupo." No doubt the first tinned goods seen in the islands were simply tinned peasoup. This would account for the extraordinary confusion of names mentioned above.

By this time we were so utterly weary that we lay down on the mats where we were, and almost slept. Iva, seeing this, chased most of the callers out with small ceremony, and got up the calico mosquito curtain that was to shelter the slumbers of all three travellers. It enclosed a space of some eight feet by six. Within, plaited pandanus-leaf mats were laid, two thick, upon the white pebble floor, and Samoan pillows offered us.

A Samoan pillow is just like a large fire-dog, being simply a length of bamboo supported on two small pairs of legs. If you are a Samoan, you lay your cheek on this neck-breaking arrangement, and sleep without moving till the daylight. We preferred our cloaks rolled up under our heads.

The invaluable little mosquito tent served as dressing-room to all of us, and very glad we were of it, for there were still a good many visitors dotted about the floor of the great guest-house, smoking and chattering; and none of them had any idea that a white woman could object to performing her evening toilet in public, any more than a Samoan girl, who simply takes her "pillow" down from the rafters, spreads her mat, and lies down just as she is.

No bed-clothes were needed, for the heat was severe. We fidgeted about on our stony couch, elbowed each other a good deal, slept occasionally, and woke again to hear the eternal chatter still going on outside our tent, and see the light still glowing through the calico. It was exactly like going to bed in the middle of a bazaar, after making a couch out of one of the stalls.

At last, however, the light went out; Iva, Pula-Ulu, and their saucy little handmaiden and relative, Kafi, got under their mosquito curtains, quite a little walk away, at the other side of the dome, all the guests departed, and there was peace.

Next morning my friends went away and I was left to study the life of a Samoan village alone, with only such aid as old Iva's very few English words could give me, since I did not know above half-a-dozen sentences of the Samoan tongue. There were no great feasts, no ceremonies or festivals while I was in Falepunu, only the ordinary everyday life of the village, which has changed extremely little since the coming of the white men, although that event is three generations old.

Perhaps the greatest change is in the native treatment of guests. Hospitable, polite and pleasant the Samoans have always been and still are; but in these days, when a white visitor stays in a native house, he is expected to give presents when parting, that fully cover the value of his stay. This is contrary to the original Samoan laws of hospitality, which still hold good in the case of natives. No Samoan ever thinks of paying for accommodation in another's house, no matter how long his stay may be; nor is there the least hesitation in taking or giving whatever food a traveller may want on his way. But the white visitors who have stayed in Samoa have been so liberal with their gifts, that the native now expects presents as a right. He would still scorn to take money for his hospitality, but money's worth is quite another matter.

Otherwise, the "faa Samoa" holds with astonishing completeness. Natives who have boxes full of trade prints, bought from the lonely little European store that every island owns, will dress themselves on ceremonial occasions in finely plaited mats, or silky brown tappa cloth. Houses on the verge of Apia, the European capital, are built precisely as houses were in the days of Captain Cook; though perhaps an incongruous bicycle or sewing-machine, standing up against the central pillars, may strike a jarring note. Men and women who have been to school, and can tell you the geographical boundaries of Montenegro, and why Charles I.'s head was cut off—who know all about the Russo-Japanese war, wear full European dress when you ask them to your house, and sing "In the Gloaming" or "Sail Away" to your piano—will take part in a native "siva" or dancing festival, dressed in a necklace, a kilt, and unlimited cocoanut-oil, and may be heard of, when the chiefs are out fighting, roaming round the mountains potting their enemies with illegally acquired Winchesters, and cutting off the victims' heads afterwards. The "faa Samoa" holds the Samoan, old and young, educated or primitive, through life and to death.

Uneventful, yet very happy, was the little week that time allowed me among the pleasant folk of Falepunu. When the low, yellow rays of the rising sun shot under the wide eaves of the great guest-house, and striped the white coral floor with gold, and the little green parrakeets began to twitter in the trees outside, and the long sleepy murmur of the surf on the reef, blown landward by the sunrise wind, swelled to a deep-throated choral song—then, I used to slip into my clothes, come out from my mosquito tent, and see the beauty of the new young day. Dawn on a South Sea Island ! The rainbow fancies of childhood painted out in real—the

> Dreams of youth come back again,
> Dropping on the ripened grain
> As once upon the flower.

Iva, Pula-Ulu, and Kafi would be awake also, and moving about. No minute of daylight is ever wasted in these tropical islands; where all the year round the dawn lingers till after five, and the dark comes down long before seven. None of my house-mates had much toilet to make. They simply got up from their mats, hung up the pillows, put the mosquito nets away, and walked forth, clad in the cotton lava-lavas of yesterday, which they had not taken off when they lay down. Taking soap and bundles of cocoanut fibre off the ever useful rafters, they went to bathe in the nearest river.

Before long they came back, fresh and clean, and wearing a new lava-lava, yesterday's hanging limp and wet from their hands—the Samoan generally washes his garments at the same time as himself. Then Iva boiled water for my tea, and produced cold baked bread-fruit and stewed fish, and I breakfasted, taking care to leave a good share of tea, butter, and any tinned food I might open, for the family to enjoy afterwards. It is a positive crime in Samoa to eat up any delicacy all by yourself—an offence indeed, which produces about the same impression on the Samoan mind as cheating at cards does upon the well-bred European. The natives themselves usually eat twice a day, about noon, and some time in the evening; but a Samoan is always ready to eat at any hour, provided there is something nice to be got. Good old Iva enjoyed my tea and tinned milk extremely, and so did her pet cronies. They used to call in now and then, in the hope of getting some—a hope liberally fulfilled by Iva, who distributed my goods among them with charming courtesy, and a total innocence of any possible objection on my part, which disarmed all criticism. I might have taken anything she had, from her Sunday lava-lava to her fattest fowl, and kept it or given it away; equally without remonstrance. Such is the "faa Samoa." That any one continues to retain anything worth having, under such circumstances, speaks well for the natural unselfishness of the people. They may be a little greedy with the whites—much as we ourselves should no doubt be greedy, if half-a-dozen millionaires were to quarter themselves in our modest mansions, or come to stay in our quiet suburbs—but among themselves they are wonderfully self-restrained, and at the same time faultlessly generous.

After my breakfast, following the agreeable Samoan

custom, I lay down on a mat and dozed a little, to feel the wind blowing over my face from the sea, as I wandered half in and half out of the lands of dreams, and saw with semi-closed eyes the sun of the hot morning hours turn the green of the bush into a girdle of burning emerald-gold, clasped round the pleasant gloom of the dark over-circling roof. Pula-Ulu was out on "ploys" of his own; Kafi had gone to fish, or to flirt; Iva, pulling a fly-cover over her body, slept like a sheeted corpse on her own mat, on the other side of the central pillars.

After an hour or two—there was never any time in Falepunu—I would rise, and call for Kafi, and we would walk slowly through the smiting sun, to a fairy-like spot in the lovely bay of Falefa—a terrace of grey rock clothed with ferns, and shaded by thick-growing palms and chestnut and mango trees. The great white waterfall, cool as nothing else is cool in this burning land, thundered within fifty yards of us, turning the salt waters of the bay to brackish freshness, and spraying the hot air with its own delicious cold. Here we swam and dived for hours at a time, getting an old canoe sometimes, and paddling it up under the very spray of the fall—upsetting it perhaps, and tumbling out while Kafi yelled as if she could not swim a stroke, and anticipated immediate death (being, of course, absolutely amphibious). A pretty little minx was Kafi, small and black-eyed and piquante, always with a scarlet hibiscus bloom, or a yellow and white frangipani flower, stuck behind her ear; always tossing her head, and swaying her beautiful olive arms, and patting her small arched foot on the ground, when she stood waiting for me under the palms, as if she could not keep her elastic little frame from dancing of itself. Pretty saucy, mischievous little Kafi, she gave me many a bad moment wickedly calling out, "S'ark!" when we were swimming far from land, in places where it was just conceivable that a shark might be; but I forgive her everything, for the sake of that unique and charming small personality of hers. Not even Fangati, the languorous sweet-eyed Taupo of Apia, can compete with her in my memories of fascinating island girls and pleasant companions.

One morning—it must have been somewhere near the middle of the day—Iva and Kafi and I were walking back from Falefa, tired out and very hungry (at least, I will answer for myself), when we were hailed from the house of a chief, and asked to come in. We did so, all saying, as we bowed our heads to step under the low eaves: "Talofa!" (my love to you), and being answered with a loud chorus: "Talofa, tamaite! (lady); Talofa, Iva; Talofa, Kafi." I took my seat cross-legged on the mats, and looked about me. All round the house in a circle were seated a number of men, about a dozen, each with a bundle of cleaned and carded cocoanut husk fibre, called sinnet, beside him, and a slender plait of sinnet in his hand, to which every minute added on an inch or so of length. It was evidently a "bee" for making sinnet plait, and it solved a problem that had perplexed me a good deal—namely, how all the thousands of sinnet used instead of nails in building Samoan houses, were ever obtained. Afterwards I learned that Samoan men occupy much of their unlimited leisure time in plaiting sinnet. The bundle of husk and the neat little coil of plait are to a Samoan man what her needle and stockings are to a Scotch housewife; he works away mechanically with them in many an odd moment, all going to swell the big roll that is gradually widening and fattening up among the rafters. Some of the sinnet thus made is as fine as fine twine, yet enormously strong.

My hosts, it seemed, were just going to knock off work for the present, and have some kava, and I was not sorry to join them, for kava is a wonderfully refreshing drink among these tropical islands, and wholesome besides. It was made Tongan fashion, by pounding the dry woody root with stones, pouring water over the crushed fragments, and straining the latter out with a wisp of hibiscus fibre. A handsome wooden bowl was used, circular in form, and supported on a number of legs—the whole being carved out of one solid block of wood. The ancient Samoan way of preparation was to chew the kava root, and deposit the chewed lumps in the bowl, afterwards pouring on the water; but this practice has died out in many parts of Samoa, though in some of the islands it is still kept up.

My kava on this occasion was not chewed, and I was thankful, as it is unmannerly to refuse it under any circumstances.

The kava made, the highest chief present called the names, according to etiquette, as in Tonga, in a loud resounding voice. I answered to my own (which came first, as a foreign chief) by clapping my hands, in the correct fashion, and drained the cocoanut bowl that was handed me. Kava, as I had already learned, quenches thirst, removes fatigue, clears the brain, and is exceedingly cooling. If drunk in excess, it produces a temporary paralysis of the legs, without affecting the head; but very few natives and hardly any whites do drink more than is good for them.

After the kava, two young men came running in from the bush, carrying between them an immense black wooden bowl, spoon-shaped, three-legged, and filled with something exactly like bread-and-milk, which they had been concocting at the cooking-pits. It was raining now, and the thrifty youths had taken off their clothes, for fear of spoiling them, yet they were dressed with perfect decency, and much picturesqueness. Their attire consisted of thick fringed kilts, made of pieces of green banana leaves (a banana leaf is often nine or ten feet long, and two or three wide), and something like a feather boa, hung round the neck, of the same material. Clad in these rain-proof garments, they ran laughing through the downpour, their bowl covered with another leaf, and deposited it on the floor, safe and hot.

A section of banana-leaf was now placed on the mat beside each person, also a skewer, made from the midrib of the cocoanut leaf. Then the servers dipped both hands generously into the food, and filled each leaf with the bread-and-milk, or "tafolo," which turned out to be lumps of bread-fruit stewed in thick white cream expressed from the meat of the cocoanut. Better eating no epicure could desire ; and the food is exceedingly nourishing. We ate with the cocoanut skewers, on which each creamy lump was speared ; and when all was done we folded the leaf-plates into a cone, and drank the remaining cream. Afterwards, Iva and Kafi and I took our leave, and I hurried back to Falepunu, feeling that my hunger and fatigue had been magically removed, and that I was ready for anything more in the way of exercise that the day might produce.

I had no watch or clock with me, and this was certainly an advantage, since it compelled me to measure time in the pleasant island fashion, which simply marks out the day vaguely by hot hours and cool hours, and the recurring calls of hunger. No one who has not tried it can conceive the limitless freedom and leisure that comes of this custom. Time is simply wiped out. One discovers, all of a sudden, that one has been groaning under an unbearable and unnecessary tyranny all one's life—whence all the hurry-scurry of civilisation ?—why do people rush to catch trains and omnibuses, and hasten to make and keep appointments, and have meals at rigidly fixed times, whether they are hungry or not? These are the things that make life short. It is illimitably long, and curiously sweet and simple, in the island world. At first one finds it hard to realise that no one is ever waiting for dinner, or wanting to go to bed—that eating and sleeping are the impulse of a moment, and not a set task—but once realised, the sense of emancipation is exquisite and complete.

The Samoan does what he wants, when he wishes, and if he does not wish a thing, does not do it at all. According to the theology of our youthful days, he ought in consequence to become a fiend in human shape; but he does nothing of the kind. He is the most amiable creature on earth's round ball. Angry voices, loud tones even, are never heard in a Samoan house. Husbands never come home drunk in the evening and ill use their wives; wives never nag at their husbands; no one screams at children, or snaps at house-mates and neighbours. Houses are never dirty; clothes are always kept clean; nothing is untidy, nothing superfluous or ugly. There is therefore no striking ground for ill-temper or peevishness; and amiability and courtesy reign supreme. The Samoan has his faults—sensuality, indolence, a certain bluntness of perception as to the white man's laws of property—but they are slight indeed compared with the faults of the ordinary European. And, concerning the tendency to exploit the latter person, which has been already mentioned, it must not be forgotten that if a white man is known to be destitute and in want, the very people who would have eagerly sought for presents from him while he was thought to be rich, will take him in, feed and lodge him, without a thought of payment, and will never turn him out if he does not choose to go.

Sometimes, in the long, lazy, golden afternoons, a woman or two would drop in, and bring with her some little dainty as a present for the stranger. "Palusani" was the favourite, made, as in Niué, of taro-tops and cocoanut; the cook grating down the meat of the nuts, and straining water through the oily mass thus produced. The cream is very cleverly wrapped up inside the leaves, and these are again enveloped in larger and tougher leaves. While baking, the cream thickens and condenses, and permeates the taro-tops completely. The resulting dish is a spinach-like mixture of dark green and white, odd to look at, but very rich and dainty to eat.

Another present was a sort of sweetmeat, also made from cocoanut cream, which was baked into small brown balls like chocolates, each containing a lump of thickened cream inside. These were generally brought tied up in tiny square packets of green banana leaf. Small dumpy round puddings, made of native arrowroot, bananas, cocoanut, and sugar-cane juice, used also to be brought, tied up in the inevitable banana-leaf; and baked wild pigeon, tender and juicy, was another offering not at all unacceptable. As a typical millionaire, possessed of several dresses, change for some sovereigns, and countless tins of salmon, I was expected to give an occasional *quid pro quo*, which usually took the form of tinned fish or meat, and was much appreciated.

I do not know how late it was, one night—the moon had been up for many hours, but no one seemed to want to go to bed—when I heard a sound of splashing and laughing from the brightly silvered lagoon beyond the belt of palms. I went out, and saw thirty or forty of the native women wading about in the shallow water inside the reef, catching fish. It looked interesting, so I shed an outer skirt or two, kilted up what remained, and ran down the white shelving beach, all pencilled with the feathery shadows of tossing palms, into the glassy knee-deep water. How warm it was! as hot as a tepid bath at home—how the gorgeous moonlight flashed back from the still lagoon, as from a huge silver shield! The whole place was as light as day; not as a Samoan day, which is too like the glare from an open furnace to be pleasant at all times, but at least, as light as a grey English afternoon.

The girls, wearing only a small lava-lava, were wading in the water, some carrying a big, wide net made out of fine fibres beaten from the bark of a Samoan tree; others trailing two long fringes of plaited palm leaves, about a yard deep, and twenty or thirty yards long. These were drawn through the water about twenty yards apart, the girls walking along for a few minutes in two parallel rows, and then quickly bringing the ends of the palm fringes together in an open V shape. The net was placed across the narrow end of the V, and from the wide end two or three splashed noisily down the enclosed space, driving before them into the net all the little silvery fish who had been gathered together by the sudden closing in of the palm-leaf fringes. Then there was laughing and crying out, and the moon shone down on a cluster of beautiful gold-bronze figures, graceful as statues, stretching out their small pretty hands and wild curly heads, diamond-gemmed with scattered drops of water, over the gathered-in net, now sparkling and quivering with imprisoned life. The captured fish were dropped into a plaited palm-leaf basket; and then the two lines of girls separated once more, and marched on through the warm silvery water, singing as they went.

I think, though I do not know, that this simple sport (which was, after all, a necessary task as well) went on nearly all the night. The Samoan is not easily bored, and no one minds losing a night's rest, when there is all the hot day to doze on the mats. I gave up an hour or so, and returned to the guest-house, loaded with presents of fish. It was quite absurd, but I wanted to go to bed, silly inferior white person that I was! so I crept under my calico tent, and "turned in," feeling amid the stir and chatter, the singing and wandering to and fro, of those moonlit small hours, exceedingly like a child that has to follow nurse and go to sleep, while all the grown-ups are still enjoying themselves downstairs.

The night before I left for Apia once more, I bought my farewell presents at the solitary little store that was marooned away down on the beach at Falefa, and bore on its house front the mysterious legend—" MISIMOA "— all in one word—translatable as " Mr. Moore ! " Advised by the trader's native wife, I got several lava-lavas for the old chief and his wife, also a " Sunday frock " piece of white muslin, and some lace, for Iva herself. Poor old Iva! she could not afford herself many clothes, being only a caretaker in the great house; and I had felt sorry for her when I saw her missionary-meeting frock—only an old blue print. All the Samoan women love to turn out in trade finery on Sundays, and a white muslin, with lace, made exactly like a British nightdress, is the height of elegance and good form. I gave Pula-Ulu, furthermore, a yellow shirt spotted with red horses; and as a final gift for Iva, I selected a large white English bath-towel, with crimson stripes and edge. This last I knew would certainly be Iva's best week-day visiting costume for some time to come.

All these splendours I tied up in a brown paper parcel, and left on my portmanteau. Samoan etiquette is very strict about the giving and receiving of presents, and prescribes absolute ignorance, on the part of the recipient, of any such intention being about; but Iva could not resist pinching the parcel, and whispering —" Misi! what 'sat?"

" Ki-ki, Iva " (food), I answered.

" You lie!" said Iva delightedly, poking me in the ribs. She had no idea that she was not expressing herself with the most perfect elegance and courtesy; the Samoan tongue has no really rude words, and Samoans often do not realise the quality of our verbal unpoliteness.

Next morning, however, when my " solofanua " (animal that runs along the ground = horse) was standing out under the bread-fruit trees, and all my goods had been tied about the saddle, till the venerable animal looked like nothing on earth but the White Knight's own horse—Iva and Pula-Ulu, bidding me good-bye with the utmost dignity, did not even glance at the parcels which I threw across the house, at their heads, narrowly escaping hitting their old grey hair. This was etiquette. In Samoa, a formal gift must be thrown high in the air at the recipient, so as to fall at his feet; and he must not pick it up at once, but simply say " Fafekai " (thank you) with a cold and unmoved accent, waiting until the giver is gone to examine the present. The inner meaning of the custom is the supposed worthlessness of the gift, when compared with the recipient's merits —it is mere rubbish, to be cast away—and the demeanour of the recipient himself is intended to suggest that in any case he is not eager for gifts.

A long, hot ride of twenty miles back to Apia and civilisation filled up the day. The pendulum of Time, held back for a whole dreamy, lazy week, had begun to swing once more; and all day I worried about the hour I should get in. I was late for *table d'hôte*; I was met by a "little bill"; and the mail had come in since I left. Thus Apia welcomed me; and thus I "took up the white man's burden" once again.

. . . . . .

"Talofa!" says a gentle yet insistent voice.

It is only half-past six, and I am exceedingly sleepy, so I bury my face in the pillow, and try not to hear.

"Talofa!" (How do you do?), repeats the voice, a little louder, and my basket armchair creaks to the sudden drop of a substantial weight. I open my eyes, and see, through the dim midst of the mosquito-curtains, the taupo, Fangati, sitting beside my bed.

Fangati is my "flennie," and that means a good deal more in Samoa than the cold English word "friend," from which it is derived. She attached herself to me upon my arrival in Apia, some weeks ago, and has ever since continued to indicate, in the gentle Samoan way, that she prefers my company to that of any other white woman on the island. There is nothing contrary to Samoan etiquette in her calling upon me at 6.30 a.m., for Samoa knows not times or seasons, save such as are pleasing to itself for the moment. If I were suffering from sleeplessness and went to call on Fangati at midnight, she would certainly awake, get up off her mat, take a fan in her hand, sit down cross-legged on the floor, ready to talk or yarn for the rest of the night—without the smallest surprise or discomposure. So, aspiring after the ideal of Samoan politeness, I feel bound to shake myself awake, and talk.

Fangati is very much "got up" this morning. She is a chief's daughter, of high rank, and her wardrobe is an extensive one. To-day she has a short tunic of tappa (native cloth, beaten out of the bark of a paper mulberry tree), satiny brown in colour, and immensely pinked and fringed. This is worn over a lava-lava, or kilt, of purple trade print, reaching a little below her knees. Her beautiful pale brown arms (all Samoan women have exquisitely shaped arms) and small arched brown feet are bare. In her thick, wavy hair she has placed one large scarlet hibiscus flower, and there are three or four long necklaces round her neck, made of the crimson rind of a big scented berry, cut into curly strips. One of these, as a matter of common courtesy, she flings over my nightdress as we talk, and smiles sweetly at the brilliant effect achieved.

"Ni—ice!" says Fangati. She can speak quite a good deal of English, but she smooths and trims it prettily to suit her own taste, and the harsh language of the black North loses all its roughness on her lips.

She has come to tell me that there will be dancing at the village of Mulinuu this afternoon, as it is the German Emperor's birthday, and a great many kegs of salt beef and boxes of biscuit have been given to the villages by the Government, to celebrate the day. (Not such a bad method of encouraging loyalty in a newly acquired colony, either.) There are to be some taupo dances, and Fangati will take a leading part. Therefore I must be certain to come and see my "flennie" perform. This matter settled, Fangati gets up and drifts to the washstand, tastes my cold cream and makes a face over it, points to a jug of cold tea and says, "You give?" shares the luxury with her ancient chaperon, who is sitting on the doormat, and then melts away down the verandah, dreamily smoking a native-made cigarette.

It is now time to explain what a taupo is, and why the dances to-day will be especially attractive.

Most Samoan villages possess a taupo, or mistress of the ceremonies, who has many duties, and many privileges as well. She is always young, pretty, and well-born, being usually the daughter of a high chief. She remains unmarried during her term of office, which may last for many years, or for only a few months. The propriety of her conduct is guaranteed by the constant presence of certain old women, who always accompany her on visits or journeys. Sometimes her train is increased by the addition of a dwarf or a cripple, who seems to act a part somewhat similar to that of a mediæval court fool. Her duties oblige her to receive and entertain all guests or travellers who pass through her village; to make kava (the universal drink of the Pacific islands) for them, welcome them to the guest-house, which is a part of every Samoan settlement, and dance for their amusement. She is treated with royal honours by the villagers, always handsomely clothed, and luxuriously fed on pig and chicken, and never required to do any hard work, while the other girls have to be content with taro-root and bread-fruit, and are obliged to work in the fields, carry water, and fish on the reef in the burning tropic sun. When there is a festival, she takes the principal part in the dances; and when the tribes are at war (as occasionally happens even to-day) the taupo, dressed as a warrior, marches out with the ceremonial parade of the troops, and acts as a *vivandière* during the fight, carrying water to the soldiers, and bringing ammunition when required. This duty is not one of the safest, for, although no Samoan warrior knowingly fires on any woman, much less on a taupo, stray bullets take no account of persons, and many a beautiful young " Maid of the Village," in times past, has justified her warrior dress by meeting with a soldier's death.

Well-mannered as all Samoan women are, the taupo is especially noted for the elegance of her demeanour. My "flennie's" bearing reminds me oddly at times of the manner of a London great lady, accustomed to constant receiving, and become in consequence almost mechanically "gracious." She never moves abruptly; her speech is calm and self-possessed, and her accent soft and *trainant*. There are, however, taupos and taupos. Vao, who lives just across the way, is by way of being an "advanced woman." She plays native cricket in a man's singlet and a kilt, dances a knife dance that tries the nerves of every one that looks on, wears her hair short and is exceedingly independent, and a little scornful. Vao does not want to marry she says ; but I have an idea, all the same, that if just the right sort of young chief came along, with just the irresistible number of baskets of food (these take the place of bouquets and chocolate boxes among Samoan wooers), Vao would renounce her dignity of taupo just as readily as other Maids of the Village have done when Mr. Right appeared. On her wedding day she would dance her last dance for the villagers, according to immemorial custom, and thenceforward live the quiet home-life of the Samoan wife and mother, all the footlights out, all the admiring audience gone, and only the little coral-carpeted, brown roofed cottage with its small home duties and quiet home affections left.

Then there is the taupo Fuamoa—but of her more anon, as the Victorian novelist used to say.

Early in the afternoon, when the sun was at its very hottest—and what that heat can be, at 13° south, in the height of the hot season, let Pacific travellers say—I made my way down to Mulinuu under a big umbrella, and took my place on the mats laid to accommodate the spectators. The dancing was in full swing. A long row of young men, dressed in short kilts of many-coloured bark strips—red, pink, green, yellow, purple—and decked out with anklets of green creepers and necklaces of big scarlet berries, which looked just like enormous coral beads, were twirling and pirouetting, retreating, advancing, and waving their arms, in wonderfully perfect time. The Samoan, man or woman, is born with a metronome concealed somewhere in his or her works, to all appearance. Certainly the exquisite sense of time and movement displayed in children's games, grown-up dances, and all the songs of the people, seems almost supernatural, as the result of unaided impulse.

The arms and hands play a remarkable part in the dance. Every finger is made a means of expression, and the simultaneous fluttering and waving of the arms of an entire *corps-de-ballet* can be compared to nothing but the petals of a bed of flowers, sent hither and thither by a capricious wind.

There is no instrumental music, for the Samoans—strange to say, for a music-loving people—have no instruments at all, unless one may count the occasional British mouth-organ. But the sonorous, full-voiced chanting of the chorus that sits cross-legged on the grass at a little distance, leaves nothing to be desired in the way of orchestra. A favourite tune, which one is sure to hear at every Samoan dance-meeting or "siva" is the following, commenced with a loud " Ai, ai ! "

It is first sung very slowly, and gradually increased

in speed until the dancers give up in despair. The faster they have danced before giving in, the louder is the applause.

By-and-by the men conclude their dance, and retire, loudly clapped, and followed by cries of " Malo ! malo ! " (well done). A short interval follows. The many-coloured crowd seated on the grass fans itself, smokes cigarettes, and chatters ; the dry palm-fronds rustle in the burning sky overhead, harshly mimicking the cool whisper of forest leaves in gentler climes. Suddenly six handsome young men, splendidly decorated, their brown skins satiny with rubbing of perfumed cocoanut-oil, rush into the middle of the green, and in the midst comes a seventh, smaller, slighter, and handsomer than the rest. What a beautiful youth ! almost too young, one would have thought, for the smart black moustache that curves above his upper lip—wonderfully active, supple, and alive in every movement—a skin like brown Lyons silk, limbs—— Why, it is a girl ! the taupo Fuamoa, dressed (or rather undressed) as a Samoan warrior, and full to the brim of mischief, sparkle, and fun. She wears a fringe of coloured bark-strips round her waist, and a very big kilt of scarlet and white striped cotton underneath. The rest of her attire consists of a necklace of whale's teeth, inestimably valuable, a string of red berries, and a tall helmet, or busby, apparently made of brilliant yellow fur. Her exquisitely moulded figure is as Nature made it, save for a rubbing of cocoanut-oil, that only serves to bring out the full beauty of every curving line. Strange to say, the black-painted moustache is wonderfully becoming, so

too is the imposing helmet; and does not Fuamoa know
it? and is not she saucy, and dainty, and kitten-like, as
she frisks and plays in the centre of the dance, making
the prettiest of eyes at the audience, and flashing her
white teeth delightedly under the wicked little black
moustache? She is a celebrated dancer, being only sur-
passed on the island by one other taupo—Vao, who is
not appearing to-day. You would never think, as her
little brown feet twinkle over the grass, and her statuesque
brown arms wave above her head, while the merry smile
ceaselessly comes and goes, that Fuamoa is suffering
positive agonies all the time, from the splendid war-
helmet that adorns her head; yet that is the truth.
One must indeed suffer to be beautiful, as a Samoan
taupo. Before the helmet is put on, the girl's long thick
hair is drawn up to the top of her head, and twisted as
tightly as strong arms can twist it, so that her very eye-
brows are pulled out of place, and every hair is a separate
torture. Then the great helmet is fastened on as firmly
as a rock, with countless tight cords, and the dancer is
ready for her part, with a scalp on fire and a torturing
headache, which will certainly last until she can take the
cruel decoration off.

There are several taupo dances this afternoon, but
only two of the girls have the courage to wear the helmet.
Fangati, my little "flennie," frankly confesses that she
cannot stand it. "He made me cly-y-y! too much!"
she says, and shows me the pretty wreath of crimson
berry peelings and green leaves that is to adorn her own
curly head.

These helmets, it may be noted, are not made of fur,
as one might suppose at a first glance. The material is
human hair, cut from the head of a Samoan girl, and
dyed bright yellow with lime. In time of war, it is a

common thing for a girl to offer up her beautiful tresses to make a helmet for father, husband, or lover; and the wearer of such a gift is as proud as a knight of Arthur's Round Table may have been, bearing on his crest his lady's little pearl-broidered glove.

It is Fangati's turn to dance now, and out she trips, wearing a valuable mat of the finest plait, her pretty wreath, countless scarlet necklaces, and a modest girdle of coloured silk. Fangati has the prettiest foot and hand in Apia, and she is a dainty little dancer—not so marvellously agile and spirited as Fuamoa, and with much less of "devil" in her composition, but a pretty and a pleasant creature to watch. She has reached the twenties, and gone nearly half-way through them, so that she is in a fair way to become an old maid, according to Samoan ideas; but she still retains her maiden state, and declares she will not marry, in spite of good offers from several chiefs. It is said in Apia that she is proud, and wishes to marry a white man—which is much as if a charming English country girl should determine to mate with nothing less than a duke. Country lasses do marry dukes, but not often; and there is not much more chance of my "flennie's" attaining her ambition, unless Providence is very kind.

The ordinary Samoan is obliged to do a little work now and then, since yam patches must be cultivated, bread-fruit plucked and cooked, banana and arrowroot puddings made, fish caught, nets woven, houses built and repaired. But all in all there is not much to do, and the real business of life in Samoa is amusement. *Le monde où l'on s'amuse*, for most people means a certain circle of London and Paris; but for all who have travelled in the South Seas, it means, once and for all, Samoa.

The taupo is of course at the head and front of every diversion, for, little as the other people have to do, she has less, having nothing at all. A day at Papaseea is one of her favourite delights. During my stay in Samoa, one of these pleasant native picnics was organised for me, and I set off on a lovely morning for the "Sliding Rock," accompanied by fifteen native and half-caste girls, stowed away in six buggies. It was a long drive in the burning sun, and afterwards a long rough walk through the bush, among wild pineapples, scarlet hibiscus, tall, creamy-flowered, pungent, scented ginger-bushes, red-fruited cacao, quaint mammee-apple trees, mangoes, Pacific chestnuts, and countless other strange tropic growths. Hot and tired as we all were, the Papaseea rock, when we reached it, seemed a perfect Paradise.

Imagine a deep gorge in the heart of green, heavily-wooded hills ; at the bottom, a narrow channel shaded by overhanging trees, where the pure mountain water runs clear and cold and deep, amber-brown pools quiver at the foot of white plunging falls—one only some seven feet high, the other a good thirty. This last was the Sliding Rock, over which we were all going to fling ourselves *à la* Sappho by-and-by, only with less melancholy consequences. It looked formidable enough, and when Fangati and the others, with cries of delight, pulled off their dresses, wound white and pink and green cotton lava-lavas over one shoulder, and round from waist to knee, crowned themselves picturesquely with woven fern-leaves, and plunged shrieking over the fall, I began to wish I had not come, or coming, had not promised to "slide." However, there was no help for it, so I got into my English bathing-dress, which excited peals of merry laughter, because of its "continuations," waded down the stream, and sitting in the rush of the water, held tightly on to a rock at each side, and looked over my own toes at the foaming, roaring thirty feet drop.

It was all over in a minute. Just an unclasping of unwilling hands from the safe black rocks, a fierce tug from the tearing stream, an exceedingly unpleasant instant when one realised that there was no going back now at any price, and that the solid earth had slipped away as it does in the ghastly drop of a nightmare dream; then nothing in the world but a loud long roar, and a desperate holding of the breath, while the helpless body shot down to the bottom of the deep brown pool and up again—and at last, the warm air of heaven filling one's grateful lungs in big gasps, as one reached the surface, and swam across to the other side of the pool, firmly resolved on no account to do it again, now that it was over.

It was pleasant, afterwards, to sit among the rocks above the fall, and watch one after another of the native and half-caste girls—including a very charming and highly educated half-American, who had been to college in San Francisco, and to smart society dances in Samoa—rush madly over the fall, leaving behind them as they went a long, loud yell, like the whistle of a train going into a tunnel. One native girl daringly went down head first; another, standing incautiously near the edge of the fall, lost her balance, and simply sat down on the pool below, dropping through the air with arms and legs outspread like a starfish. Fangati seized a friend in her arms and tumbled over the verge with her, in a perfect Catherine wheel of revolving limbs. It was hours before the riotous party grew tired, and even then, only the sight of large green leaves being laid out on the stones, and palm-leaf baskets being opened, brought them out of the water, and got them into their little sleeveless tunics and gracefully draped kilts. By this time, the pretty Samoan-American's mother had laid out the "ki-ki"—baked fowl and pig, taro-root, yams, bananas, pineapples, guavas, European delicacies such as cake and pies, and native dainties, including the delicious, *palusami* of which I have spoken before. The drinking cocoanuts had been husked and opened by the boy who brought the food, and there they stood among the stones, rows of rough ivory cups, lined with smooth ivory jelly of the young soft meat, and filled with fresh sweet water, such as is never to be tasted out of the cocoanut-land. Our plates were sections of green banana-leaf; our forks were our fingers. And when every one had fed, and felt happy and lazy, we all lay among the rocks above the fall, in the green shadow of the trees, and did nothing whatever till evening. Then we climbed back to the road, and drove home, six buggies full of laughing brown and white humanity, crowned and wreathed with green ferns, and singing the sweet, sad song of Samoa—"Goodbye, my flennie"—the song that was written by a native only a few years ago, and has already become famous over the whole Pacific. It is the farewell song of every island lover, the melody that soars above the melancholy rattling of the anchor chains on every outward-bound schooner that spreads her white wings upon the breast of the great South Seas. And for those who have known the moonlight nights of those enchanted shores, have smelt the frangipani flower, and listened to the soft singing girls in the endless, golden afternoons, and watched the sun go down upon an empty, sailless sea, behind the weird pandanus and drooping palms—the sweet song of the islands will ring in the heart for ever. In London rush and rain and gloom, in the dust and glitter of fevered Paris, in the dewy cold green woods of English country homes, the Samoan air will whisper, calling, calling, calling—back to the murmur of the palms, and the singing of the coral reef, and the purple tropic night once more.

"GOOD-BYE, MY FLENNIE."

(Song, with Samoan words, English beginning to each verse.)

CHAPTER XV

Southward to New Zealand—Into the Hot-Water Country—Coaching Days come back—The Early Victorian Inn—The Fire and Snow of Ruapehu—A Hotel run wild—Hot Lakes and Steaming Rivers—The Devil's Trumpet—The Valley of the Burning Fountains—Waking up the Champagne Lake.

OF the other island groups that I visited during that pleasant year or two of wandering—Strange Fiji, exquisite Norfolk Island, the wicked, unknown New Hebrides—I have told elsewhere. But before the great P. & O. liner carried me away from Sydney on the well-known track across the seas to England and home, I had a journey through New Zealand that was second to nothing in the world, for pure enjoyment, but the unsurpassable Islands themselves.

New Zealand is not yet fully opened up—that was what the geography books said in my school days. The saying, like most geography-book information, slipped through my mind easily, and did not create any marked impression. The marked impression came later, when I went half round the world to see New Zealand, and discovered that I could not take train to just anywhere I chose. It seemed incredible, in a country as highly civilised as France or Germany, that coaches—not the ornamental tourist brand, run as an accompaniment to railways, but real Early Victorian coaches, with "no frills on them" of any sort or kind—were the only

THE HOT LAKE DISTRICT 339

means of transit, save boats, to a great part of the famous hot lake and river district of the North Island. One could go to Rotorua, the most remarkable collection of geysers and hot lakes, direct by rail from Auckland. But the lovely Wanganui River, the beautiful up-country bush, and whole duchies of hot-water and mud-volcano land, could only be "done" by coach and boat.

This made the journey more interesting, on the whole, though it was a little amazing at first to leave the railway far behind, and strike out right into the early nineteenth century. One should have worn side-curls, a spencer, and a poke bonnet, instead of the ordinary tourist coat and skirt and useful straw hat, to feel quite in character with the mud-splashed coach, its six insides, two outsides, and four struggling straining horses; the days of wind and shower, the hurried meals eaten at lonely little wayside inns, and the nights spents in strange barrack-like, barn-like places, where the stable was of more importance than the house, and every one always arose and fled like a ghost at the early dawn of day.

But first, after the railway town and railway hotel were left behind, came Wanganui River, a whole day of it; nearly sixty miles of exquisite loveliness, viewed in perfect comfort from the canopied deck of a river steamer. The Wanganui has been called New Zealand's Rhine, but it no more resembles the Rhine than it resembles a garden-party or an ostrich farm. It has nothing whatever in common with Germany's great historic river but its beauty; and the beauty of the Wanganui is of an order very far indeed removed from that of the ancient castle-crowned streams of Europe which are strewn with records of dead and decaying æons of human life. Solitude, stillness, absolute, deathly loneliness are the keynotes of Wanganui scenery. Shut in by fold on fold of great green mountain peaks, scarp on scarp of fern-wreathed precipice, one can almost fancy that the swift little paddle-steamer is churning her way for the first time into solitudes never seen of man. Now and then a Maori dug-out canoe, long and thin and upturned at the ends, may be sighted riding under the willows, or gliding down-stream to the swift paddle-strokes of its dusky-faced occupant. At rare intervals, too, the spell of silent loneliness is broken by the sight of some tiny river-side settlement perched on a great green height—half a dozen wooden houses, and a tin-roofed church: the whole being labelled with some extraordinarily pretentious name. One of our passengers that day got in at London, and went on to Jerusalem; another was booked from Nazareth to Athens!

All New Zealanders are *not* Maories, despite the hazy ideas as to colour which exist at home. There is a little trifle of nine hundred thousand full-blooded white settlers, to compare with the few thousand native Maories still left, in the land they once owned from sea to sea. Still, the Maori in New Zealand is an unmistakable fact, and a most picturesque fact into the bargain. To see a family taking deck passage on the boat—handsome dark-eyed women, with rosy cheeks in spite of their olive skins, and beautifully waved black hair; bright elfish little children; dogs and cats and a sack or two for luggage—is an interesting spot in the day's experience, especially when some patronising passenger, accustomed to "natives" in other countries, gets one of the delightful set-downs the Maori can give so effectively. For all their shapeless clothing and heavy blankets, hatless heads and tattooed lips and chins, the New Zealand

Maories are very much "all there"; and when the patronising saloon passenger struts up to one, and remarks: "Tenakoe (good-day), Polly! You got ums nicey little fellow there, eh?" "Polly" will probably reply in excellent English: "My name happens to be Te Rangi, not Polly; and as for the child you are referring to, I believe it belongs to the lady in the yellow plaid sitting aft!"

At the end of the day comes an hotel, standing on a wooded cliff above the river, and looking down upon a long lovely stretch of winding water and high-piled forest. The night is spent here, and in the morning comes the coach, with its team of four fine satin-skinned bays, its many-coated driver, its portmanteaux on the roof, mysterious little parcels in the "boot," and confidential letters in coachman's hat, for all the world like something in Charles Dickens. There is no bugle and no guard, and the coach itself is a high, long-legged, spidery thing enough, not even painted red, and though it is "Merry Christmas" time, it is a warm summer day, with some prospect of thundery rain, but not the faintest of any typical Dickensesque Christmas weather. Still, the sentiment is there, so one may as well make the most of it.

All day, muddy roads and straining horses; all day, a long pull up-hill; half the day rain in the wet lovely bush, starring and sparkling the exquisite tree-ferns, those fine ladies of the forest; crystal-dropping the thick coat of ferns that tapestries the tall cliffs, shutting in our road. Beneath the wheel curve innumerable black-green gorges, deep and dark as Hades, gurgling in their mysterious depths with unseen full-throated streams and half-glimpsed waterfalls. About and above us rises the impenetrable "bush"—tall green trees, feathery, cedary, ferny, flowery, set as close together as the spires of moss on a velvet-cushioned stone, shutting out half the sky; marking off an unmistakable frontier between the territory of still unconquered Nature and the regions wrested from her by toiling Man. Wood-pigeons flash their blue-grey wings across the valleys; the merry mournful *tui* flutes " piercing sweet by the river," undisturbed by our rattling wheels. There are wild creatures in plenty, further back in the bush—wild boars, wild cattle, wild cats, and " dingoes " or dogs—all originally escaped from civilisation, but now as wild as their own savage ancestors. The feathery bracken, that carpets all the banks by the wayside, was, and indeed still is, a staple food of the Maories. Its young roots are excellent eating, being rather like asparagus, and reasonably nourishing when nothing better can be had—and the white-flowered tea-tree—one of the tree-heath family—has often furnished a " colourable imitation " of China tea, to the benighted bush-wanderer run out of the genuine leaf. This bush about us is all Maori land. Maories alone can find their way easily and safely through its pathless mysteries. No, there is no avoiding the Maori, anywhere in the North Island!

Dinner, warm and grateful and unspeakably comforting, is met with at a little inn in a little settlement whose name (of course) begins with Wai. The towns in North New Zealand that do not begin with Wai begin with Roto. There are a few others, but they hardly count. We are all amazingly cheerful when we issue forth warmed and fed; and the cold wind that is beginning to blow down from the icy mountain peaks just out of sight, is encountered without any British-tourist grumbling. The driver explains that the wind ought not to be so cold—never is, in December (the New Zealand June); but somehow, this is "a most exceptional season," and there has been a lot of rain and cold that they don't generally have. Across twelve thousand miles of sea my mind leaps back to home; I feel the raspy air of the English spring nipping my face, and hear the familiar music of the sweet old English lie about the weather. It is a dear home-like lie, and makes me feel that New Zealand is indeed what it claims to be—the Britain of the Southern Cross.

The effect of dinner is wearing off, and the insides are saying things about the weather that make a lonely wanderer like myself long to clasp the speakers warmly by the hand—because they sound so English. Now I understand what puzzled me a good deal at first—the difference between the Americanised, Continentalised Australians and the perfectly British New Zealander. The Briton cannot retain his peculiar characteristics in a climate like that of Australia; deprived of his natural and national grumble about the changeable weather, he is like a dog without a bark—an utterly anomalous being. But the New Zealand climate is windy and showery, given to casting autumn in the lap of spring and throwing winter into the warm, unexpecting arms of summer. So the Briton of the South, settled among his familiar weather "samples," remains like the Briton of the North; and the travelling Englishman or Englishwoman, visiting New Zealand, feels more entirely at home than in any other quarter of the globe. It is only fair to New Zealand, however, to add that the average summer, beginning in December, is at worst very much warmer and pleasanter than the English spring or winter, and at best, a season of real delight.

Late and dark and cold is the evening when we

rattle up to the accommodation house planted in a strange desert spot, where the night is to be passed. Another coach comes in and discharges its load by-and-by. The Dickensonian flavour increases, as we of the earlier coach sit round the great ingle-nook fire of blazing logs in the coffee-room, silently surveying the new comers, while they shed their many wraps and crowd about the blaze. To how many Early Victorian tales—Dickens, Bulwer Lytton, G.P.R. James—have not the lonely inn and the late arriving guest been the familiar commencement!

But the three Maories, man and two women, alighting from the coach and taking their place in the warm room, break through the illusion of Victorian romance at a touch, as a passing figure breaks through a gossamer cobweb stretched across a furzy path. Even G.P.R. could have had no dealings with those tall bundled-up, black-eyed, self-possessed beings from the bush. He would have turned them out in despair, or turned himself out, and gone back to his mysterious, Spanish-complexioned gentlemen in furred riding-cloaks.

A nipping early morning sees us off at seven o'clock, the discontented innkeeper, with (apparently) a dark crime on his conscience, seeing us go with obvious relief. It is too evident that like rather many backwoods hotel-keepers, he regards the harmlesss necessary traveller in the unflattering light of "the pig that pays the rint."

Ruapehu's giant cone, covered with dazzling snow, soars 3,000 feet into heaven above us. We are high up ourselves, for we pass the 4,000 foot level later on, rather cold and cross, and inclined to regard the little flag of hot smoke creeping out of the crest of Ngaurhoe, a smaller volcano ahead, as the most desirable thing in nature. Brumbies (wild horses) skim the plains below us, quick-moving little dots of black against the buff-colour of river valleys and flats of sand. "There's a fellow hunting those at present," volunteers the driver —"catches and breaks them, and gets thirty shillings apiece for them for youngsters to ride to school. The kids must have something, you know, and the brumbies are wiry little brutes."

No one walks on two legs in New Zealand, apparently. I recollect a picture that the coach passed only yesterday evening—a man on horseback, and two dogs, fetching home a cow and her calf from a pasture a quarter of a mile away from the homestead. In England the whole outfit of man, horse, and dogs would have been represented by one small child with a pinafore and a stick. Other countries, other manners.

One o'clock, forty-two miles out, with a stop for a fresh team; and we now enter a valley where we are met by the strange sight of a puff of steam rising from a bushy dell, and a little river that glides along with smoky vapours curling up from its surface. We are in the hot-water country at last; this is Tokaanu, and from here to Rotorua, ninety miles away, the earth is dotted, every now and then, with boiling springs, erupting geysers, hot lakes, and warm rivers. In all this country you need never light a fire to cook, unless you choose; never heat water to wash your pots and pans, or to bathe yourself. The Maories, and many of the whites, steam all their food instead of boiling or baking it; and as for hot baths, an army might enjoy them all day long.

The valley is warm and pleasant; Lake Taupo lies before us, thirty miles long, wide and blue and beautiful as the sea, sentinelled by tall peaks of dazzling white and purest turquoise, and all embroidered about the shores with gold braiding of splendid *Planta Genista* scattered in groves and hedges of surpassing richness. Three hours in a tiny steamer brings us to the other side ; and here the sights of the hot-water country fairly begin.

The Spa Hotel, at Taupo (where one passes the night and as many days as one has time for), is a museum, an exhibition, and very good joke, all in itself. One might fairly describe it as hashed hotel, served up with excellent sauce. You find bits of it lost in a wilderness of rose and rhododendron, at the end of a garden path ; half a dozen bedrooms run away all along among the honeysuckles to play hide-and-seek ; a drawing-room isolated like a light-house in a sea of greenery ; a dining-room that was once a Maori assembly-house, and is a miracle of wildly grotesque carvings, representing the weirdest of six-foot goblin figures, eyed and toothed with pearl shell, and carved in the highest of alto relievo, all down the walls. White sand pathways run between the various fragments of the hotel ; a hot stream, breathing curly vapour as it goes, meanders about the grounds, captured here and there in deep wooden ponds under rustic roofs, or hemmed in by walls and concealing trees, to make the most attractive of baths. There is sulphur and soda and free sulphuric acid in these waters ; one spring, welling up all by itself, has iodine. For rheumatism, skin diseases, and many blood diseases, these constantly running pools are almost a certain cure. It seems a shocking waste of golden opportunities to let this chance go by without being healed of something ; but I can only collect a cold in the head, a grazed ankle, and a cracked lip, to meet the occasion—of all which evils the baths at once relieve me, offering in their place an appetite which must seriously impair my popularity

THE OPEN-AIR SYSTEM 347

with the proprietress, though I am bound to say she hides her feelings nobly.

There is a celebrated "porridge pot," or mud volcano, near this hotel. I have not time to see it; therefore I leave it with gentle reproaches ringing in my ears, and hints to the effect that I shall be haunted on my deathbed by unavailing regret. But I meet the Waikato River directly after, and at once forget everything else. Never anywhere on this earth, except in the hues of a peacock's breast shining in the sun, have I seen such a marvellous blue-green colour as that of this deep, gem-like, splendid stream. And the golden broom on its banks, the golden broom on the heights, the golden broom everywhere—bushes eight and ten feet high, all one molten flame of burning colour, with never a leaf to be seen under the conflagration of riotous blossom—what is the English broom, or the English gorse, compared to this?

All the six miles to Wairakei, we follow the Waikato River; watch it sink into a deep green gorge; break into splendid foam and spray down a magnificent fall, that alone might make the fortune of any hotel in a less richly dowered country; wind underneath colossal tree-clad cliffs, in coils and streaks of the strange emerald-blue that is the glory of the river, and finally bend away towards the Arateatea Rapids. Another hotel built after the charming fashion of the Taupo hostelry, receives the coach occupants. The style of architecture sets one thinking. Where, twenty years ago, did out-of-the-way New Zealand light upon the "pavilion" system, that is the very latest fancy of all modern-built sanatoria? Has the liability to occasional small earthquake tremors anything to do with it? Whatever the cause may be, the result is that the fresh-air system is in full swing in nearly all the New Zealand thermal resorts; that doors and windows are always open, paths take the place of passages, and everybody acquires the complexion of a milkmaid and the appetite of a second-mate.

The hot outdoor swimming bath is a toy with which one really cannot stop playing. It is something so new and so amusing to dive into a bath 90 feet long and 102° Fahrenheit as to heat; swim about like marigolds in broth, in a temperature that would cook an egg in a few minutes, and all the time see the exquisite weeping willows wave overhead, the tall grasses stand on the bank, the wild clematis tremble in the trees above the pool. After the hot dip, one steps over a partition into another bathful of cool spring water, only 68° in heat, to cool down; and then comes dressing in a little bathing-box (shut off from the grounds, like all the bath, by a high board fence), followed by a two minutes' walk back to the house. But again, when night comes on, and the moon silvers the weeping willows to the semblance of pale frost-foliage on an icy pane, and the dim wraith-like vapours of the pool float up in ghostly shapes and shadows about the darkness of the inner boughs, one is tempted to come down once more, gliding hurriedly through the chill night air to the pool, locking the door, and floating for an hour or more in the dim, warm, drowsy waters. Cold? No one ever gets cold from the thermal waters, even if the cool dip is left out. That is one of their chiefest charms.

With the morning, I am informed that life will not be worth living to me any more, if I do not see the Geyser Cañon. Some one declares that it is the most beautiful sight in New Zealand; some one else says that it frightens you most delightfully, in the safest possible way; and "one low churl, compact of thankless earth," says that it is extremely instructive. This last calumny I

AN INTERESTING GUIDE   349

must at once deny. Interesting, to the deepest degree, the Wairakei Geysers are; suggestive also beyond any other geological phenomena in New Zealand; but instructive, after the tedious scientific-evenings fashion of our childhood, they are not. They are too beautiful for that, and too fascinating. One ought, no doubt, to absorb a great deal of geological information during the tour of the valley, but one is so busy having a good time that one doesn't. Which is exactly as it should be.

Coming round the corner of the path that leads to the geysers, one sees a column of white steam rising over the shoulder of the hill, among the greenery of tea-tree and willow, exactly like the blowing-off steam of some railway engine, waiting at a station. It is indeed an engine that is blowing off steam; but the engine is rather a big one—nothing less, indeed, than that admirable piece of work, Mother Earth herself. Ingle, the guide, now comes out of a tin-roofed cottage at the entrance to the valley, and starts to show us the wonders of the place.

Now be it known that Mr. Ingle is a very remarkable character, and second only to the geysers themselves, as a phenomenon of singular interest. He is one of the very few men in the world who know all about geysers, and quite the only one who can literally handle and work them. Ingle knows how to doctor a sick geyser as well as any stableman can doctor a horse; he can induce it to erupt, keep it from doing so, or make it erupt after his fashion, and not after its own. He is the author of at least two scientific discoveries of some importance, combining the effects of steam pressure on rocks and the incidence of volcanoes along certain thermal lines. In fact, what Ingle does not know about the interior of the earth, and the doings down there, is not worth knowing; and he tells us much of it as he takes us over the cañon.

Instructive? Certainly not. It is all gossip about volcanoes and geysers—personal, interesting, slightly scandalous gossip (because the behaviour of some of them, at times, and the tempers they exhibit, *are* simply scandalous); but not "instructive"; assuredly not.

The average tourist likes to have every sight named—romantically or comically named, if possible—and his tastes have been fully considered in the Geyser Cañon. I am not going to quote the guide-book titles of the dozen or two thermal wonders exhibited by Ingle. Staircases of pink silica, with hot water running down them; boiling pools of white fuller's earth, with miniature volcanoes and geysers pock-marked all over them: sapphire-coloured ponds, where one can see fifty feet of scalding depths; the great Wairakei Geyser, casting up huge fountains of boiling steam and spray every seven minutes; twin geysers living in one pool of exquisite creamy stalactites, and erupting every four minutes with the punctuality of a watch; geysers that throb exactly like the paddles of a steamer, or beat like the pulse of an engine; geysers that throw up great white balls of steam through crystal funnels of hot water; geysers that cast themselves bodily out of their beds at regular intervals, leaving you with exactly nine minutes in which to scramble down the hot wet rock of the funnel, stagger through the blinding steam that rises from the rents and fissures at the bottom, and climb up the other side again, into coolness and safety, to wait and watch the roaring water burst up through the rock once more; geysers that make blue-green pools on the lip of milky and ruddy terrace of carven silica; that explode like watery cannon, in definite rows, one after another; that build themselves nests like birds, send boiling streams under rustic bridges, scatter hot spray and steam over richly drooping ferns, and plant rainbow haloes on a scalding cloud of mist, high above the clustering trees of the valley—these are the sights of the cañon, and they need no childish names to make them interesting. When a visitor gets into the Geyser Cañon he is like a fly in a spider's web. He cannot get away from this colossal variety entertainment. He runs from a nine-minute geyser to see a four-minute geyser do its little "turn," and by this time the number is up for the seven-minute performance of the great star, so he hurries there; and after that he must just go back and see the twin geysers do another four-minute trick, and then there is quite another, which will do a splendid "turn" in twenty-seven minutes' time, if he only waits—and so half a day is gone, without any one noticing the flight of time, until the sudden occurrence of a "passionate vacancy," not at all connected with the geysers or their beds, informs the traveller that another meal-time has, unperceived, come round.

    The Arateatea Rapids fill in the afternoon. From the high road where the open coach stands waiting, down through a pretty woodland of greenery and shadow and thick soundless moss, one follows a narrow pathway towards an ever-increasing sound of rushing, tumbling, and thundering, out, at last, on to a projecting point where one stands right over a rocky cañon filled almost to the brim with a smother of white rolling foam, woven through with surprising lights of clear jade green and trembling gold. And here, on the brink of this half-mile of rapids, over the roaring water, I give it up. I do not attempt to describe it. When you take a great river, exceptionally deep and swift, and throw it over half a mile of sloping cliff, things are bound to happen that are somewhat beyond the power of pen and ink to render. Who has ever read a description of a waterfall, anywhere, written by any one that conveyed an impression worth a rotten nut? Every one who goes to see Arateatea must manufacture his own sensations on the spot. Sheer fright will certainly be one of them; not at anything the innocent rapids are doing to the beholder, but at the bare notion of what they might do, one foot nearer—one step lower down—one—— Let me have a couple of trees to hold on to, please. Thank you, that is better.

Many years ago, a party of twenty Maories had a narrow escape from the cruel embraces of snow-white Arateatea.' They were canoeing on the upper river; and, partly because the trout in the Waikato are the biggest trout in the world, partly because some of the rowers had had too much fun at a "tangi," or wailing party, the night before, and were not very clear-headed, they forgot to think of the current until it had them fairly in its clutch, whirling them along only a mile or two above the terrible rapids. They could not reach the shore, and they dared not swim. One would have supposed that nothing could save them from being beaten to pieces against the cruel rocks in the rapids—yet they escaped that fate.

They went over the Huka Falls, which come a mile or two above the rapids (the Maories had forgotten all about that) and were decently drowned instead.

I am sorry that the above is not a better story; but the fact is, that tourists are not very plentiful about Wairakei, and the natives have not yet learned to invent the proper tourist tale. That is about the best they can do as yet. It will hardly be credited, but there is not even a Lover's Leap in the whole valley; not a story of an obstinate father who got opportunely boiled in a geyser, while his daughter eloped down a scalding river in a motor-boat worked by the steam from the

IN THE VOLCANIC ZONE 353

surface—nor a tale of a flying criminal pursued by executioners, who leaped from side to side of a gorge some thirty feet across and got away. This is certainly remiss of the authorities; but I have no doubt the Government Tourist Department would take the matter up, and supply the necessary fiction, if suitably approached. In the meantime travellers must be satisfied with the rather bald and uninteresting tale of a Maori maiden named Karapiti, who jumped into the steam blow-hole bearing her name, because her *fiancé* did not meet her there on Sunday afternoon as arranged to take her to afternoon tea at the Wairakei Hotel. At least, that is one version of the tale, and it is quite enough for the Smith family from London, and other representative tourists.

"You should have given yourself more time." "Whatever you are going to do later on, this place really requires at least a week." "You cannot possibly miss so-and-so, or this and that!" Such are the reproaches that haunt the hasty traveller through the Hot-Water Country—reproaches fully deserved in nearly every case, for very few tourists who journey to New Zealand realise the amount of time that should be spent in seeing the miracles of the volcanic zone, if nothing really good is to be omitted.

It results in an unsatisfactory compromise as a rule—some "sights" being seen; many passed over. There is always something fascinating just ahead, calling the traveller on, and something wonderful close at hand, which demands the sacrifice of yet another day, before moving. Such a superfluity of beautiful and wonderful sights can assuredly be found nowhere else on earth. Iceland is far inferior; the famous Yellowstone Park of America has only a stepmother's helping of what might be New Zealand's "left-overs." The lovely, lamented Pink and White Terraces are by many supposed to have been the only great thermal wonder of the country. This is so far from being the truth that only a good-sized volume could fairly state the other side of the question. I have never met any traveller through the thermal districts, who had succeeded in seeing everything of interest. All whom I saw were as hard at work as the very coach-horses themselves—walking, driving, climbing, scrambling, each hour of every day, and often thoroughly overdoing themselves, in the plucky attempt to carry away as much as possible from this over-richly spread banquet of Nature's wonders.

I squeezed out an afternoon for Karapiti (the "Devil's Trumpet") and the Valley of the Coloured Lakes. By this time I was a little jaded with sight-seeing, disposed to talk in a hold-cheap tone of anything that was not absolutely amazing, and to taste all these weirdly impressive marvels with a very discriminating palate. Karapiti, however, is cayenne to any jaded taste. It is known as the "Safety-Valve of New Zealand," and the term is peculiarly fitting. The whole of the Hot-Water Country is only one plank removed from the infernal regions; it almost floats upon the scalding brow of molten rock, liquid mineral, and vaporised water, that composes the earth interior immediately below. That it is perfectly safe to live in (a constant wonder to outsiders) is very largely due to just those steam blow-holes and geysers which excite the fears of the nervous-minded—and the colossal dragon-throat of Karapiti is the most important safety-valve of all.

Walking up the hill to the blow-hole, many hundred yards off, one hears its loud unvarying roar, like the steam-thunder that comes from an ocean liner's huge

NEW ZEALAND'S SAFETY VALVE 355

funnel, when the ship is ready to cast loose from shore. The ground as one gets nearer is jutted and uneven, and perceptibly warm in certain spots. Rounding a corner, one comes suddenly upon the Devil's Trumpet, a funnel-shaped opening, ten feet across at the lip, in the bottom of a cup-shaped hollow. A fierce jet of steam rushes out from the Trumpet, thick and white as a great marble column, and roaring horribly as it comes forth. The pressure is no less than 180 lb. to one square inch, and the rush of this gigantic waste-pipe never slackens or ceases, night or day ; nor has it done so within the memory of man.

"If it did, I'd look for another situation pretty sharp, for it wouldn't be 'ealthy to stay around Wairakei no more," observes one guide, who is showing off, the monster to us by throwing a kerosene can into the jet, and catching it as it is violently flung back to him, many yards away. "I can throw a penny the same," he says, and does so, getting back the coin promptly, a good deal hotter than it went in.

One of the ladies of our party is nearly reduced to tears by the sinister aspect, the menacing horror of the spot. She begs to be taken away, because she knows she will dream about it. She does dream about it ; I know that, because I do myself, that night ; and the dreams are not nice. Still, I would face them again for another look at roaring Karapiti. It is a wonder of wonders, a horror of horrors, unlike anything else in the world. On the whole, I am glad of that last fact. Too much Karapiti would certainly get on one's nerves.

There have never been any accidents to travellers here. No one could fall down the hole, because the funnel narrows rapidly, and is only about two feet across in the inner part. All the same, one cannot safely approach very near, for there is an in-rush as well as an out-rush, and if any one did fall victim to it, and stumble into the funnel, the highly condensed steam would strip the flesh from his bones as quickly as a cherry is shelled off its stone.

The Valley of the Coloured Lakes came next. I wonder what the inhabitants of Brighton or Bath would do—how they would advertise, how they would cry for visitors—if they had a valley at their very gates which contained a scalding hot river, tumbling over pink and cream-coloured cascades of china-like silica, in clouds of steamy spray—a great round pond, set deep in richest forest, and coloured vivid orange, with red rocks round the brim; another, crude Reckitt's blue; another, staring verdigris green; another, raspberry pink; others still, yellow as custard and white as starch! All these ponds are hot; they are coloured by the various minerals they hold in solution, but they have not yet been chemically analysed, so it is only possible to speculate as to the exact cause of the colours. Seen from a height above, the ponds resemble nothing so much as a number of paint-pots; and that, indeed, is one of the names by which the valley is generally known.

Leaving behind me, unlooked at, still more than I had seen, I took coach again next morning for Rotorua. It was an early and a chilly start, for we had over thirty miles to do before lunch. The light, springy coach, with its leather-curtain sides, was filled with a cheerful party, all young, all enjoying themselves heartily, and all full of the genial good spirits that come of much open air and a holiday frame of mind. *New* New Zealand at its best was represented there, much as Old New Zealand was represented by the silent bearded men, with the lonely looking eyes, who travelled in the Pipiriki and Waiouru stages of the journey.

How fast the spanking team swings in along the road! How lovely the changing panorama of the encircling hills, now velvet-brown with rich green dells and valleys, now far-off pansy-purple, now palest grey, seamed with crimson streaks of hematite! The air is very clear to-day, with that strange New Zealand clearness that changes every distance to sea-blue crystal, and pencils every shadow sharp and square.

We have left the royal gold broom behind us; but the beautiful manuka scrub of the valleys is in full blossom, exquisitely tipped and touched with white lace-like blossoms. It is almost as if a heavy hoar-frost had misted over every delicate green bough with finest touches of silver. Arum lilies bloom in the ditches; the Maori flax, like tall iris leaves, wanders wildly over hill and valley; great fields of Pampas grass wave their creamy plumes over the shot green satin of thick-growing leaves. Wild horses, as the coach goes by, look warily out from behind some woody knoll, or canter away across the plains with their long-legged foals. Some of them are fine creatures, too, worth catching and breaking, and many are taken there from time to time. What a happy land, where a man can go out and pick a fine horse in a mountain meadow, much as you pick a daisy at home!

Lunch-time befalls at another of the inevitable Wais—Waiotapu, this time—and before the coach starts on the last stretch of eighteen miles to Rotorua, I go across the road to see the only one of Waiotapu's sights for which I have time—the Champagne Pool and Alum Cliffs.

These are to be found on a most extraordinary

milk-coloured plain, which looks exactly as if a careless giant had been mixing colours and trying brushes on it, and left everything lying about. The rocks and heights, the deep dells with boiling pools and grumbling geysers at the bottom, the narrow pathways leading here and there, are spotted and streaked with carmine, rose madder, scarlet, primrose, bright yellow, and amber. The "Cliffs" are a succession of rocky heights, composed of something very like cream fondant, which is mostly alum. At their feet opens out a fascinating succession of bays and inlets full of variously coloured water, at which I can only glance as I pass. There are two mustard-coloured pools, and one pale green, among them. Close at hand the overflow from the Champagne Pool rushes, steaming fiercely, over a fall of rocks which appear to have been very newly and stickily painted in palest primrose colour. Alum, sulphur, and hematite are responsible, I am told, for most of these strange hues. Sulphur and arsenic have coloured the Champagne Pool itself—a great green lake, almost boiling, and of a most amazing colour—something between the green of a peridot and that of Chartreuse. It has never been bottomed; the line ran out at 900 feet when tried. The edge of all the lake is most delicately wrought into a coralline border of ornamental knobs and branches, canary yellow in colour. Its name is derived from the curious effect produced in the depths of the pond by a handful of sand. The water begins to cream and froth at once, like champagne or lemonade, and continues to do so in places for at least half an hour.

And now we hurry back to the coach once more, and on to Rotorua, wonder of wonders, and thermal temple of every healing water known to the medical world,

CHAPTER XVI

From Heaven to Hades—Gay Rotorua—Where One lives on a Piecrust—The Birth of a River—Horrible Tikitere—In the Track of the Great Eruption—Where are the Pink and White Terraces?—A Fountain fifteen hundred Feet high—Foolhardy Feat of a Guide—How the Tourists were killed—A Maori Village—Soaping a Geyser—The End.

RED roofs and white verandahs; straight sandy streets of immense width, planted with green trees, and spindling away into unnaturally bright blue distances; omnibuses, phætons, motor-cars, and four-in-hands passing at long intervals towards the shining lakes that lie beside the town; puffs of white steam rising up among green gardens and open fields; a ring of amethyst-coloured hills surrounding the whole bright scene, bathed in such a white, pure, crystalline sun as never shines on misty England. That is Rotorua, a half-day's journey from Auckland, and the centre of the wonderful geyser region of New Zealand.

Every one now-a-days knows that New Zealand possesses wonderful geysers, but not quite everybody knows what a geyser is; and certainly very few are aware of the extraordinary richness and variety of the geyser country. Geysers are intermittent fountains of boiling water, in height from a couple of feet up to fifteen hundred—the enormous altitude reached by Waimangu the Terrible, greatest geyser of the whole world. They consist of a shaft reaching down from the surface of the earth to deep, very highly heated reservoirs of steam and boiling water below; and (usually) of a siliceous basin surrounding the shaft-opening, and full of hot water. Some geysers open in the centre of a cone of siliceous sinter, built up by the deposits from the water, and have no basin.

The periodic explosions of active geysers are due to the following facts—water under heavy pressure requires a much higher temperature to boil than water free from pressure. While the water high up in the geyser pipe may be a little under 212 degrees, that in the lower levels may be standing at 50 or 60 degrees higher, and only kept from expanding into steam by the weight of the column above it. If anything lessens that weight or increases the temperature of the lower water, this latter will explode into steam, and drive the upper waters high into air with the force of its exit from the shaft. This, briefly, is the theory of geyser action.

Rotorua itself, the great focus of the healing forces of Nature in the geyser district, is simply a crust over a mass of hot springs, charged with various minerals. Three feet under earth you will find hot water, in nearly any part of the town. There are hundreds of hot springs in the neighbourhood that have never been analysed. Of the many that are in use in the Government Sanatorium, the "Priest's Water" and "Rachel Water" are the most famous. The former cures rheumatism, gout, and blood diseases, while "Rachel" makes her patrons "beautiful for ever" by curing all forms of skin trouble, and bestowing a lovely complexion, not to speak of the remarkable effects of the spring on nervous affections. There are also wonderful hot swimming baths, much patronised by the casual tourist; baths of hot volcanic mud, and baths of hot sulphur vapour rising direct from the burning caverns under the earth.

But for people who are in good health, it is the "sights" of Rotorua that are the chief attractions, and these are very many. One of the loveliest, and a welcome change from the countless hot-water springs, is Hamurana, surely the most beautiful river source in the world. It is reached by a journey across one of the lakes in a steamer. All the way the great lake ripples purest turquoise under a high, clear, cloudless sky; green islands rise bright and cool from its shining surface, sharply peaked and shadowed mountains, on the distant shores, stand out in strange hues of crystalline hyacinth unknown to our northern climes. By-and-by the little steamer leaves us on a green wooded shore, and we take boat up a fairy river to a region of enchanted beauty. Blossoming trees line the sun-steeped banks; the water is of the strangest colours—jade-green, clear molten sapphire, silver, emerald, and transparent as a great highway of rock crystal. Enormous trout, weighing up to twenty pounds, rush from under our keel; grass-green and rose-red water weeds quiver far beneath the oar. Wild fuchsias, wild cherries, loaded with scarlet fruit, snowy-flowered tea-tree, arum lilies, yellow broom, and pink dog-roses, hang out over the water. But a few hundred yards, and the big lovely river comes to a sudden end, walled in by blossoming bushes, and apparently cut short in the strangest of *cul-de-sacs*. In reality it is the source we have reached; here the whole Hamurana stream springs full-grown from the earth. A great rift in the bed of the glassy river is visible, where the water wells up under our keel in wavering masses of amber, aquamarine, and deep blue, shot with glancing arrows of prismatic light. Five million gallons are poured forth from this deep cold cavern every twenty-four hours—each drop as clear as a diamond, and as pure. The force of the upspringing stream is so great that pennies can be thrown in from the boat without sinking to the bottom of the cavern—the water sends them back, and casts them out into the shallows about the edge of the rift. Sometimes a small silver coin will slip down into depths, and lie glittering many fathoms below, magnified conspicuously by the transparent water. The Maori natives, who are marvellous divers, have tried time and again to reach this tempting store of treasure; but no man can stem the uprushing torrent of water, and if the coins were gold, they would be as safe as they are now from being taken by human hands. The most determined suicide could not drown himself in the Hamurana River source, for the stream about the source is shallow, and the cavern water itself would not permit him to sink, however willing he might be.

The Valley of Tikitere, some ten miles from Rotorua, is the greatest contrast that could possibly be conceived to Hamurana's enchanted loveliness. Enchanted indeed this valley also might be, but by a spell of evil. It is the nearest possible approach to the familiar conception of hell. A stretch of white siliceous soil, streaked here and there with the blood-coloured stains of hematite, or the livid yellow of sulphur, is pitted all over with lakes, pools, and small deep pot-holes of boiling mud, sometimes thick, sometimes thin, but always scalding, bubbling, spirting, and threatening. Chief of all the horrors is the well-named lake, "Gates of Hell." Standing upon a bank of white earth that is warm underfoot, and seamed with steaming cracks, one looks down upon a ghastly hell-hole of a seething cauldron, slimy black in colour, and veiled with stinging mists that only now and then lift sufficiently to show the hideous surface of the lake. The foul broth of which it is composed bubbles and lifts ceaselessly, now and then rising into ominous heights and waves that seem about to break upon the banks above. The heat reaches our faces, as we stand half-stifled on the pathway. Just beside us, a large pool of bubbling mud, which stands constantly at 212° Fahrenheit—ordinary boiling point —seems almost cool in comparison. Little wonder that is so; for the "Gates of Hell" is largely composed of sulphuric acid, and its surface temperature is 232°.

Beyond lies a perfect wilderness of boiling mud-holes of every kind. Here, there is a pond of mud as thick as porridge; there, one fluid as cream. Here, the deadly, scalding surface lies innocently smooth and unrippled; there, it leaps and thunders like a young volcano in action. At one corner we come suddenly upon an ugly black archway, leading to no inviting interior; nothing can be seen within; but the loud gurglings and chokings of the seething depths inside restrain any desire for closer observation. "The Heavenly Twins," derisively so-named, are two boiling mud-holes not a foot apart, but quite unconnected; one boils the thickest of brews, while its twin concocts the thinnest.

One must follow the guide closely and carefully about these ghastly wonders. One step off the pathway, and a horrible death awaits the careless walker. Even the path itself is only cool and solid on the outside skin. The guide stops now and then to dig his stick into the whitey-brown earth for a couple of inches, and turn up a clod all glittering on the under-side with fresh crystals of sulphur. This under-side is so hot that one can hardly touch it with the unprotected hand!

From one deep mud-hole, of a comparatively reasonable temperature, mud is taken out for medical uses. It is wonderfully effective as a bath, for soothing pain and curing sleeplessness. Further on, on safe ground, one can see a hot waterfall about twenty feet high, in temperature about 100°, which is used as a douche bath by invalids of many kinds, with remarkable results.

On the edges of the valley, I see for the first time in detail exactly how the "fumarole," or steam blow-hole, is used for cooking purposes. Over the opening of a small manageable blow-hole, an inch or two across, is placed a box without a bottom. The food to be cooked is placed in the box, either in a pot, or wrapped in leaves. The lid is then put on, and covered with clay. In an hour or so the meat or stew is done to a turn; and even if left too long, it cannot be burned. One blow-hole, in constant use by the Maories, is not steam at all, but hot sulphur vapour, which deposits a crust of sulphur on everything it touches. This does not trouble the Maori, however; he eats his food quite contentedly, with a strong sulphurous flavour added to its natural taste, and says it does him good. Certainly, the natives living about Tikitere are unusually strong and hearty in appearance, and never troubled with any kind of illness.

People of middle age will doubtless remember vividly the impression created all over the world in 1886 by the eruption of the great volcano Tarawera, and the destruction of New Zealand's most cherished natural wonder—the peerless Pink and White Terraces of Rotomahana. Countless marvels have been left, and one new one that far outstrips the Terraces in sheer wonder and magnificence—Waimangu, the greatest geyser in the world; but New Zealand still laments her beautiful

THE ERUPTION OF 1886

Terraces, and shows the spot where they lie deep, buried under ninety feet of volcanic débris, as though pointing out the grave of something loved and lost.

A day of wonderful interest is that spent in seeing the track of the great eruption. Leaving Rotorua early in the morning, I saw, as the coach wound up the hilly road outside the town, many traces of that awful night and day of darkness, thunder, and terror, eighteen years ago. Although Rotorua is fifteen miles or more from the site of the Terraces, the sky was dark all the day of the eruption, and only three or four miles from the town black volcanic dust fell so densely as to leave a stratum several inches thick over the country. This is clearly visible in the cuttings at the side of the road, where the black stratum can be seen underlying the more recent layer of ordinary soil. Where the great coach-road to Rotomahana once ran, a chasm some sixty feet deep scars the mountain side, caused by the fearful rush of water that took place down the road-track. An earthquake crack, thirty feet deep, runs close to the road for a long distance. All the way up to the buried village of Wairoa, similar traces can be seen. But before the village is reached, two gems of scenic loveliness are passed—the Blue and Green Lakes, lying side by side, each enclosed by steep rugged hills, reflected clearly on its glassy surface. One is of the strangest, most delicate Sèvres blue—a colour not depending on any reflection from above, for I saw it on a grey and cloudy day—the other is a bright verdigris green. "Chemicals in the water" is the very vague reason given by inhabitants of the district for these remarkable beauties of colour.

I must note here that in no case have I succeeded in obtaining any satisfactory reason for the remarkable blues and greens so common in both the cold and hot waters of the thermal district. The Waikato River, a great, cold stream, full of immense trout; Taupo Lake (cold); the coloured lakes of Wairakei and Waiotapu (hot); Hamurana Springs (cold), and many others, display these remarkable tints, under every sky and in every depth of water. Varying reasons are given, but none seem satisfactory. The beauty of the colouring is, at all events, certain, and the cause may safely be left to geologists.

Wairoa Village is now a green, silent waste of young forest and rich grass, broken only by the ruins of the old hotel that stood there before the eruption, and by a few scattered traces of other human occupation—a fragment of wall, the rusty skeleton of an iron bedstead, lying in a gully; the remains of a shattered buggy. In 1886 it occupied the place now held by Rotorua, and was visited by numbers of tourists, all anxious to see the Terraces, which lay not far away at the other end of the chain of lakes now united in one, and called Rotomahana. On the day of the eruption, the roof of the hotel was broken in by red-hot falling stones and mud, and eleven people were killed. Some, who escaped, ran out and took refuge in a native "warry" or hut, which, strange to say, remained uninjured. Over a hundred people in all—mostly Maories—were killed by the eruption, which destroyed millions of acres of good land, swept away several native villages, and utterly altered the face of the whole country.

Lake Tarawera, which must be crossed to see the site of the lost terraces, lies under the shadow of the great volcanic cone of Tarawera, 8,000 feet high, from which much of the molten rock and burning ashes came. It is as lovely, in its own strange way, as the famous lakes of Italy and Switzerland. The water is intensely blue, and the high hills closing it in are of a colour unknown to most other scenery in the world—a strange pale barren grey, so nearly white as to be slightly suggestive of snow. Like snow, too, is the distribution of this coloured matter; it lies on the crests and projections of the hills, and is streaked thinly down the sides. It is ash, volcanic ash, cast out by the surrounding craters on that fatal night of June 1886, and lying unchanged on the hills about the lake ever since. Tarawera itself towers above the lake, grim and dark and ominous; a mountain not yet tamed by any means, and still hot, though not molten, in the interior of the cone.

On the shores of the lake, as the launch carries us past, can be seen, at one spot, the whitened bones of some of the natives who perished in the eruption. The name and titles of one, who was a great chief, are painted on a rock that overhangs the shore.

Rotomahana, the second lake, is also surrounded by ash-whitened hills. At the far end, as our second oil-launch starts to cross, we can see thick columns of steam rising against the grey of the cliffs. These are the gravestones of the lost Pink Terrace; these tall pillars of cloud alone mark the spot where one half of the world's greatest wonder once stood. Just where the launch starts, the White Terrace was buried, under a hundred feet of earth and mud, deep in the bed of the lake.

What were the Terraces like? New Zealand has many oil paintings of them, so that a clear idea of their loveliness can be formed even to-day. They consisted of two immense terraced slopes, formed by the action of downward dropping hot water heavily loaded with silicon. Every terrace was a succession of fairy-like baths and basins, filled with bright blue water. One was pure ivory-white, the other, tinged with hematite, was bright pink. The exquisite natural carvings and flutings of the silicon, the beautiful tints of the terraces, the blue sky above and blue lakes below, together formed a picture the like of which does not exist on earth to-day.

Our oil-launch, sailing now over water which is actually boiling, close in shore, though the main body of the lake is cold, allows us to land on the very spot where the Pink Terrace once stood. It is a dangerous task, even with the aid of a guide, to pick one's way about this stretch of ground, for it is nothing but a crumbling honey-comb of boiling-water ponds, and narrow ridges as brittle as piecrust. Over these latter we take our perilous way, planting each footstep slowly and carefully, but never standing still, for the ground is so exceedingly hot that the soles of one's boots are scorched, if planted long in one place. The earth is choked and clouded with steam, the ponds roar and bubble about our feet, the blow-holes rumble. The ground is full of raw cracks, old and new, and as our small party steps over one of these, on the way back, it is seen to be visibly wider than it was on the previous coming! To-morrow the whole of this narrow ridge may have crumbled in and disappeared. No one is sorry to reach the launch again, and glide away from those threatening shores.

A little further on, where we land for the walk up to Waimangu Geyser, there is a hot iodine spring, unique among medical waters, and most useful in many diseases. Arrangements are now being made to have the water collected and sent to Rotorua; up to the present, it has only been used by the Maories.

All the three-mile walk up to the geyser is crowded with tokens of the great eruption. Mud cliffs a hundred

SMOULDERING GEYSERS

feet in height were created by the terrible outburst, and for miles about the whole country was covered yards deep with the boiling slimy mass. Not only Tarawera, but three other craters (all visible in the high distance above the lake) were erupting together, for a night and a day. The eruption took place without the least warning of any kind, about ten o'clock at night. The chain of lakes about Tarawera's foot suddenly exploded like colossal bombs, blowing their entire contents, and all the mud from their bottoms, over the whole countryside. Tarawera and the neighbouring craters cast out huge jets of flame, and scattered burning masses of rock, ashes, and scoriæ, for many miles. The noise was terrible, and the sky for twenty miles around was dark at noonday. It is supposed that the eruption was caused by the falling in of the lake bottom, which allowed the water to drop into the underlying fires, and exploded the lakes instantly into steam.

Up a great earthquake chasm, among deep volcano craters that were formed at the time of the eruption, we climb towards the Great Geyser. These craters are for the most part still in a more or less heated state, though grass and ferns grow in the interior of nearly all, and no apprehension is felt as to future outbursts. One has a hot mudpool at the bottom; a second spits steam from many cracks and blow-holes; a third, the largest of all, erupted slightly in August 1904, and threw a quantity of hot mud and stones out over the top.

Waimangu Geyser itself, which is really more a volcano than a geyser, is supposed to have been formed at the time of the eruption. It did not, however, commence its present activity until 1900, when an enormously high "shot" was seen by one or two explorers camping in the neighbourhood, and the source at once investigated.

It became apparent that New Zealand, in the place of the lost Terraces, had acquired the largest and most magnificent geyser in the whole world. The exchange is by no means a bad one. Waimangu attracts hundreds of travellers to the pretty little hotel planted on a cliff not far from the crater; and those who have been fortunate enough to see the geyser play, one and all utterly lose themselves in attempting to express the extraordinary majesty, wonder, and terror of the sight.

The geyser is somewhat irregular in action, but generally plays every day or so. The water in the huge basin heaves and lifts; then an enormous cloud of steam rushes up, and then a column of black water, charged with mud and stones, flings itself upward in repeated leaps or "shots" through the steam, to an almost incredible height—at times as high as fifteen hundred feet. More than a quarter of a mile in sheer height is Waimangu's biggest "shot." On such occasions, the sky is darkened by the tremendous spread of the leaping waters, the earth trembles with the concussion, and the watching spectators, perched high above the crater by the shelter hut, feel as though the terrors of the Last Day itself were falling upon them, unprepared.

In the summer of 1903 two girls and a guide were killed during the explosion of the geyser. The girls had been repeatedly warned, even entreated, not to stand near the crater, as it was momentarily expected to "play"; but they hovered close by the verge, anxious to secure a photograph. Without warning, Waimangu suddenly rose and hurled itself bodily skyward out of its bed. The enormous backfall of the boiling water caught and swept away the luckless three, and they were carried down the outflow valley in the flood that succeeds every eruption. When found, the bodies were terribly mutilated, and stripped of all clothing. The mother of the girls, standing higher up, saw the whole awful disaster, and had to be forcibly held back from rushing into the crater, in a wild effort to save her children. Since that melancholy day, the geyser basin has been railed off, in such a manner that no one can approach near enough to incur the slightest danger. Warbrick, the head guide of the district, was present, and nearly lost his life in a daring attempt to save the girls and the guide, who was his own brother. He rushed into the midst of the falling stones and water, to try and drag the luckless victims back, but was too late to save them, and narrowly escaped being carried away himself.

Warbrick is the best-known guide in New Zealand, and a character of considerable interest. He is a half-caste Maori, decidedly more intelligent than the average white man, and speaking English perfectly. In company with a sailor, he lately made what was probably the most daring boat-trip ever attempted on earth—nothing less then a voyage over Waimangu's boiling basin, undertaken with the object of sounding the depths of the geyser. The monster often erupts without the least warning, sending the whole contents of its huge basin bodily skyward; so that the feat was one likely to shake the strongest nerve. Warbrick took a lead line with him, and noted the various depths of the crater basin. In the centre, where the great throat of the geyser opens up, no bottom could be found. The boat came safely to shore, after some minutes spent in performing one of the most perilous feats ever attempted, even by a Maori.

Visitors generally stay at the Government accommodation house near the geyser for a day or two, on the chance of seeing a good " shot," and they seldom go away unrewarded. It is well worth while to cut short one's stay in some other place by a couple of days, to have a chance of seeing the world's greatest thermal wonder in full action, for Waimangu, when playing, is the sight of a lifetime. I was not fortunate enough to see the geyser in action, as it was undergoing a period of "sulks" at the time of my visit; but if it had been playing as it played some weeks after I left, nothing would have tempted me away from its neighbourhood until I had seen an eruption.

One of the great charms of the geyser country about Rotorua is its absolute unlikeness to anything that can be found on the other side of the Line. To the much-travelled wanderer, nearly all famous show-places, after a time, display a distressing similarity. The two or three leading types of peasant to be found on the Continent of Europe, grow familiar by-and-by. Giuseppe of Italy is not very novel to the traveller who still remembers Ignacio of Spain; German Wilhelm recalls Dutch Jan; Belgian Françoise is sister to French Mathilde. As for the "sights"—well, one waterfall is very like another, and lakes and ruined castles pall, taken in bulk. Even if the traveller wanders further away, he does not find much in Egypt, India, or Japan, that has not been greatly spoiled for him beforehand, by the countless descriptions he has heard and read ever since childhood. It seems almost as though the illimitable flood of sightseers, past and present, rushing through all the famous beauty-spots of the old world, had washed away something of their charm—as if the air about such places were drained dry of the ozone of fresh delight which every lovely and wonderful spot should give, leaving only an atmosphere of feeling that is stale and used-up in the last degree.

THE ORDINARY MAORI 373

New Zealand's "sights," however, are (to vary the metaphor) new gems in a new setting. Not even the most experienced traveller can look on the wonders of the thermal region with an eye dulled and indifferent by other experiences, since there is hardly anything similar the whole world over. And the setting of the gems—the strange, unfamiliar country, oddly reversed seasons, and wild brown Maori folk, taking the place of European peasantry, is perhaps the greatest charm of all.

For myself, the carefully revived native dances of the Maories, performed for money, in civilised concert halls; the "haka," or war dance, done by children on the roads for pennies, and the modern native carvings, done with English tools, which are all among the most striking features of daily life in Rotorua, were not the real attractions of the place. Those lay in the common features of ordinary Maori existence, seen here, there, and everywhere, without pose or preparation. When one strolls out along the country roads near the town, it is an adventure to meet a party of wild-eyed, brown-faced men and women, galloping madly up and down hill on their rough "brumbies" (wild horses, broken in)—both sexes alike wrapped in heavy blankets, and sitting astride. Wandering about on a bicycle, it pleasantly increases the "go-abroady" feeling that most travellers welcome, to come upon a woman taking a fat fowl out of the steam-hole cooker, that Nature has provided just at the door of her thatch-roofed, reed-built "warry," and to stop and talk for an interesting quarter of an hour with a barefooted, half-clad savage, who speaks English as good as one's own, reads the daily papers, and has his opinions on Mr. Seddon's fiscal policy. The Maori guides and hangers on, about the best-known sights, are naturally more or less spoiled by the visitors. But the real Maori, of whom one gets an occasional sight, even about such a civilised town as Rotorua, is attractive enough to make one fully understand the strong regard that most New Zealanders have for their native friends. Dignity, pride, and the manners of an exiled royalty are his natural heritage. His mind is as keen as the white man's, though perhaps somewhat narrower in scope; he has a vivid sense of humour, strong feelings about honour and faithfulness, the courage of a bull-dog, and the reckless daring of an Irish dragoon. Worth knowing, and well worth liking when known, are the brown men and women of North New Zealand.

The little village of Ohinemutu, less than a mile from Rotorua, is astonishingly Maori still, in spite of the development of the district for tourist travel. Go down towards the shores of the lake at the back of the big hotel, and you step at once into a native "pah," built in the haphazard fashion peculiar to Maori settlements. There are no streets, and no definite beginnings or endings. The houses face every way, and are of many fashions; here a reed-built warry, there a house with a front splendidly carved and painted in old native fashion, further on a wooden dwelling about as large as a bathing-box, with a full-sized bay-window fastened on to it. Most are wooden huts with iron roofs—a compromise between native and European styles.

Everywhere one goes, there are steaming pools with newly washed clothes drying on the edge, or small brown bodies happily disporting themselves in the water. Cooking-boxes are erected over countless steam-holes; and every here and there, one meets a tall brown man or woman, looking extremely clean and damp, and wrapped in a big coloured blanket and nothing else, stalking housewards from a refreshing bath. Try to take a photograph, and if the Maori is accustomed to tourists, he will ask a shilling for the labour of posing; but if he has recently come down from the wilds, and is still unspoiled, he will reject an offer of coin with quiet dignity. Taken as nature made him, the Maori is not greedy of money. It is only a very few months since the Maories of the King country (a wild, half-claimed district in the " back blocks ") have allowed gold prospectors to pass through their lands. Until recently, they admitted tourists and sportsmen freely, but refused to allow any one to look for gold, giving as a reason their belief that the finding of gold did no country any good.

Whakarewarewa, a couple of miles outside the town of Rotorua, has a very interesting model of a typical Maori fortified "pah," lately completed by the Government. The large space of grass enclosed by the fort is guarded by high earth breastworks and a deep ditch. Beyond the ditch is an open wooden paling, apparently more for ornament than use, on which are placed at intervals carved wooden figures of a threatening and terrifying character. All of them are native work, but of modern date.

The geysers of Whakarewarewa are many and famous. The most famous of all was the great twin geyser Waikite, whose double throat opens at the top of a high terraced cone, built up of siliceous sinter, deposited by the geyser water during long ages of action. Waikite has ceased to play since 1886, when the railway from Auckland to Rotorua was completed. On the day when the line was opened for traffic, the geyser ceased playing, and its fountains have never ascended since.

Wairoa (Maori, " Long Water ") is now the lion of Whakarewarewa. It plays very seldom of its own accord, but on special occasions the local authorities permit it to be dosed with soap, which always produces an eruption. A geyser constantly physicked in this manner often gives up playing altogether in the end; so careful restrictions hedge round the operation, in the case of Wairoa. It is first necessary to procure consent from the Government Tourist Department in Wellington, and then to arrange a day, and give notice to the town. The Government authorities in Wellington were kind enough to send an order to Rotorua to have Wairoa soaped for me during my stay; and I took advantage of the opportunity to enjoy the novel sensation of starting the geyser myself.

On a Sunday afternoon of December 1904, all Rotorua assembled in a black crowd at "Whaka" to see Wairoa play. Rows of cameras were placed upon the hillocks commanding the spot; bets were freely made about the height and quality of the coming performance, and every one scuffled politely for a front place when the ceremony began. The caretaker of the grounds and the head guide solemnly removed the wooden cover (pierced to allow the escape of steam) which is padlocked over the geyser's stony lips, and handed me a bag containing three bars of soap, cut up into small pieces. I stood on the edge of the geyser-mouth, looking down a great black well full of steam, and rumbling with deep, groaning murmurs from below, until the guide gave the word, and then emptied the bag down Wairoa's throat.

Almost immediately, white lather began to form in the depths of the well, and rose rapidly to the verge. The guide now ordered me away from the geyser; for, although Wairoa generally takes some minutes to play after being soaped, one can never be absolutely certain that it will not respond with inconvenient swiftness. I went back to a neighbouring hillock from which an excellent view could be obtained, and waited with the eager crowd. Every now and then a small rush of water lifted over the geyser rim, and once or twice the fountain seemed about to start; but it was not until seventeen minutes after I had put in the soap that Wairoa choked, gurgled, and finally broke into a roar like a ten thousand ton liner throwing off steam. In another instant, still roaring, the geyser shot up silvery white water, dissolving at the top, full 140 feet above ground, into a crest of delicate streamy feathers all sparkling in the sun. The display lasted about a couple of minutes, and then sank gradually away; but for long afterwards, Wairoa mumbled and grumbled and frothed at the mouth, not settling down into quiet for at least an hour.

Of Auckland—" last, loneliest, loveliest, exquisite, apart," as Kipling has called it—thus compelling all later travellers to see, or at least pretend to see, exquisite loveliness in prosaic Queen Street, and go a-hunting for poetic solitudes along the quays—I have nothing to say. Great ports are all alike, the wide world over, and hotel is as like unto hotel as pebble unto pebble. And when the story is done, why linger?

I have set forth to tell something of Britain of the South Seas, and such as it is, my say has been said.

www.ingramcontent.com/pod-product-compliance
Lightning Source LLC
Chambersburg PA
CBHW032058090426
42743CB00007B/160